THE PEARL

Third of four full-page illustrations in color which occupy the opening pages of the *Pearl* (folios 37-39). Although crudely drawn and inaccurate in detail, these pictures add a mediaeval charm to the anonymous poet's work, as do the blue initial letters ornamented in red which mark the opening of each stanza. (Reproduced by courtesy of the Trustees of the British Museum from MS. Cotton Nero A. x, f.38.)

THE DREAMER AND THE PEARL-MAIDEN CONVERSE ACROSS THE STREAM

THE PEARL

MEDIAEVAL TEXT WITH A LITERAL TRANSLATION AND INTERPRETATION

by
SISTER MARY VINCENT HILLMANN, PH.D.
Professor of English

COLLEGE OF SAINT ELIZABETH PRESS

For information, write University Publishers Incorporated,
239 Park Avenue South, New York City 3, sole distributors.

Nihil obstat:
Henry J. Zolzer
Censor Librorum

April 19, 1959

Imprimatur:
James A. McNulty
Bishop of Paterson

April 24, 1959

Library of Congress Catalog Card Number: 61:8731

*Manufactured in the United States of America by
Quinn & Boden Company, Inc., Rahway, New Jersey.*

To

MOTHER ELLEN MARIE, LL. D.

and the

SISTERS OF CHARITY OF SAINT ELIZABETH

this book was dedicated on its completion
in the centennial year of
the founding of our Order

1859-1959

Preface

The Pearl is one of four long alliterative poems contained in a faded manuscript (MS. Cotton Nero A. x) preserved in the British Museum. The date of the manuscript, whose author is unknown, is approximately sometime between 1360 and 1400. The dialect is generally that of the North-West Midlands. The text of the present edition has been made from a photographic copy of the original manuscript, collated with the texts of Richard Morris, Sir Israel Gollancz, and Charles G. Osgood, and checked by the work of other scholars, especially O. F. Emerson, E. V. Gordon, H. J. Hulbert, R. J. Manner, and J. P. Oakden.

The poem has been introduced to readers unacquainted with Middle English through several translations, most of them very free. One even omits the religious passages which constitute the major portion of the work. Such free translations, though sincerely intended, no doubt, to enlarge the audience of the poet and to reveal his remarkable beauty of expression and nobility of mind, depart somewhat from the imperatives of justice in minimizing what to him must have been superlatively important—his underlying idea. The general content of *The Pearl* was quite sensibly indicated in the earliest extant description of it, written in Latin by Richard James, librarian to Sir Robert Cotton: [1] *Vetus poema Anglicanum, in quo sub insomnii figmento multa ad religionem et mores spectantia explicantur* ("An old English poem, in which,

[1] A noted bibliophile and littérateur, Sir Robert Cotton (1571-1631) lived and died in the family manor house at Denton, Conington, Huntingdonshire, England. Famed for his collection of manuscripts and rare books, he was founder of one of England's earliest antiquarian societies and a member of Parliament from Newtown.

under the figure of a dream, many things relating to religion and morals are explained").

Richard Morris' classification of the poem as an elegy [2]—the lamentation of a poet-father over the death of his two-year-old daughter—captivated scholars and held them until 1904, when Morris' interpretation was challenged by W. H. Schofield,[3] who offered thoroughly logical arguments against it. Thenceforth, in the face of somewhat acrimonious opposition on the part of the elegy devotees, scholarship looked toward other possible interpretations.

Most of those offered, however, appeared to lean rather heavily on the text and translation provided in 1891 by Israel Gollancz,[4] both of which, it must be admitted, were very free and misleading. Such inexact readings of the original text often played havoc with the meaning of separate lines or of the poem as a whole because of unnecessary or fantastic emendations.

The remedy for further multiplication of conjecture as to the unknown poet's message would seem to be a new, literal translation drawn from the manuscript itself. The present study offers such a translation. The interpretation presented is derived from close study of the language, with punctuation introduced to clarify the meaning, and is one more attempt to prove that *The Pearl* is not an elegy, but an homiletic poem teaching that the soul must not be attached to earthly treasure if it is to attain the Kingdom of God.

> They are happen þat han in hert pouerté,
> For hores is þe heuen-ryche to holde for euer.[5]
>
> *Blessed are the poor in spirit*
> *For theirs is the Kingdom of Heaven to hold forever.*

[2] *Early English Alliterative Poems,* ed. Richard Morris (London: Trübner, 1864), *E.E.T.S.,* No. 1, p. ix.

[3] W. H. Schofield, "The Nature and Fabric of *The Pearl,*" *PMLA,* XIX (1904), 154-215; see also his "Symbolism, Allegory, and Autobiography in *The Pearl,*" *PMLA,* XXIV (1909), 585-675, wherein his views appear as somewhat modified, although not changed entirely.

[4] Pearl: *An English Poem of the 14th Century (with Modern Rendering . . .)* ed. Sir Israel Gollancz (London: David Nutt, 1891; Chatto & Windus, 1921).

[5] *Patience,* ed. Hartley Bateson, B.A. (Manchester University Press, 1912).

Since the present edition of *The Pearl* is a development of a doctoral dissertation presented at Fordham University, it remains for me here gratefully to acknowledge my debt to Dr. Charles Donahue, Professor of English at the University, for his scholarly and generous direction of the original work and for his further kindness in consenting to read the proofs of this book.

I wish also to thank the Reverend Edwin D. Cuffe, S.J., dean of the Jesuit Novitiate at St. Andrew-on-Hudson, Poughkeepsie, N. Y., for reading the galley proofs and for his helpful comments thereon.

M. V. H.

College of Saint Elizabeth
Convent Station, New Jersey

Interpretation

A jeweler, owner of a peerless Oriental pearl, loses it one day in a garden. His grief over the loss impels him frequently to visit the garden in the hope that he may find his treasured jewel. One day, on the hillock down which his pearl had rolled away from him, he sees a lovely growth of spice-blooms. Beneath those flowers, fittingly, he is sure, his treasure must abide. Recollection of it moves him to inordinate grief, a culpable grief because it is wilful and contrary to both reason and Christian teaching. In this state of mind he falls prostrate upon the flower-grown hill. There, overcome by the fragrance of the spice-flowers, he slips into a deathlike sleep or trance.

His spirit, after an interval, enters into a dream-vision land, the jewel-like beauty of which causes him, passionate lover of beauty that he is, straightway to forget all sorrow. He walks on in bliss until he reaches a stream flowing along between banks of beryl, the bed of it a mass of emeralds, sapphires, and other gems. He thinks he must be in Paradise, or near it. Suddenly, glancing across the stream, he is aware of a maiden robed in glittering white, seated at the foot of a crystal cliff. As a dreamer might, he immediately identifies her with that which had absorbed his thoughts just before he fell asleep, that which he loved most in this world and for which he had searched in vain—his lost pearl. The shock of beholding his treasure (as he believes the maiden to be) there in that lovely land renders him quite speechless. The radiant beauty of the apparition bewilders him. Awe follows upon bewilderment. As he stands, silently surmising some spiritual purpose in the vision, the maiden, in royal array of pearl-adorned robes and crown of pearl, comes down the bank to a position which permits conversation, and calls out to him a word of greeting. Recovering himself, he asks her whether or not she is his pearl—that pearl which had gone glittering away from him into the grass.

The maiden's answer is indirect. She does not identify herself with the material pearl, but tells the dreamer that his pearl (i.e., as she ultimately reveals, his soul) is there in this garden. If he were a noble jeweler, she adds, this beautiful garden would indeed be a treasure chest for him. Grief, she explains, for a transitory thing like his material pearl—not a "pearl of great price" but perishable as a rose—is irrational. The jeweler fails to understand. He still clings to the fancy that she is his lost jewel, and expresses a desire to cross the stream that he may be with her. She rebukes him for his presumption, forbidding him to cross and reminding him that he like all men must pass through death before he may enter Eternity to be judged by God.

After some debate, she begins at his request an exposition of the state of the soul in Heaven. She reminds him that at the time when he lost the material pearl, his soul—which she symbolizes—was extremely young (see Explanatory Notes, 411-12). But despite its immaturity, the dreamer's soul, like every soul, has been called to union with God. Attainment to that mystical union is represented in the poem not as something that has taken place, an actuality, but as a potentiality. Her words show the dreamer what might be his were he to practice the renunciation to which all Christians are called—were he to renounce the inordinate affection for a creature (the material pearl) that now renders him unmindful of God.

Yet the dreamer is represented by the poet as failing to grasp the truth that the maiden is indeed the soul, the *sponsa Christi.* And this attitude of mind in the dreamer is necessary if the poem is to go on. If at this point he clearly understood her words, there would be no further debate, no further opportunity for the poet to transmit the other lessons of his homily. Accordingly, the dreamer is represented as puzzled by the circumstance of the maiden's queenly estate, and as receiving necessary instruction upon that and kindred subjects.

Gradually the jeweler begins to perceive something of the spiritual significance of the visionary maiden. Her beauty, unlike that of the lost pearl, is supernatural (745-54). He requests her to explain her office in Heaven. She further expounds the doctrine of the mystical union of the soul with God, then leads the way to a hilltop whence the jeweler is privileged to behold the New Jerusalem as it is described in the Apocalypse. Suddenly, in the procession following the Lamb, the jeweler again beholds the maiden, whom he had last seen standing across from him in the dale. He is so overpowered by her beauty and by his wish to be with her that, despite her previous warning (289-300), he lawlessly yields to an impulse to cross the mysterious stream. On the very point of plunging into the water, however, he is roused from his deathlike sleep and finds himself in the garden, his head upon the hillock down which his precious material pearl had rolled away from him.

Disturbed at first, he quickly realizes the spiritual import of the dream: If the immortal soul, that pearl of rich renown (1182), is destined to abide in so beautiful a place, like a jewel in a garland (1186), then it is to his advantage while he abides in this prison of sorrow, the earth (1187), that his soul be pleasing to God. Therefore, to God the jeweler willingly gives up the material pearl, renouncing it as a symbol of earthly treasure, which causes man to forget his high destiny. It was Christ Who made our high destiny possible, Who granted us (by His Passion and Death) to be of His fellowship, souls bought at an infinite price and pleasing to Him as precious pearls to a prince.

Contents

THE PEARL

The Pearl

I

1 Perle, plesaunte to prynces paye!
To clanly clos in golde so clere,
Oute of Oryent, I hardyly saye,
Ne proued I neuer her precios pere.
So rounde, so reken in vche araye,
So smal, so smoþe her sydeȝ were,
Queresoeuer I jugged gemmeȝ gaye,
I sette hyr sengeley in synglure.
Allas, I leste hyr in on erbere—
Þurȝ gresse to grounde hit fro me yot!
I dewyne, fordolked of luf-daungere
Of þat pryuy perle wythouten spot.

2 Syþen in þat spote hit fro me sprange,
Ofte haf I wayted, wyschande þat wele
Þat wont watȝ whyle deuoyde my wrange,
& heuen my happe & al my hele—
Þat dotȝ bot þrych my hert þrange,
My breste in bale bot bolne & bele.
Ʒet þoȝt me neuer so swete a sange
As stylle stounde let to me stele;
Forsoþe þer fleten to me fele
To þenke hir color so clad in clot.
O moul, þou marreȝ a myry iuele,
My priuy perle wythouten spotte!

The Pearl

I

1 Pearl, pleasing to the fancy of a prince!
To set without flaw in gold so clear,
Out of the Orient, confidently I say,
I never tested its precious peer.
So round, so perfect in every array,
So fine, so smooth its surfaces were,
Wheresoever I bright gems appraised,
I set it apart in particular.
Alas, I lost it in a garden—
Through grass to earth it went from me!
I pined away, sore-wounded by the love-dominion
Of that pearl of mine without a spot.

2 Since then, in that spot where it sprang from me,
Oft have I watched, wishing for that wealth
That was wont for a while to make nought of my sin,
And exalt my fortune and my entire well-being—
Which doth but crushingly afflict my heart,
But swells and burns my breast with grief.
Yet never imagined I so sweet a song
As a quiet hour let steal to me;
Indeed, many drifted to me there,
Musing on its color so clad in clay.
O earth, thou marrest a lovely jewel,
My own pearl without a spot!

3 Þat spot of spyseȝ [mo]t nedeȝ sprede
Þer such rycheȝ to rot is runne;
Blomeȝ blayke & blwe & rede
Þer schyneȝ ful schyr agayn þe sunne.
Flor & fryte may not be fede
Þer hit doun drof in moldeȝ dunne;
For vch gresse mot grow of grayneȝ dede;
No whete were elleȝ to woneȝ wonne.
Of goud vche goude is ay bygonne!
So semly a sede moȝt fayly not
Þat spryg ande spyceȝ vp ne sponne
Of þat precios perle wythouten spotte.

4 To þat spot þat I in speche expoun
I entred in þat erber grene,
In Auguste in a hyȝ seysoun
Quen corne is coruen wyth crokeȝ kene.
On huyle, þer perle hit trendeled doun,
Schadowed þis worteȝ, ful schyre & schene—
Gilofre, gyngure, & gromylyoun,
& pyonys powdered ay bytwene.
Ȝif hit watȝ semly on to sene,
A fayr reflayr ȝet fro hit flot.
Þer wonys þat worþyly, I wot & wene,
My precious perle wythouten spot.

5 Bifore þat spot my honde I spenn[e]d
For care ful colde þat to me caȝt;
A deuely dele in my hert denned
Þaȝ resoun sette myseluen saȝt.
I playned my perle þat þer watȝ spenned
Wyth fyrte skylleȝ þat faste faȝt,
Þaȝ kynde of Kryst me comfort kenned.
My wreched wylle in wo ay wraȝte;
I felle vpon þat floury flaȝt.
Suche odour to my herneȝ schot,
I slode vpon a slepyng-slaȝte
On þat prec[i]os perle wythouten spot.

3 That spot with spice-blooms needs must be o'erspread
Where such wealth to rot is run;
Blossoms pale and blue and red
There will shine full bright against the sun.
Flower and fruit can not be withered
Where into dark molds it hurried down;
For from dead grains each blade of grass must grow;
No wheat would else be won for homes.
From good every good thing is ever begun!
So lovely a seed could not come to nought
So that sprig and spice-blooms would not grow up
From that precious pearl without a spot.

4 At that spot which I in speech set forth
I entered into that garden green,
In August in the season high
When corn is cut with sickles keen.
One hillock, where the pearl went rolling down,
These plants shadowed, full bright and fair—
Gillyflower, ginger, and gromwell,
And peonies powdered everywhere.
If it was lovely to look upon,
A fair fragrance also floated from it.
There fittingly that abides, I know,
My precious pearl without a spot.

5 Before that spot my hands I wrung
For the care full cold that seized on me;
A wicked grief lodged in my heart
Though understanding would have brought me peace.
I mourned my pearl which there was locked
With violence which swiftly reasonings fought,
Though the nature of Christ would have taught me comfort.
My wretched will in woe aye tossed;
I fell upon that flowery sward.
Such fragrance to my senses shot,
I fell upon a deathlike sleep
O'er that precious pearl without a spot.

II

6 Fro spot my spyryt þer sprang in space;
My body on balke þer bod in sweuen,
My goste is gon, in Godeȝ grace,
In auenture þer meruayles meuen.
I ne wyste in þis worlde quere þat hit wace,
Bot I knew me keste þer klyfeȝ cleuen.
Towarde a foreste I bere þe face,
Where rych rokkeȝ wer to dyscreuen.
Þe lyȝt of hem myȝt no mon leuen—
Þe glemande glory þat of hem glent—
For wern neuer webbeȝ þat wyȝeȝ weuen
Of half so dere adubmente.

7 Dubbed wern alle þo downeȝ sydeȝ
Wyth crystal klyffeȝ so cler of kynde;
Holte-wodeȝ bryȝt aboute hem bydeȝ
Of bolleȝ as blwe as ble of Ynde;
As bornyst syluer þe lef onslydeȝ
Þat þike con trylle on vch a tynde.
Quen glem of glodeȝ agaynȝ hem glydeȝ,
Wyth schymeryng schene ful schrylle þay schynde.
Þe grauayl þat on grounde con grynde
Wern precious perleȝ of Oryente,
Þe sunnebemeȝ bot blo & blynde
In respecte of þat adubbement.

8 The adubbemente of þo downeȝ dere
Garten my goste al greffe forȝete.
So frech flauoreȝ of fryteȝ were
As fode hit con me fayre refete.
Fowleȝ þer flowen in fryth in fere,
Of flaumbande hweȝ, boþe smale & grete;
Bot sytole-stryng & gyternere
Her reken myrþe moȝt not retrete,
For quen þose bryddeȝ her wyngeȝ bete,
Þay songen wyth a swete asent.
So grac[i]os gle couþe no mon gete
As here & se her adubbement.

II

6 At once my spirit from the spot sprang thither;
My body on the bank there stayed in sleep,
My soul gone forth, through grace of God,
Upon adventure, where wondrous things occur.
I knew not where in this world it was,
But I knew myself cast where cliffs cleaved the air.
Toward a forest I turned my face,
Where rich rocks were to be descried.
The light from them no man could believe—
The gleaming glory that from them shone—
For never were webs which mortals weave
Of half so precious an adornment.

7 Adorned were all the margins of the down
With crystal cliffs exceeding clear of kind;
Forests bright around them stand
With boles as blue as color of Ind;
Like burnished silver slip away the leaves
Which quiver thick on every branch.
When the gleam of the glades against them glides,
With a glittering glimmer full brilliantly they shone.
The gravel which underfoot did grind
Was precious pearls of the Orient,
The beams of the sun but dark and dim
As compared with that adornment.

8 The resplendency of those precious downs
Caused my soul all grief to forget.
So fresh were the fragrances of the fruits
Like food they did fairly revive me.
There in the woodland birds flew in flocks,
Of flaming colors, both small and great;
But citole string and gittern player
Could not reproduce their perfect joy,
For when those birds their wings did beat,
With a sweet harmony they sang.
Joy so gracious could no man attain
As to hear and see their splendor.

9 So al watȝ dubbet on dere asyse
Þat fryth þer Fortwne forth me fereȝ.
Þe derþe þerof for to deuyse
Nis no wyȝ worþe þat tonge bereȝ.
I welke ay forth in wely wyse—
No bonk so byg þat did me dereȝ.
Þe fyrre in þe fryth, þe fei[r]er con ryse
Þe playn, þe plontteȝ, þe spyse, þe pereȝ,
& raweȝ & randeȝ & rych reuereȝ—
As fyldor fyn her b[o]nkes brent.
I wan to a water by schore þat schereȝ—
Lorde, dere watȝ hit adubbement!

10 The dubbemente of þo derworth depe
Wern bonkeȝ bene of beryl bryȝt.
Swangeande swete þe water con swepe,
Wyth a rownande rourde raykande aryȝt.
In þe founce þer stonden stoneȝ stepe,
As glente þurȝ glas þat glowed & glyȝt,
A[s] stremande sterneȝ quen stroþe-men slepe
Staren in welkyn in wynter nyȝt.
For vche a pobbel in pole þer pyȝt
Watȝ emerad, saffer, oþer gemme gente,
Þat all þe loȝe lemed of lyȝt,
So dere watȝ hit adubbement!

III

11 The dubbement dere of doun & daleȝ,
Of wod & water & wlonk playneȝ,
Bylde in me blys, abated my baleȝ,
Fordidden my stresse, dystryed my payneȝ.
Doun after a strem þat dryȝly haleȝ,
I bowed in blys, bredful my brayneȝ.
Þe fyrre I folȝed þose floty valeȝ,
Þe more strenghþe of ioye myn herte strayneȝ.
As Fortune fares þer-as ho frayneȝ;
Wheþer solace ho sende oþer elleȝ sore,
Þe wyȝ to wham her wylle ho wayneȝ
Hytteȝ to haue ay more & more.

9 Thus was all-adorned in splendid manner
That wooded down where Fortune leads me on.
To describe the glory thereof
No mortal is worthy who has a tongue.
I walked always onward in happy wise—
No rise so great that it troubled me.
The farther into the region, the fairer did rise
The plain, the plants, the spice, the pears,
And hedgerows and borders and rivers royal—
As fine thread of gold their banks did glow.
I came to a current that winds over the strand—
Lord, precious was its adornment!

10 The adornment of those precious depths
Was beautiful banks of beryl bright.
Swinging sweetly the water did sweep,
Coursing straight on with a murmuring sound.
In the river bed there stood glistening stones,
Which glowed and gleamed like light through glass,
As radiant stars when mortals sleep
Shine in the sky on a winter night.
For every pebble in the stream there set
Was emerald, sapphire, or noble gem,
So that all the water glanced with light,
So precious was its adornment!

III

11 The adornment precious of hill and dales,
Of wood and water and splendid plains,
Aroused in me bliss, abolished my woes,
Dispelled my distress, put an end to my pains.
Following a stream which unceasingly flows,
In bliss I went, brimful my brain.
The farther I followed those undulating vales,
The more strength of joy my heart constrains.
So Fortune continues whenever she tries us;
Whether solace she send or else sorrow,
The mortal for whom she gains her intent
Is likely to have ever more and more.

12 More of wele watȝ in þat wyse
Þen I cowþe telle þaȝ I tom hade,
For vrþely herte myȝt not suffyse
To þe tenþe dole of þo gladneȝ glade.
Forþy I þoȝt þat Paradyse
Watȝ þer oþer gayn þo bonkeȝ brade;
I hoped þe water were a deuyse
Bytwene myrþeȝ by mereȝ made.
Byȝonde þe broke, by slente oþer slade,
I hope þat mote merked wore;
Bot þe water watȝ depe, I dorst not wade,
& euer me longed, a more & more.

13 More & more & ȝet wel mare
Me lyste to se þe broke byȝonde;
For if hit watȝ fayr þer I con fare,
Wel loueloker watȝ þe fyrre londe.
Abowte me con I stote & stare;
To fynde a forþe faste con I fonde,
Bot woþeȝ mo iwysse þer ware
Þe fyrre I stalked by þe stronde.
& euer me þoȝt I schulde not wonde
For wo þer weleȝ so wynne wore.
Þenne nwe note me com on honde,
Þat meued my mynde ay more & more.

14 More meruayle con my dom adaunt!
I seȝ byȝonde þat myry mere
A crystal clyffe ful relusaunt;
Mony ryal ray con fro hit rere.
At þe fote þerof þer sete a faunt,
A mayden of menske, ful debonere.
Blysnande whyt watȝ hyr bleaunt—
I knew hyr wel, I hade sen hyr ere!
As glysnande golde þat man con schere,
So schon þat schene anvnder schore.
On lenghe I loked to hyr þere—
Þe lenger, I knew hyr more & more.

12 More happiness of that sort there was
Than I could tell though I leisure had,
For earthly heart may not suffice
For the tenth part of that joyance glad.
Therefore I thought that Paradise
Was there, or facing those broad banks;
I supposed the water was a division
Between joyances with boundaries made.
Beyond the stream, near slope or dale,
I guessed that a city would be reached;
But the water was deep, I durst not cross,
And ever I longed—aye more and more.

13 More and more and yet still more
I longed to see beyond the stream;
For if fair it was where I journeyed,
Much lovelier was the farther land.
Around me I did pause and stare;
To find a ford quickly I did try,
But further searchings there truly were
The farther I stole along the shore.
And ever I felt I should not turn back
Because of failure where joys so blessèd were.
Then a new wonder to my attention came,
Which moved my mind ever more and more.

14 A greater marvel did my mind o'erpower!
I saw beyond that lovely mere
A most relucent crystal cliff;
Many a royal ray did from it rise.
At the foot thereof there sat a youthful being,
A maiden of dignity, of high estate,
Gleaming white was her garment rich—
I knew her well, I had seen her before!
Like glistening gold that man doth grave,
So shone that bright one 'neath the hill.
For an interval long I gazed toward her there—
The longer, I recognized her more and more.

15 The more I frayste hyr fayre face,
Her fygure fyn quen I had fonte,
Suche gladande glory con to me glace
As lyttel byfore þerto watȝ wonte.
To calle hyr lyste con me enchace,
Bot baysment gef myn hert a brunt—
I seȝ hyr in so strange a place.
Such a burre myȝt make myn herte blunt!
Þenne vereȝ ho vp her fayre frount,
Hyr vysayge whyt as playn yuore.
Þat stonge myn hert ful stray atount,
& euer þe lenger, þe more & more.

IV

16 More þen me lyste my drede aros;
I stod ful stylle & dorste not calle.
Wyth yȝen open & mouth ful clos,
I stod as hende as hawk in halle—
I hope þat gostly watȝ þat porpose.
I dred onende quat schulde byfalle—
Lest ho me eschaped þat I þer chos.
Er I at steuen hir moȝt stalle,
Þat gracios gay wythouten galle,
So smoþe, so smal, so seme slyȝt,
Ryseȝ vp in hir araye ryalle,
A prec[i]os pyece in perleȝ pyȝt.

17 Perleȝ pyȝte of ryal prys,
Þere moȝt mon by grace haf sene
Quen þat, frech as flor-de-lys,
Doun þe bonke con boȝe bydene.
Al blysnande whyt watȝ hir beaumys,
Vpon at sydeȝ & bounden bene
Wyth þe myryeste margarys, at my deuyse,
Þat euer I seȝ ȝet with myn yȝen,
Wyth lappeȝ large, I wot & I wene,
Dubbed with double perle & dyȝte—
Her cortel of self sute schene,
Wyth precios perleȝ al vmbepyȝte.

15 The more I searched her features fair,
After her slender figure I had scanned,
Such gladdening glory upon me flashed
As a short while ago was wont thereto.
A wish to call her did impel me,
But amazement gave my heart a jolt—
I saw her in so strange a place.
Such a shock might my heart benumb!
Then lifts she up her forehead fair,
Her face as white as ivory clear.
It pierced my heart, to distraction stunned,
And ever the longer, the more and more.

IV

16 More than I wished, my dread arose;
I stood full still and dared not call.
With eyes open and mouth tight closed,
I stood as alert as hawk in hall—
That the import was spiritual I surmised.
I feared concerning what would befall—
Lest she might escape me whom I there discerned.
Ere I could anticipate her by a call,
That beautiful bright one from blemish free,
So flawless, so graceful, so pleasingly slight,
Arises in her royal array,
A precious person adorned in pearls.

17 Pearls of royal price set in place,
There by grace might one have seen
When she, fresh as a fleur-de-lis,
Came forthwith down the bank.
All glistening white her mantle was,
Open at the sides and beautifully bound
With the loveliest pearls, in my judgement,
That ever I saw yet with my eyes,
With ample folds, I wot and I ween,
Decked with double pearl and ornamented—
Her kirtle in the same fair mode,
With precious pearls set all around.

18 A pyȝt coroune, ȝet, wer þat gyrle
Of mariorys & non oþer ston,
Hiȝe pynakled, of cler quyt perle,
Wyth flurted flowereȝ perfet vpon.
To hed hade ho non oþer werle.
Her lere leke al hyr vmbe gon,
Her semblaunt sade for doc oþer erle,
Her ble more blaȝt þen whalleȝ bon.
As schorne golde schyr her fax þenne schon,
On schyldereȝ þat leghe vnlapped lyȝte;
Her depe colour, ȝet, wonted non
Of precios perle in porfyl pyȝte.

19 Pyȝt watȝ poyned & vche a hemme,
At honde, at sydeȝ, at ouerture,
Wyth whyte perle & non oþer gemme,
& bornyste quyte watȝ hyr uesture.
Bot a wonder perle wythouten wemme
In myddeȝ hyr breste watȝ sette so sure.
A manneȝ dom moȝt dryȝly demme
Er mynde moȝt malte in hit mesure.
I hope no tong moȝt endure
No sauerly saghe say of þat syȝt,
So watȝ hit clene & cler & pure,
Þat precios perle þer hit watȝ pyȝt.

20 Pyȝt in perle, þat precios p[ec]e
On wyþer half water com doun þe schore.
No gladder gome heþen into Grece
Þen I quen ho on brymme wore;
Ho watȝ me nerre þen aunte or nece.
My joy forþy watȝ much þe more.
Ho p[ro]fered me speche, þat special sp[e]ce,
Enclynande lowe in wommon lore,
Caȝte of her coroun of grete tresore,
& haylsed me wyth a lote lyȝte.
Wel watȝ me þat euer I watȝ bore
To sware þat swete in perleȝ pyȝte!

18 That maiden also wore a crown, adorned
With margarites and no other stone,
High pointed, of clear white pearl,
With figured flowers perfect on (it).
On her head she had no other circlet.
Her face-radiance all 'round her beamed,
Her expression grave, like duke's or earl's,
Her complexion whiter than bone of whale.
As carved gold bright her hair then shone,
Which, unbound, lightly on her shoulders lay;
Also, her collar deep had no lack
Of precious pearl in border set.

19 Adorned was cuff and every hem,
At hands, at sides, at opening,
With white pearl and no other gem,
And lustrous white was her vesture.
But a wondrous pearl without a flaw
Securely in the center of her breast was set.
A man's judgment must in exhaustion stop
Before the mind dissolve in appraisal of it.
I suppose no tongue would be able to last
To utter an appreciative statement of that sight,
So flawless it was and clear and pure,
That precious pearl where it was set.

20 Adorned with pearls, that precious one
Across the stream came down the bank.
No gladder man from here to Greece
Than I when she was at the brink;
She was nearer to me than aunt or niece.
My joy, therefore, was much the more.
She proffered me speech, that being rare,
In woman-fashion bowing low,
Caught off her crown of value great,
And greeted me with a cheerful word.
Fortunate for me that I was born
To answer that sweet one in pearls adorned!

V

21 'O perle,' quod I, 'in perleȝ pyȝt,
Art þou my perle þat I haf playned,
Regretted by myn one on nyȝte?
Much longeyng haf I for þe layned
Syþen into gresse þou me aglyȝte.
Pensyf, payred, I am forpayned,
& þou in a lyf of lykyng lyȝte
In Paradys-erde, of stryf vnstrayned!
What wyrde hatȝ hyder my iuel vayned
& don me in þys del & gret daunger?
Fro we in twynne wern towen & twayned,
I haf ben a joyleȝ juelere.'

22 That juel þenne in gemmeȝ gente
Vered vp her vyse wyth yȝen graye,
Set on hyr coroun of perle orient,
& soberly after þenne con ho say:
'Sir, ȝe haf your tale myse tente
To say your perle is al awaye,
Þat is in cofer so comly clente
As in þis gardyn gracios gaye,
Hereinne to lenge for euer & play,
Þer mys nee mornyng com neuer here.
Her were a forser for þe, in faye,
If þou were a gentyl jueler.

23 'Bot, jueler gente, if þou schal lose
Þy ioy for a gemme þat þe watȝ lef,
Me þynk þe put in a mad porpose,
& busyeȝ þe aboute a raysoun bref;
For þat þou lesteȝ watȝ bot a rose
Þat flowred & fayled as kynde hyt gef;
Now þurȝ kynde of þe kyste þat hyt con close,
To a perle of prys hit is put in pref.
& þou hatȝ called þy wyrde a þef,
Þat oȝt of noȝt hatȝ mad þe cler,
Þou blameȝ þe bote of þy meschef.
Þou art no kynde jueler!'

V

21 'O pearl,' said I, 'in pearls adorned,
Art thou my pearl that I have mourned,
Grieved over alone at night?
Much longing for thee have I concealed
Since into the grass thou glittered away from me.
Pensive, worn, tormented am I,
And thou arrived at a life of joy
In Paradise-land, from strife set free!
What fate has brought my jewel hither
And put me in this grief and great duress?
Since we were forced apart and separated,
I have been a joyless jeweler.'

22 That jewel then in noble gems
Lifted her face with eyes of gray,
Put on her crown of Orient pearl,
And after that she did seriously say:
'Sir, you have ill considered your speech
In saying your pearl is utterly gone,
Which is in a coffer so beautiful secured
As in this garden charmingly gay,
Herein to dwell forever and play,
Since loss or mourning never come here.
Here would be a treasure chest for thee, in faith,
If thou wert a noble jeweler.

23 'But, noble jeweler, if thou must lose
Thy joy for a gem that was dear to thee,
Methinks thou art set on a mad intent,
And busieth thyself about a transient cause;
For what thou didst lose was but a rose
Which, as nature granted, flowered and failed;
Now, through the character of the chest which doth enclose it,
As a pearl of price it is put to the test.
If thou hast called thy fate a thief,
Which something from nothing hath clearly made for thee,
Thou blamest the cure of thy misfortune.
Thou art no rightful jeweler!'

24 A juel to me þen watʒ þys geste,
& iueleʒ wern hyr gentyl saweʒ.
'Iwyse,' quod I, 'my blysfol beste,
My grete dystresse þou al todraweʒ;
To be excused I make requeste.
I trawed my perle don out of daweʒ;
Now haf I fonde hyt, I schal ma feste
& wony wyth hyt in schyr wod-schaweʒ,
& loue my Lorde & al His laweʒ,
Þat hatʒ me broʒ þys blys ner.
Now were I at yow byʒonde þise waweʒ,
I were a ioyfol jueler.'

25 'Jueler,' sayde þat gemme clene,
'Wy borde ʒe men? So madde ʒe be!
Þre wordeʒ hatʒ þou spoken at ene;
Vnavysed, forsoþe, wern alle þre.
Þou ne woste in worlde quat on dotʒ mene;
Þy worde byfore þy wytte con fle.
Þou says þou traweʒ me in þis dene
Bycawse þou may wyth yʒen me se;
Anoþer þou says—in þys countre
Þyself schal won wyth me ryʒt here;
Þe þrydde—to passe þys water fre—
Þat may no ioyfol jueler.

VI

26 'I halde þat iueler lyttel to prayse
Þat l[e]ueʒ wel þat he seʒ wyth yʒe,
& much to blame & vncortoyse
Þat leueʒ Oure Lorde wolde make a lyʒe,
Þat lelly hyʒte your lyf to rayse,
Þaʒ fortune dyd your flesch to dyʒe.
Ʒe setten hys wordeʒ ful west ernays,
Þat l[e]ueʒ noþynk bot ʒe hit syʒe,
& þat is a poynt o sorquydryʒe
Þat vche god mon may euel byseme—
To leue no tale be true to tryʒe
Bot þat hys one skyl may dem.

24 Then was this guest a jewel to me,
And jewels were her gentle words.
'Truly,' said I, 'my blissful best,
My great distress thou removest quite;
To be pardoned I make request.
I believed my pearl utterly gone;
Now I have found it, I shall rejoice
And dwell with it in bright woodlands,
And praise my Lord and all His laws,
Who has brought me near this happiness.
Now were I with you beyond these waves,
I would be a joyful jeweler.'

25 'Jeweler,' said that jewel pure,
'Why do ye mortals mock? So foolish ye be!
Three statements hast thou uttered at one time;
All three, in truth, were ill-advised.
Thou knowest not what on earth one doth mean;
Thy word ahead of thy wit doth flee.
Thou sayest thou believest me in this vale
Because with eyes thou canst me see;
Another thing thou sayest—in this country
Thou thyself wilt dwell with me right here;
The third—to pass this noble stream—
That may no joyful jeweler.

VI

26 'I hold that jeweler little to praise
Who well believes what he sees with the eye,
And much to blame and discourteous
Who believes Our Lord would invent a lie,
Who faithfully promised your life to raise,
Though destiny caused your flesh to die.
You make His words a quite empty pledge,
Who nothing believe unless you see it,
And that is a mark of presumption
Which every good man may ill befit—
To believe no tale be true to trust
Save that which his reason alone may judge.

27 'Deme now þyself if þou con dayly,
As man to God wordeȝ schulde heue.
Þou saytȝ þou schal won in þis bayly.
Me þynk þe burde fyrst aske leue,
& ȝet of graunt þou myȝteȝ fayle.
Þou wylneȝ ouer þys water to weue.
Er moste þou ceuer to oþer counsayl:
Þy corse in clot mot calder keue,
For hit watȝ forgarte at Paradys-greue;
Oure ȝore-fader hit con mysseȝeme.
Þurȝ drwry deth boȝ vch ma dreue
Er ouer þys dam hym Dryȝtyn deme.'

28 'Demeȝ þou me,' quod I, 'my swete,
To dol agayn? Þenne I dowyne!
Now haf I fonte þat I forlete,
Schal I efte forgo hit er euer I fyne?
Why schal I hit boþe mysse & mete?
My precios perle dotȝ me gret pyne!
What serueȝ tresor bot gareȝ men grete
When he hit schal efte wyth teneȝ tyne?
Now rech I neuer for to declyne,
Ne how fer of folde þat man me fleme,
When I am parteleȝ of perleȝ myne!
Bot durande doel what may men deme?'

29 'Thow demeȝ noȝt bot doel-dystresse,'
Þenne sayde þat wyȝt. 'Why dotȝ þou so?
For dyne of doel of lureȝ lesse,
Ofte mony mon forgos þe mo.
Þe oȝte better þyseluen blesse,
& loue ay God, & wele & wo,
For anger gayneȝ þe not a cresse.
Who nedeȝ schal þole, be not so þro!
For þoȝ þou daunce as any do,
Braundysch & bray þy braþeȝ breme,
When þou no fyrre may, to ne fro,
Þou moste abyde þat he schal deme.

27 'Judge now thyself if thou didst lightly speak,
As if man should hurl up words at God.
Thou sayest in this dominion thou wilt dwell.
Methinks it behooved thee first to ask leave,
And yet of permission thou mightest fail.
Thou wishest to move across this stream.
Thou must first submit to another plan:
Thy body in clay must colder sink,
For it was stricken in Paradise-grove;
Our first father did fail to value it.
Through dreary death must each man pass
Ere beyond this stream God judges him.'

28 'Doomest thou me, my sweet,' said I,
'To sorrow again? Then I pine away!
Now I have found that which I lost,
Must I again forego it ere ever I die?
Why must I both lose and find it?
My precious pearl causes me anguish great!
What use is treasure but to make one weep
When he with sufferings must again lose it?
Now care I never about wasting away,
Nor how far from earth they may banish me,
When I am deprived of my peerless one!
What can man expect but lasting grief?'

29 'Thou thinkest of nothing but grief's distress,'
Then said that being. 'Why dost thou so?
Through clamor of grief about minor losses,
Oft many a man doth forego the more.
Thou oughtest rather bless thyself,
And praise God ever, come weal or woe,
For anger gains thee not a cress.
Who needs must suffer, be not so fierce!
For though thou mayst prance like any doe,
Threaten and shout thy furies wild,
When thou canst no farther, to or fro,
Thou must await what He shall decree.

30 'Deme Dryȝtyn, euer hym adyte—
Of þe way a fote ne wyl he wryþe,
Þy mendeȝ mounteȝ not a myte.
Þaȝ þou for sorȝe be neuer blyþe,
Stynst of þy strot & fyne to flyte,
& sech hys blyþe ful swefte & swyþe;
Þy prayer may hys pyte byte
Þat mercy schal hyr crafteȝ kyþe.
Hys comforte may þy langour lyþe
& þy lureȝ of lyȝtly leme,
For, marre oþer madde, morne & myþe,
Al lys in hym to dyȝt & deme.'

VII

31 Thenne demed I to þat damyselle:
'Ne worþe no wrathþe vnto my Lorde
If rapely [I] raue, spornande in spelle;
My herte watȝ al wyth mysse remorde,
As wallande water gotȝ out of welle.
I do me ay in hys myserecorde!
Rebuke me neuer wyth wordeȝ felle,
Þaȝ I forloyne, my dere endorde,
Bot lyþeȝ me kyndely your coumforde,
Pytosly þenkande vpon þysse:
Of care & me ȝe made acorde,
Þat er watȝ grounde of alle my blysse.

32 'My blysse, my bale, ȝe han ben boþe,
Bot much þe bygger ȝet watȝ my mon
Fro þou watȝ wroken fro vch a woþe—
I wyste neuer quere my perle watȝ gon.
Now I hit se, now leþeȝ my loþe.
& quen we departed we wern at on,
God forbede we be now wroþe—
We meten so selden by stok oþer ston.
Þaȝ cortaysly ȝe carp con,
I am bot mol & mare reȝ mysse.
Bot Crystes mersy & Mary & Jon—
Þise arn þe grounde of alle my blysse.

30 'Judge God, constantly accuse Him—
From the way He will not turn one foot,
Thy opinions amount to not a mite.
Though thou for sorrow be never glad,
Desist from thy strife and cease to dispute,
And full swiftly and earnestly seek His favor;
Thy prayer His pity may secure
So that mercy will its powers reveal.
His comfort can relieve thy suffering
And through thy losses gently gleam,
For, obstruct or rage, mourn and hide away,
All lies with Him to dispose and judge.'

VII

31 Then said I to that demoiselle:
'Let it not be counted anger toward my Lord
If recklessly I rave, resisting in speech;
My heart was all with loss disturbed,
As welling water goes out of a spring.
In His mercy always I place myself!
Rebuke me never with cruel words,
Though I be in error, my dear adored,
But kindly yield your comfort to me,
In pity reflecting upon this:
Of care and me you made accord,
Who were once the ground of all my bliss.

32 'My bliss, my grief, you have been both,
But much the greater yet was my woe
From the time thou wast cut off from every search—
I never knew where my pearl was gone.
Now I see it! Now my woe is assuaged.
If when we parted we were in accord,
God forbid we now be wroth—
We meet so seldom, by stock or stone.
Though you are able to speak with courteous wit,
I am but dust and great eloquence lack.
But Christ's mercy, and Mary, and John—
These are the ground of all my bliss.

33 'In blysse I se þe blyþely blent,
& I a man al mornyf mate.
Ȝe take þeron ful lyttel tente,
Þaȝ I hente ofte harmeȝ hate.
Bot now I am here in your presente,
I wolde bysech wythouten debate
Ȝe wolde me say in sobre asente
What lyf ȝe lede erly & late.
For I am ful fayn þat your astate
Is worþen to worschyp & wele iwysse;
Of alle my joy þe hyȝe gate
Hit is in grounde of alle my blysse.'

34 'Now blysse, burne, mot þe bytyde!'
Þen sayde þat lufsoum of lyth & lere,
'& welcum here to walk & byde,
For now þy speche is to me dere.
Maysterful mod & hyȝe pryde,
I hete þe, arn heterly hated here.
My Lorde ne loueȝ not for to chyde,
For meke arn all þat woneȝ hym nere.
& when in hys place þou schal apere,
Be dep deuote in hol mekenesse;
My Lorde þe Lamb loueȝ ay such chere,
Þat is þe grounde of alle my blysse.

35 'A blysful lyf þou says I lede;
Þou woldeȝ knaw þerof þe stage.
Þow wost wel, when þy perle con schede
I watȝ ful ȝong & tender of age.
Bot my Lorde þe Lombe, þurȝ hys Godhede,
He toke my self to hys maryage,
Corounde me quene, in blysse to brede
In lenghe of dayeȝ—þat euer schal wage—
& sesed in alle hys herytage
Hys lef is! I am holy hysse!
Hys prese, hys prys, & hys parage
Is rote & grounde of alle my blysse.'

33 'In bliss I see thee blithely blent,
And I a man all mournful balked.
Thereof you take full little heed,
Though oft I meet with burning wrongs.
But now that I am in your presence here,
I would beseech without debate
That you would tell me with serious accord
What life you lead, early and late.
For I am most glad that your estate
Has been truly changed to honor and bliss;
The exalted state of all my joy
Is at the ground of all my bliss.'

34 'Now must blessedness befall thee, noble sir,'
Then said she, lovely in form and face,
'And welcome here to walk and bide,
For now thy speech is dear to me.
Masterful mood and haughty pride,
I assure thee, are strongly hated here.
My Lord loves not at all to chide,
For meek are all who near Him dwell.
And when in His house thou shalt appear,
In all meekness be deeply reverent;
Such mien my Lord the Lamb ever loves,
Who is the ground of all my bliss.

35 'A blissful life thou sayest I lead;
Thou wishest to know thereof the state.
Thou knowest well, when thy pearl did fall
I was full young and tender of age.
But my Lord the Lamb, through His Godhead,
Did receive my self for His marriage,
Crowned me queen, in bliss to flourish
For the duration of time—He Who will ever keep faith—
And possessed of all His heritage
Is His beloved! I am wholly His!
His virtue, His worth, and His nobility
Are root and ground of all my bliss.'

VIII

36 'Blysful,' quod I, 'may þys be trwe?
Dysplese3 not if I speke errour.
Art þou þe quene of heuene3 blwe
Þat al þys worlde schal do honour?
We leuen on Marye þat Grace of grewe,
Þat ber a Barne of vyrgynflor;
Þe croune fro hyr quo mo3t remwe
Bot ho hir passed in sum fauour?
Now for synglerty o hyr dousour
We calle hyr Fenyx of Arraby,
Þat freles fle3e of hyr Fasor
Lyk to þe Quen of Cortaysye.'

37 'Cortayse Quen!' þenne s[a]yde þat gaye,
Knelande to grounde, folde vp hyr face,
'Makele3 Moder & Myryest May,
Blessed Bygyn[n]er of vch a grace!'
Þenne ros ho vp & con restay
& speke me towarde in þat space:
'Sir, fele here porchase3 & fonge3 pray,
Bot supplantore3 none wythinne þys place.
Þat Emperise al heuen[e]3 hat3
& vrþe & helle in her bayly;
Of erytage 3et non wyl ho chace,
For ho is Quen of Cortaysye.

38 'The court of þe kyndom of God alyue
Hat3 a property in hyt self beyng:
Alle þat may þerinne aryue
Of alle þe reme is quen oþer kyng
& neuer oþer 3et schal depryue;
Bot vchon fayn of oþere3 hafyng,
& wolde her coroune3 wern worþe þo fyue,
If possyble were her mendyng.
Bot my Lady, of quom Jesu con spryng,
Ho halde3 þe empyre ouer vus ful hy3e;
& þat dysplese3 non of oure gyng,
For ho is Quene of Cortaysye.

VIII

36 'Blessed one,' said I, 'can this be true?
Be not displeased if error I speak.
Art thou the Queen of heaven's blue
To whom all this world must honor do?
We believe in Mary from whom sprang Grace,
Who bore a Child in virginity;
Who may remove the crown from her
Unless she excelled her in some grace?
Now for the singularity of her sweetness
We call her Phoenix of Araby,
Which flawless flew from its Creator
Like to the Queen of Courtesy.'

37 'Courteous Queen!' then said that bright one,
Kneeling on the ground, her face concealed,
'Matchless Mother and loveliest Maid,
Blessed Beginner of every grace!'
Then she arose and was able to restrain
And contradict me in that interval:
'Sir, many here seek and receive reward,
But usurpers none within this place.
That Empress holdeth all the heavens
And earth and hell within her sway;
Yet from heritage she will no one drive,
For she is Queen of Courtesy.

38 'The court of the kingdom of the living God
Hath a property of its own being:
Each one who thither may arrive
Of the whole realm is queen or king
And yet shall never dispossess another;
But each one is glad of the others' having
And would their crowns were then worth five
If possible were their enhancement.
But my Lady, from whom Jesus sprang,
She holds the empire over us full high;
And of our company that displeases none,
For she is Queen of Courtesy.

39 'Of courtaysye, as saytȝ Saynt Poule,
Al arn we membreȝ of Jesu Kryst;
As heued & arme & legg & naule
Temen to hys body ful trwe & t[r]yste,
Ryȝt so is vch a Krysten sawle
A longande lym to þe Mayster of Myste.
Þenne loke what hate oþer any gawle
Is tached oþer tyȝed þy lymmeȝ bytwyste.
Þy heued hatȝ nauþer greme ne gryste
On arme oþer fynger þaȝ þou ber byȝe;
So fare we alle wyth luf & lyste,
To kyng & quene, by cortaysye.'

40 'Cortayse,' quod I, 'I leue,
& charyte grete be yow among.
Bot my speche þat yow ne greue—

*   *   *   *   *

Þyself in heuen ouer hyȝ þou heue!
To make þe quen þat watȝ so ȝonge!
What more honour moȝte he acheue
Þat hade endured in worlde stronge,
& lyued in penaunce hys lyueȝ longe,
Wyth bodyly bale hym blysse to byye?
What more worschyp moȝt h[e] fonge
Þen corounde be kyng by cortayse?

IX

41 'That cortayse is to fre of dede,
Ȝyf hyt be soth þat þou coneȝ saye.
Þou lyfed not two ȝer in oure þede—
Þou cowþes neuer God nauþer plese ne pray,
Ne neuer nawþer Pater ne Crede—
& quen mad on þe fyrst day!
I may not traw—so God me spede!—
Þat God wolde wryþe so wrange away.
Of countes, damysel, par ma fay,
Wer fayr in heuen to halde asstate,
Oþer elleȝ a lady of lasse aray—
Bot a quene! Hit is to dere a date!'

39 'Through courtesy, as says Saint Paul,
We all are members of Jesus Christ;
As head and arm and leg and navel
Connect to His body full true and tried,
Just so is every Christian soul
A limb belonging to the Master of Might.
Then look whether any hate or rancor
Is fixed or fastened among thy limbs.
Thy head hath neither wrath nor irritation
Though on arm or finger thou wearest ring;
Thus fare we all in love and joy,
As king and queen, with courtesy.'

40 'Courtesy,' said I, 'I do believe,
And charity great exist among you.
But that my speech may grieve you not—

* * * * *

Thou dost lift thyself in Heaven over high!
To make thee queen who was so young!
What more honor might he achieve
Who in the world had strongly endured,
And lived in penance his life's length
With bodily suffering to buy himself bliss?
What more honor might he attain
Than be crowned king by courtesy?

IX

41 'That Courteous One is too liberal of deed,
If it be truth that thou dost utter.
Thou livedst not two years in our land—
Thou couldst never either please God or pray,
Not ever either Pater or Creed—
And queen made on the first day!
I cannot believe—so God me speed!—
That God would deviate so unjustly.
As countess, damsel, by my faith,
'Twere fair in heaven to hold estate,
Or else a lady of lesser degree—
But a queen! 'Tis a term too highly rated!'

42 'Þer is no date of hys godnesse,'
Þen sayde to me þat worþy wyȝte,
'For al is trawþe þat he con dresse
& he may do noþynk bot ryȝt.
As Mathew meleȝ in your messe,
In sothfol Gospel of God Almyȝt,
In sample he can ful grayþely gesse
& lykneȝ hit to heuen lyȝte:
"My regne," he saytȝ, "is lyk on hyȝt
To a lorde þat hade a uyne I wate.
Of tyme of ȝere þe terme watȝ tyȝt;
To labor vyne watȝ dere þe date.

43 ' "Þat date of ȝere wel knawe þys hyne;
Þe lorde ful erly vp he ros
To hyre werkmen to hys vyne,
& fyndeȝ þer summe to hys porpos.
Into acorde þay con declyne
For a pene on a day, & forth þay gotȝ,
Wryþen & worchen & don gret pyne,
Keruen & caggen & man hit clos.
Aboute vnder þe lorde to marked totȝ,
& ydel men stande he fyndeȝ þerate.
'Why stande ȝe ydel?' he sayde to þos,
'Ne knawe ȝe of þis day no date?'

44 ' " 'Er date of daye hider arn we wonne.'
So watȝ al samen her answar soȝt.
'We haf standen her syn ros þe sunne,
& no mon byddeȝ vus do ryȝt noȝt.'
'Gos into my vyne, dotȝ þat ȝe conneȝ.'
(So sayde þe lorde, & made hit toȝt
What resonabele hyre be naȝt be runne.)
'I yow pray in dede & þoȝte.'
Þay wente into þe vyne & wroȝte,
& al day þe lorde þus ȝede his gate,
& nw men to hys vyne he broȝte
Wel-neȝ wyl day watȝ passed date.

42 'There is no termination of His goodness,'
Then said to me that noble one,
'For all is truth which He establishes
And He can nothing do but right.
As Matthew in your Mass relates
In truthful Gospel of Almighty God,
Full readily He doth improvise in a parable,
And likens it to Heaven bright:
"My kingdom," He says, "is like on high
To a lord who had a vineyard I know.
The end of the season was at hand;
Time was precious the vineyard to work.

43 ' "These householders well know that time of year;
The master very early up he rose
Workmen into his vineyard to hire,
And some there to his purpose finds.
Unto agreement they did submit
For a penny a day, and forth they go,
Twist and toil and endure much pain,
Cut and bind and gather the harvest.
About the third hour, the lord to the market goes,
And idle men he findeth standing there.
'Why stand ye idle?' he said to them,
'Know ye not the hour of this day?'

44 ' " 'Ere break of day hither are we come.'
So, all in unison, was their answer murmured.
'We have stood here since the sun arose,
And no man bids us do aught at all.'
'Go into my vineyard, do what ye can.'
(So said the lord, and made agreement
What just wage would be accrued by night.)
'I call on you through bond and intent.'
Into the vineyard they went and worked,
And all day long the lord pursued his way,
And new men to his vineyard he brought
Until almost time past was the day.

45 ‘ “At þe day of date of euensonge,
On oure byfore þe sonne go doun,
He seȝ þer ydel men ful stronge,
& sade to he[m] wyth sobre soun,
‘Wy stonde ȝe ydel þise dayeȝ longe?’
Þay sayden her hyre watȝ nawhere boun.
‘Gotȝ to my vyne, ȝemen ȝonge,
& wyrkeȝ & dotȝ þat at ȝe moun.’
Sone þe worlde bycom wel broun;
Þe sunne watȝ doun & & hit wex late,
To take her hyre he mad sumoun.
Þe day watȝ al a passed date.

X

46 ‘ “The date of þe daye þe lorde con knaw,
Called to þe reue: ‘Lede, pay þe meyny.
Gyf hem þe hyre þat I hem owe.
& fyrre, þat non me may repren[y],
Set hem alle vpon a rawe,
& gyf vchon inlyche a peny.
Bygyn at þe laste þat standeȝ lowe,
Tyl to þe fyrste þat þou atteny.’
& þenne þe fyrst bygonne to pleny,
& sayden þat þay had trauayled sore.
‘Þese bot on oure hem con streny;
Vus þynk vus oȝe to take more.

47 ‘ “ ‘More haf we serued, vus þynk so,
Þat suffred han þe dayeȝ hete,
Þenn þyse þat wroȝt not houreȝ two,
& þou dotȝ hem vus to counterfete!’
Þenne sayde þe lorde to on of þo:
‘Frende, no wanig I wyl þe ȝete.
Take þat is þyn owne & go.
& I hyred þe for a peny agrete,
Quy bygynneȝ þou now to þrete?
Watȝ not a pene þy couenaunt þore?
Fyrre þen couenaunde is noȝt to plete.
Wy shalte þou þenne ask more?

45 '"On that day at time of evensong,
One hour before the sun went down,
He saw there idle men quite strong,
And said to them in serious tone,
'Why stand ye idle this day's length?'
Nowhere, they said, was their wage prepared.
'Go to my vineyard, yeomen young,
And work and do that which ye can.'
Soon the world became very dark;
The sun was down, and when it grew late,
To get their wages he made summoning.
The day was completely a time gone by.

X

46 '"The time of the day the lord did perceive,
Called to the reeve: 'Pay the company, man.
Give them the wage that I owe them.
And, further, that none may reproach me,
Draw them all up in a row,
And give each one a penny in full.
Begin with the last who standeth low,
Until to the first thou dost arrive.'
And then the first began to complain,
And said that they had sorely toiled.
'These but one hour did themselves exert;
It seems to us we ought to get more.

47 '" 'More have we served, so to us it seems,
Who have endured the heat of the day,
Than these who labored not two hours,
And thou dost make them to equal us!'
Then said the lord to one of them:
'Friend, I will not concede thee lacking.
Take what is thine own and go.
If I hired thee for a penny agreed,
Why dost thou now begin to rebuke?
Was not a penny thy contract then?
Further than contract there is nought to plead.
Why, then, shalt thou ask more?

48 '"'More, weþer louyly is me my gyfte—
To do wyth myn quat so me lykeȝ?
Oþer elleȝ þyn yȝe to lyþer is lyfte
For I am goude & non byswykeȝ?'
"Þus schal I," quod Kryste, "hit skyfte:
Þe laste schal be þe fyrst þat strykeȝ,
& þe fyrst þe laste, be he neuer so swyft;
For mony ben calle þaȝ fewe be mykeȝ."
Þus pore men her part ay pykeȝ
Þaȝ þay com late & lyttel wore;
& þaȝ her sweng wyth lyttel atslykeȝ,
Þe merci of God is much þe more.

49 'More haf I of ioye & blysse hereinne,
Of ladyschyp gret & lyueȝ blom,
Þen alle þe wyȝeȝ in þe worlde myȝt wynne
By þe way of ryȝt to aske dome,
Wheþer welnygh now I con bygynne!
In euentyde into þe vyne I come.
Fyrst of my hyre my Lorde con mynne;
I watȝ payed anon of al & sum.
Ȝet oþer þer werne þat toke more tom,
Þat swange & swat for long ȝore,
Þat ȝet of hyre noþynk þay nom,
Paraunter noȝt schal toȝere more.'

50 Then more I meled & sayde apert:
'Me þynk þy tale vnresounable.
Goddeȝ ryȝt is redy & euermore rert,
Oþer Holy Wryt is bot a fable.
In Sauter is sayd a verce ouerte,
Þat spekeȝ a poynt determynable:
"Þou quyteȝ vchon as hys desserte,
Þou Hyȝe Kyng ay Pretermynable."
Now he þat stod þe long day stable,
& þou to payment com hym byfore,
Þenne þe lasse in werke, to take more able,
& euer þe lenger þe lasse, þe more!'

48 ‘“‘Moreover, is not my right to bestow lawful to me—
To do with mine own whatsoever I like?
Or else is thine eye to evil raised
Because I am good and none deceive?’
“Thus,” said Christ, “shall I arrange it:
The last shall be the first that goes,
And the first the last, be he never so swift;
For many are called though few be chosen ones.”
Thus poor men always gather their share
Though they may come late and lowly may be;
And though their stroke with little glides off,
The mercy of God is much the more.

49 ‘More of joy have I and bliss herein,
Of ladyship great and bloom of life,
Than all the people in the world might win
Through asking judgment by way of right,
Yet almost now did I begin!
At eventide into the vineyard I came.
First did my Lord take care of my wage;
I was paid forthwith, wholly and fully.
Yet others there were who spent more time,
Who toiled and sweated for long in the past,
Who yet of wages have nought received—
Perchance nought shall anymore this year.’

50 Then further I spoke and frankly said:
‘Methinks thy account unreasonable.
God’s justice is prompt and forever fixed,
Or Holy Writ is but a fable.
In the Psalter is said an explicit verse,
Which expresses a point determinable:
“Thou requitest each according to his desert,
Thou High King ever Infinite.”
Now he that stood the long day firm,
If thou came for payment ahead of him,
Then the less the work, the more able to get,
And ever the longer the less, the more!’

XI

51 'Of more & lasse in Godeȝ ryche,'
Þat gentyl sayde, 'lys no joparde,
For þer is vch mon payed inlyche,
Wheþer lyttel oþer much be hys rewarde.
For þe gentyl Cheuentayn is no chyche,
Queþersoeuer he dele nesch oþer harde;
He laueȝ hys gyfteȝ as water of dyche,
Oþer goteȝ of golf þat neuer charde.
Hys fraunchyse is large þat euer dard
To Hym þat matȝ in synne rescoghe;
No blysse betȝ fro hem reparde,
For þe grace of God is gret inoghe.

52 'Bot now þou moteȝ me for to mate,
Þat I my peny haf wrang tan here;
Þou sayȝ þat I þat come to late
Am not worþy so gret lere.
Where wysteȝ þou euer any bourne abate,
Euer so holy in hys prayere,
Þat he ne forfeted by sum kyn gate
Þe mede sumtyme of heueneȝ clere?
& ay þe ofter þe alder þay were
Þay laften ryȝt & wroȝten woghe.
Mercy & grace moste hem þen stere,
For þe grace of God is gret innoȝe.

53 'Bot innoghe of grace hatȝ innocent;
As sone as þay arn borne, by lyne
In þe water of babtem þay dyssente;
Þen arne þay boroȝt into þe vyne.
Anon—þe day wyth derk endente—
Þe myȝt of deth dotȝ to enclyne
Þat wroȝt neuer wrang er þenne þay wente.
Þe gentyle Lorde þenne payeȝ hys hyne.
Þay dyden hys heste, þay wern þereine;
Why schulde he not her labour alow?
Ȝys, & pay hym at the fyrst fyne?
For þe grace of God is gret innoghe.

XI

51 'Of more and less in the Kingdom of God,'
That gentle one said, 'lies no uncertainty,
For there is each one fully paid,
Whether little or much be his reward.
For the noble Chieftain is no niggard,
Whether He dealeth mild or hard;
He pours out His gifts as water from dike,
Or as streams from bay which never swerved.
Ample is his heritage who always reverence paid
To Him Who makes rescue in the case of sin;
No happiness is from such withheld,
For the grace of God is great enough.

52 'But now thou dost argue me to defeat,
That I have taken my penny unjustly here;
Thou sayest that I who came too late
Am not worthy of so large a recompense.
Where knewest thou ever any man to lose zeal,
However holy in his prayer,
That he did not forfeit in some kind of way
The reward sometime of Heaven's brightness?
And ever the oftener the older such were
They abandoned right and evil wrought.
Mercy and grace must guide them then,
For the grace of God is great enough.

53 'But enough of grace have the innocent;
As soon as they are born, in order of birth
Into the water of Baptism they descend;
Then into the vineyard are they brought.
Forthwith—that day with darkness marked—
The might of death causes to bow low
Those who never wrought evil ere thence they went.
The noble Lord thereupon payeth His servants.
They did His behest, they were therein;
Why should He not their labor allow?
Yes, and pay them at the first furrow's end?
For the grace of God is great enough.

the newborn or very young who die

54 'Inoȝe is knawen þat mankyn grete
Fyrste watȝ wroȝt to blysse parfyt;
Oure forme fader hit con forfete
Þurȝ an apple þat he vpon con byte.
Al wer we dampned for þat mete
To dyȝe in doel out of delyt,
& syþen wende to helle hete,
Þerinne to won wythoute respyt.
Bot þeron com a bote as tyt:
Ryche blod ran on rode so roghe,
& wynne water; þen, at þat plyt,
Þe grace of God wex gret innoghe.

55 'Innoghe þer wax out of þat welle,
Blod & water of brode wounde.
Þe blod vus boȝt fro bale of helle,
& delyuered vus of þe deth secounde;
Þe water is baptem, þe soþe to telle—
Þat folȝed þe glayue so grymly grounde—
Þat wascheȝ away þe gylteȝ felle
Þat Adam wyth inne deth vus drounde.
Now is þer noȝt in þe worlde rounde
Bytwene vus & blysse bot þat he wythdroȝ,
& þat is restored in sely stounde,
& þe grace of God is gret innogh.

XII

56 'Grace innogh þe mon may haue
Þat synneȝ þenne new, ȝif hym repente;
Bot wyth sore & syt he mot hit craue,
& byde þe payne þerto is bent.
Bot resoun of ryȝt, þat con not raue,
Saueȝ euermore þe innossent.
Hit is a dom þat neuer God gaue
Þat euer þe gyltleȝ schulde be schente.
Þe gyltyf may contryssyoun hente,
& be þurȝ mercy to grace þryȝt;
Bot he to gyle þat neuer glente,
At inoscente is saf, & ryȝte.

54 'Well enough 'tis known that mankind great
First was fashioned for perfect bliss;
Our first father did forfeit it
Through an apple that he bit upon.
We were all condemned because of that food
To die in sorrow, away from bliss,
And then to go to heat of hell,
Therein without surcease to dwell.
But for that, at once, a remedy came:
Precious Blood flowed on the rood so rough,
And blessèd water; then, at that plight,
The grace of God grew great enough.

55 'Enough there flowed forth from that well,
Blood and water from wide wound.
The blood bought us from bale of hell,
And delivered us from the second death;
The water is Baptism, the truth to tell—
That followed the lance so cruelly ground—
Which washes away the deadly sins
With which Adam drowned us in death.
Now there is nothing in the whole world
Between us and bliss, except what he took away,
And that is restored in a blessèd hour,
And the grace of God is great enough.

XII

56 'Grace enough that man may have
Who sins then anew, if he repent;
But with sorrow and grief he must implore it,
And endure the penance which is bound thereto.
But sentence of justice, which cannot err,
Saves evermore the innocent.
It is a doom which God never allotted,
That ever the guiltless should be confounded.
The guilty may contrition grasp,
And be through mercy impelled to grace;
But he who never glanced at guile,
With the innocent is safe, and justly.

57 ‘Ry3t, þus, þus I knaw wel in þis cas,
Two men to saue is God by skylle:
Þe ry3twys man schal se hys fa[c]e,
Þe harmle3 haþel schal com hym tylle.
Þe Sauter hyt sat3 þus in a pace:
“Lorde, quo schal klymbe þy hy3 hylle,
Oþer rest wythinne þy holy place?”
Hymself to onsware he is not dylle:
“Hondelynge3 harme þat dyt not ille,
Þat is of hert boþe clene & ly3t,
Þer schal hys step stable stylle.”
Þe innosent is ay saf by ry3t.

58 ‘The ry3twys man also sertayn
Aproche he schal þat proper pyle—
Þat take3 not her lyf in vayne,
Ne glauere3 her nie3bor wyth no gyle.
Of þys ry3twys, sa3 Salamon playn
How kyntly on[o]re con aquyle.
By waye3 ful stre3t h[o] con hym strayn
& scheued hym þe rengne of God a whyle,
As quo says, “Lo, 3on louely yle!
Þou may hit wynne if þou be wy3te.”
Bot hardyly, wythoute peryle,
Þe innosent is ay saue by ry3te.

59 ‘Anende ry3twys men 3et sayt3 a gome—
Dauid in Sauter, if euer 3e se3 hit:
“Lorde, þy seruaunt dra3 neuer to dome,
[F]or non lyuyande to þe is justyfyet.”
Forþy to corte quen þou schal com,
Þer alle oure cause3 schal be tryed,
Alegge þe ry3t þou may be innome
By þys ilke spech I haue asspyed.
Bot He on rode þat blody dyed,
Delfully þur3 honde3 þry3t,
Gyue þe to passe, when þou arte tryed,
By innocens & not by ry3te.

57 'Just, therefore, as in this case I know well,
Is God through judgment to save two men:
The righteous man shall see His face,
The guiltless man shall come to Him.
The Psalter in a passage says it thus:
"Lord, who shall ascend Thy high hill
Or rest within Thy holy place?"
Himself to answer He is not slow:
"He who with hands did not wickedly harm,
Who is of heart both pure and guiltless,
There shall his footstep firmly rest."
The innocent is always justly saved.

58 'The just man, too, undoubtedly
He shall approach that city fair—
Such as consume not their life in vanity,
Nor deceive their neighbor with any guile.
As to this just man, Solomon clearly saw
How fittingly honor (he) did receive.
By ways full straight she did him constrain
And showed him briefly the kingdom of God,
As one who says: "Lo, yon lovely isle!
Thou mayest win it if thou be brave."
But assuredly, without peril,
The innocent is always justly saved.

59 'Concerning righteous men, still says a man—
David in Psalter, if ye ever noted it:
"Lord, Thy servant never to judgment draw,
For to Thee no one living is justified."
Thus when to court thou shalt come,
Where all our causes shall be tried,
If thou plead virtue for thyself, thou mayst be denied
In accordance with this very speech I have espied.
But may He Who died bloody on the rood,
Grievously through the hands pierced,
Grant thee to pass, when thou art tried,
Through innocence and not through right.

60 'Ry3twysly quo con rede
He loke on bok & be awayed
How Jesus Hym welke in areþede,
& burne3 her barne3 vnto Hym brayde
For happe & hele þat fro Hym 3ede;
To touch her chylder þay fayr Hym prayed.
His dessypele3 wyth blame let be Hym bede,
& wyth her resoune3 ful fele restayed.
Jesus þenne hem swetely sayde,
"Do way! Let chylder vnto Me ty3t;
To suche is heuenryche arayed."
Þe innocent is ay saf by ry3t.

XIII

61 'Jesus con calle to Hym Hys mylde,
& sayde Hys ryche no wy3 my3t wynne
Bot he com þyder ry3t as a chylde,
Oþer elle3 neuer more com þerinne.
Harmle3, trwe, & vndefylde,
Wythouten mote oþer mascle of sulpande synne,
Quen such þer cnoken on þe bylde,
Tyt schal hem men þe 3ate vnpynne.
Þer is þe blys þat con not blynne,
Þat þe jueler so3te þur3 perre pres,
& solde alle hys goud, boþe wolen & lynne,
To bye hym a perle wat3 mascelle3.

62 'This makele3 perle, þat bo3t is dere—
Þe joueler gef fore alle hys god—
Is lyke þe reme of heuenesse clere:
So sayde þe Fader of folde & flode.
For hit is wemle3, clene, and clere,
& endele3 rounde, & blyþe of mode,
& commune to alle þat ry3twys were.
Lo, euen in mydde3 my breste hit stode!
My Lorde þe Lombe, þat schede Hys blode,
He py3t hit þere in token of pes.
I rede þe forsake þe worlde wode,
& porchace þy perle maskelles.'

60 'Let him who can rightly read
Look into the Book and be informed
How Jesus walked in an ancient land,
And people quickly drew their children to Him
For the blessing and healing that went forth from Him;
To touch their children they gently prayed Him.
His disciples with reproach bade let Him alone,
And with their objections full many restrained.
Jesus then to them sweetly said,
"Forbear! Suffer children to come unto Me;
For such the Kingdom of Heaven is prepared."
The innocent is always justly saved.

XIII

61 'Jesus called to Him His tender ones,
And said His kingdom no man might win
Unless he came thither just as a child,
Else never more might he come therein.
Sinless, true, and undefiled,
Without speck or spot of polluting sin,
When such knock there at the dwelling,
Quickly for them shall men unbolt the gate.
There is the bliss which doth not cease,
Which the jeweler sought through a mass of gems,
And sold all his goods, both woolen and linen,
To buy him a pearl that was spotless.

62 'This peerless pearl, which is dearly bought—
The jeweler gave all his goods for it—
Is like the Kingdom of Heaven's brightness:
So said the Father of earth and sea.
For it is spotless, pure, and clear,
And round without end and bright of tone,
And common to all who righteous were.
Lo, exactly in the center of my breast its place!
My Lord the Lamb, Who shed His blood,
Firmly He fixed it there in token of peace.
I counsel thee to renounce the foolish world,
And purchase thy pearl spotless.'

63 'O maskeleȝ perle in perleȝ pure,
Þat bereȝ,' quod I, 'þe perle of prys,
Quo formed þe þy fayre fygure,
Þat wroȝt þy wede, He watȝ ful wys.
Þy beaute com neuer of nature;
Pymalyon paynted neuer þy vys;
Ne Arystotel nawþer by hys lettrure
Of carpe þe kynde þese properteȝ.
Þy colour passeȝ þe flour-de-lys,
Þyn angel-hauyng so clene corteȝ—
Breue me, bryȝt, quat kyn offys
Bereȝ þe perle so maskelleȝ?'

64 'My makeleȝ Lambe þat al may bete,'
Quod scho, 'my dere Destyne,
Me ches to Hys make alþaȝ vnmete
Sumtyme semed þat assemble.
When I wente fro yor worlde wete,
He calde me to Hys bonerte:
"Cum hyder to Me, My lemman swete,
For mote ne spot is non in þe."
He gef me myȝt & als bewte;
In Hys blod He wesch my wede on dese
& coronde clene in vergynte,
& pyȝt me in perleȝ maskelleȝ.'

65 'Why, maskelleȝ bryd, þat bryȝt con flambe,
Þat reiateȝ hatȝ so ryche & ryf,
Quat kyn þyng may be þat Lambe
Þat þe wolde wedde vnto Hys vyf?
Ouer alle oþer so hyȝ þou clambe
To lede wyth Hym so ladyly lyf!
So mony a comly onvnder cambe
For Kryst han lyued in much stryf;
& þou con alle þo dere outdryf,
& fro þat maryag al oþer depres,
Al only þyself so stout & styf—
A makeleȝ may & maskelleȝ!'

63 'O spotless pearl in pearls pure,
That wearest,' said I, 'the pearl of price,
He Who fashioned for thee thy fair form,
Who wrought thy raiment, He was all-wise.
Thy beauty from nature never came;
Pygmalion painted never thy face;
Nor did Aristotle either in his writings
Speak of the nature of these properties.
Thy color surpasses the fleur-de-lis,
Thy angel-manner so completely courteous—
Tell me, bright one, what sort of rank
Holdeth the pearl so spotless?'

64 'My peerless Lamb Who can vanquish all,'
Said she, 'my dear Destiny,
Chose me as His spouse, although undeserved
That union formerly did appear.
When I went from your world's woe,
He called me to His blessedness:
"Come hither to Me, my sweet belovèd,
For mote nor speck there is none in thee."
He gave me strength and beauty too;
In His blood He washed my robes at the dais
And crowned me, pure in virginity,
And adorned me in pearls spotless.'

65 'Why, spotless bride, who bright dost shine,
Who hast marks of royalty so rich and rife,
What sort of Being can that Lamb be
Who thee would wed as His wife?
Over all the others thou didst climb so high
To lead with Him so noble a life!
So many a beautiful one wearing comb
For Christ has lived in much conflict;
And thou didst drive all those dear ones out,
And from that marriage push all others down,
All alone thyself so proud and strong—
A peerless maid and spotless!'

XIV

66 'Maskelles,' quod þat myry quene,
'Vnblemyst I am, wythouten blot,
& þat may I wyth mensk menteene.
Bot "makeleȝ quene" þenne sade I not.
Þe Lambes vyueȝ in blysse we bene,
A hondred & forty þowsande flot,
As in þe Apocalyppeȝ hit is sene.
Sant John hem syȝ al in a knot
On þe hyl of Syon, þat semly clot.
Þe apostel hem segh in gostly drem,
Arayed to þe weddyng in þat hyl coppe,
Þe nwe cyte o Jerusalem.

67 'Of Jerusalem I in speche spelle.
If þou wyl knaw what kyn He be—
My Lombe, my Lorde, my dere Juelle,
My Joy, my Blys, my Lemman fre—
Þe profete Ysaye of Hym con melle,
Pitously of Hys debonerte:
"Þat gloryous Gyltleȝ þat mon con quelle
Wythouten any sake of felonye,
As a schep to þe slaȝt þer lad watȝ He,
& as lombe þat clypper in lande [n]e[m],
So closed He Hys mouth fro vch query
Quen Jueȝ Hym iugged in Jerusalem."

68 'In Jerusalem watȝ my Lemman slayn,
& rent on rode wyth boyeȝ bolde.
Al oure baleȝ to bere ful bayn,
He toke on Hymself our careȝ colde.
Wyth boffeteȝ watȝ Hys face flayn
Þat watȝ so fayr on to byholde.
For synne He set Hymself in vayn,
Þat neuer hade non Hymself to wolde.
For vus He lette Hym flyȝe & folde
& brede vpon a bostwys bem.
As meke as lomp þat no playnt tolde,
For vus He swalt in Jerusalem.

XIV

66 'Spotless,' said that lovely queen,
'Unblemished am I, without a blot,
And that may I with dignity maintain.
But "peerless queen" then said I not.
The Lamb's spouses in bliss are we,
A hundred and forty thousand flock,
As in the Apocalypse it is seen.
Saint John saw them all in a throng
On the Hill of Sion, that beautiful mount.
The Apostle saw them in ghostly dream,
Arrayed for the wedding on that hilltop,
The new City of Jerusalem.

67 'Of Jerusalem I in speech discourse.
If thou wilt know what kind He is—
My Lamb, my Lord, my dear Jewel,
My Joy, my Bliss, my noble Love—
The prophet Isaias did speak of Him,
Of His meekness, compassionately:
"That glorious guiltless One Whom men did kill
Without any cause of felony,
As a sheep to the slaughter there led was He,
And as lamb that the shearer seizes on heath,
So closed He His mouth against each questioning
When Jews judged Him in Jerusalem."

68 'In Jerusalem was my Belovèd slain,
And, with malefactors, rent on rood.
Full ready all our woes to bear,
He took on Himself our cares cold.
With buffets was His face flayed
Which was so fair to look upon.
Because of sin He set Himself at nought,
Who never Himself had any to subdue.
For us He let Himself be scourged and bent
And stretched upon a rude cross.
As meek as lamb which uttered no plaint,
For us He died in Jerusalem.

69 'Jerusalem, Jordan, & Galalye—
Þer as baptysed þe goude Saynt John,
His wordeȝ acorded to Ysaye.
When Jesus con to hym warde gon,
He sayde of Hym þys professye:
"Lo, Godeȝ Lombe as trwe as ston,
Þat dotȝ away þe synneȝ dryȝe
Þat alle þys worlde hatȝ wroȝt vpon,
Hymself ne wroȝt neuer ȝet non
Wheþer on Hymself He con al clem.
Hys generacyoun quo recen con,
Þat dyȝed for vus in Jerusalem?"

70 'In Jerusalem þus my Lemman swatte,
Twyeȝ for lombe watȝ taken þare,
By trw recorde of ayþer prophete,
For mode so meke & al Hys fare.
Þe þryde tyme is þerto ful mete,
In Apokalypeȝ wryten ful ȝare:
In mydeȝ þe trone, þere saynteȝ sete,
Þe apostel John Hym saytȝ as bare
Lesande þe boke with leueȝ sware,
Þere seuen syngnetteȝ wern sette in seme;
& at þat syȝt vche douth con dare,
In helle, in erþe, & Jerusalem.

XV

71 'Thys Jerusalem Lombe hade neuer pechche
Of oþer huee bot quyt jolyf.
Þat mot ne masklle moȝt on streche
For wolle quyte so ronk & ryf.
Forþy vche saule þat hade neuer teche
Is to þat Lombe a worthyly wyf,
& þaȝ vch day a store He feche,
Among vus commeȝ non oþer strot ne stryf,
Bot vchon enle we wolde were fyf—
Þe mo þe myryer, so God me blesse!
In compayny gret our luf con þryf
In honour more, & neuer þelesse.

69 'Jerusalem, Jordan, and Galilee—
There as the good Saint John baptized,
His words accorded with Isaias.
When Jesus did toward him go,
He uttered of Him this prophecy:
"Behold the Lamb of God, as true as stone,
Who doth take away the iniquities
Which all this world hath committed,
Yet He Himself wrought never one
Which on Himself He did wholly smear.
His generation who can recount,
Who died for us in Jerusalem?"

70 'In Jerusalem thus my Belovèd bled,
Twice as a Lamb was accounted there,
By record true of each prophet,
Because of spirit so meek and all His ways.
The third time is fully equal thereto,
In the Apocalypse written quite clearly:
In the midst of the throne, where sat the saints,
The Apostle John most plainly reports Him
Opening the Book with pages square,
Where seven seals were set in line;
And at that sight each creature worshipped Him,
In hell, in earth, and Jerusalem.

XV

71 'This Jerusalem Lamb had never a shred
Of other hue save beautiful white.
Him neither spot nor speck could reach
Because of the white wool so rich and rife.
Therefore each soul that had never a mark
Is to that Lamb a worthy spouse,
And though each day He may fetch a great number,
Among us comes neither confusion nor strife,
But each one singly we would were five—
The more the merrier, so God me bless!
In a company large our love doth thrive
In honour more, and never the less.

72 'Lasse of blysse may non vus bryng
Þat beren þys perle vpon oure bereste,
For þay of mote couþe neuer mynge
Of spotleȝ perleȝ þa beren þe creste.
Alþaȝ oure corses in clotteȝ clynge,
& ȝe remen for rauþe wythouten reste,
We þurȝoutly hauen cnawyng.
Of o[n] deth ful oure hope is drest.
Þe Lo[m]be vus gladeȝ, oure care is kest,
He myrþes vus alle at vch a mes.
Vchoneȝ blysse is breme & beste,
& neuer oneȝ honour ȝet neuer þeles.

73 'Lest les þou leue my tale farande,
In Appocalyppece is wryten in wro:
"I seghe," says John, "þa Loumbe Hym stande
On þe mount of Syon ful þryuen & þro,
& wyth Hym maydenneȝ an hundreþe þowsande,
& fowre & forty þowsande mo.
On alle her forhedeȝ wryten I fande
Þe Lombeȝ Nome, Hys Fadereȝ also.
A hue fro heuen I herde þoo,
Lyk flodeȝ fele laden runnen on resse,
& as þunder þroweȝ in torreȝ blo,
Þat lote, I leue, watȝ neuer þe les.

74 ' "Nauþeles, þaȝ hit schowted scharpe,
& ledden loude alþaȝ hit were,
A note ful nwe I herde hem warpe.
To lysten þat watȝ ful lufly dere!
As harporeȝ harpen in her harpe,
Þat nwe songe þay songen ful cler,
In sounande noteȝ a gentyl carpe!
Ful fayre þe modeȝ þay fonge in fere
Ryȝt byfore Godeȝ chayere;
& þe fowre besteȝ þat Hym obes,
& þe aldermen so sadde of chere,
Her songe þay songen, neuer þe les.

72 'Less of bliss no one can recall to us
Who bear this pearl upon our breast,
For with a trifle they could never be concerned
Who wear the best of spotless pearls.
Although in clods our corpses decay,
And ye lament in grief without repose,
We throughout have consciousness.
Our hope of one death is established fully.
The Lamb gladdens us, our care is cast away,
He rejoices us all at every course of the feast.
Each one's happiness is glorious and best,
And yet never one's honor any the less.

73 'Lest thou believe less my fitting account,
In Apocalypse it is written in a passage:
"I saw," says John, "the Lamb take His stand
On the Mount of Sion, full vigorous and strong,
And with Him maidens one hundred thousand,
And four and forty thousand more.
On all their foreheads written I found
The Lamb's Name, His Father's also.
A cry from Heaven I then did hear,
Like the sound of many waters run together in a rush,
And as thunder rolls in blue-black tors,
That sound, I believe, was never the less.

74 ' "Nevertheless, though it shouted piercingly,
And outcry loud although it was,
I heard them sound forth a note quite new.
To hear *that* was most pleasingly dear!
As harpers harp upon their harps,
That new song they sang full clear,
In resounding tones—a noble utterance!
Full fair in unison they caught the modes
Right before the throne of God;
And the four beasts that Him obey,
And the ancients so serious of mien,
Their song they sang, nevertheless.

75 '"Nowþelese, non watȝ neuer so quoynt,
For alle þe crafteȝ þat euer þay knewe,
Þat of þat songe myȝt synge a poynt
Bot þat meyny. Þe Lombe þay swe,
For þay arn boȝt fro þe vrþe aloynte
As newe fryt to God ful due,
& to þe gentyl Lombe hit arn anioynt
As lyk to Hymself of lote & hwe,
For neuer lesyng ne tale vntrwe
Ne towched her tonge for no dysstresse."
Þat moteles meyny may neuer remwe
Fro þat maskeleȝ Mayster—neuer þe les.'

76 'Neuer þe les let be my þonc,'
Quod I, 'my perle, þaȝ I appose.
I schulde not tempte þy wyt so wlonc
To Krysteȝ chambre þat art ichose.
I am bot mokke & mul among,
& þou so ryche a reken rose
& bydeȝ here by þys blysful bonc,
Þer lyueȝ lyste may neuer lose.
Now, hynde, þat sympelnesse coneȝ enclose,
I wolde þe aske a þynge expresse,
& þaȝ I be bustwys as a blose,
Let my bone vayl, neuer þe lese.

XVI

77 'Neuer þe lese cler I yow bycalle—
If ȝe con se hyt be to done—
As þou art gloryous, wythouten galle,
Wythnay þou neuer my ruful bone.
Haf ȝe no woneȝ in castel-walle,
Ne maner þer ȝe may mete & won?
Þou telleȝ me of Jerusalem, the ryche ryalle,
Þer Dauid dere watȝ dyȝt on trone;
Bot by þyse holteȝ hit con not hone,
Bot in Judee hit is, þat noble note.
As ȝe ar maskeleȝ vnder mone,
Your woneȝ schulde be wythouten mote.

75 ' "Nevertheless, none was ever so skilled,
Despite all the arts that ever they knew,
Who of that song might sing a note
Except that company. They follow the Lamb,
For they are purchased from the earth afar
As first fruit to God full due,
And to the gentle Lamb are they united
As like to Him in appearance and hue,
For never lie nor tale untrue
Ever touched their tongue because of any distress."
That spotless company can never depart
From that spotless Master—never the less.'

76 'Never the less let my pardon be,
My pearl,' said I, 'though I questions pose.
I should not test thy wit so fine
Who to Christ's chamber art elect.
I am but mingled with muck and mold,
And thou so rich a perfect rose
And abidest here near this blissful bank,
Where joy of life may never die.
Now, gracious one, who dost simplicity enshrine,
I would ask thee an explicit thing,
And though I be rude as a clod,
Let my prayer avail nevertheless.

XVI

77 'Nevertheless clearly I call upon you,
Whether you can see that it be fulfilled.
Since thou art glorious, without spite,
Deny thou never my wistful prayer.
Have ye no homes within castle wall,
Nor manor where ye may meet and dwell?
Thou tellest me of Jerusalem, the kingdom royal,
Where David dear was established on throne;
But by these groves it did not stand,
But in Juda it is, that noble city.
Since ye are spotless under the moon,
Your dwellings should be without a flaw.

78 'Þys motele3 meyny þou cone3 of mele,
Of þousande3 þry3t so gret a route,
A gret cete—for 3e arn fele—
Yow byhod haue, wythouten doute.
So cumly a pakke of joly juele,
Wer euel don schulde ly3 þeroute.
& by þyse bonke3 þer I con gele—
& I se no bygyng nawhere aboute—
I trowe alone 3e lenge & loute
To loke on þe glory of þys grac[i]ous gote.
If þou hat3 oþer lygynge3 stoute,
Now tech me to þat myry mote.'

79 'That mote þou mene3 in Judy londe,'
Þat specyal spyce þen to me spakk,
'Þat is þe cyte þat þe Lombe con fonde
To soffer inne sor for mane3 sake—
Þe olde Jerusalem to vnderstonde,
For þere þe olde gulte wat3 don to slake;
Bot þe nwe, þat ly3t of Gode3 sonde,
Þe apostel in Apocallypce in theme con take.
Þe Lompe þer wythouten spotte3 blake
Hat3 feryed þyder Hys fayre flote;
& as Hys flok is wythouten flake,
So is Hys mote wythouten moote.

80 'Of motes two, to carpe clene,
& Jerusalem hy3t boþe, nawþeles—
Þat nys to yow no more to mene
Bot "Cete of God" oþer "Sy3t of Pes."
In þat on oure pes wat3 mad at ene;
Wyth payne to suffer þe Lombe hit chese.
In þat oþer is no3t bot pes to glene,
Þat ay schal laste wythouten reles.
Þat is þe bor3 þat we to pres
Fro þat oure f[l]es[c]h be layd to rote;
Þer glory & blysse schal euer encres
To þe meyny þat is wythouten mote.'

78 'This flawless company thou speakest of,
Of thousands massed, so great a throng,
A great city—for ye are many—
You ought to have, without a doubt.
So beautiful a collection of jewels fair,
'Twere ill done should they lodge outside.
And along these banks where I do tarry—
And I see no buildings anywhere about—
I suppose alone you linger and bend
To gaze upon the glory of this gracious stream.
If thou hast other lodgings strong,
Now direct me to that joyous city.'

79 'That city thou meanest in Juda-land,'
That peerless one then said to me,
'That is the city which the Lamb sought out
To suffer in sorely for mankind's sake—
The *old* Jerusalem, that is to say,
For there the ancient sin was made to subside;
But the *new*, which descended through God's command,
The Apostle in Apocalypse as theme did take.
There the Lamb without black flecks
Has thither led His beauteous train,
And as His flock is without blemish,
So is His city without defect.

80 'Of cities, *two*, to speak precisely,
And both called Jerusalem, nevertheless—
Which is to you no more in meaning
Than "City of God" or "Vision of Peace."
In the one our peace was formerly made;
With pain to suffer, the Lamb did choose it.
In the other is nought but peace to glean,
Which shall last forever without surcease.
That is the city toward which we hasten
From the time our flesh is laid to rot;
There glory and bliss shall ever increase
For the company which is without a spot.'

81 'Moteleȝ may so meke & mylde,'
Þen sayde I to þat lufly flor,
'Bryng me to þat bygly bylde,
& let me se þy blysful bor.'
Þat schene sayde: 'Þat God wyl schylde!
Þou may not enter wythinne Hys tor;
Bot of þe Lombe I haue þe aquylde
For a syȝt þerof, þurȝ gret fauor.
Vtwyth to se þat clene cloystor
Þou may, bot inwyth not a fote
To strech in þe strete þou hatȝ no vygour
Bot þou wer clene, wythouten mote.

XVII

82 'If I þis mote þe schal vnhyde,
Bow vp towarde þys borneȝ heued,
& I anendeȝ þe on þis syde
Schal sve tyl þou to a hil be veued.'
Þen wolde [I] no lenger byde,
Bot lurked by launceȝ so lufly leued,
Tyl on a hyl þat I asspyed,
& blusched on þe burghe as I forth dreued.
Byȝonde þe brok fro me warde keued,
Þat schyrrer þen sunne wyth schafteȝ schon;
In þe Apokalypce is þe fasoun preued,
As deuyseȝ hit, þe apostel John.

83 As John þe apostel hit syȝ wyth syȝt,
I syȝe þat cyty of gret renoun,
Jerusalem so nwe & ryally dyȝt,
As hit watȝ lyȝt fro þe heuen adoun.
Þe borȝ watȝ al of brende golde bryȝt,
As glemande glas burnist broun,
Wyth gentyl gemmeȝ anvnder pyȝt,
Wyth banteleȝ twelue on basyng boun,
Þe foundementeȝ twelue of riche tenoun;
Vch tabelment watȝ a serlypeȝ ston.
As derely deuyseȝ þis ilk toun
In Apocalyppeȝ, þe apostel John.

81 'Spotless maid so meek and mild,'
Then said I to that lovely flower,
'Bring me to that pleasant dwelling,
And let me see thy glad abode.'
That shining one said: '*That* God will thwart!
Thou mayest not enter within His tower;
But from the Lamb I have acquired for thee permission
For a sight thereof, by favor great.
Outside to see that pure enclosure
Thou mayest, but within, not a foot
Hast thou any power to extend in the street
Except thou wert stainless, without a spot.

XVII

82 'If I this city am to reveal to thee,
Bend upward toward this river's head,
And I on this side opposite thee
Shall follow till thou be in sight of a hill.'
Then no longer would I delay,
But stole on through the branches so beautifully leaved,
Till on a hill I espied it,
And gazed on the city as I forward pressed.
Beyond the brook from me low-placed,
It shone with rays brighter than the sun;
In the Apocalypse is the manner shown,
As describes it the Apostle John.

83 As John the Apostle saw it in a vision,
I saw that city of great renown,
Jerusalem so new and royally adorned,
As it was descended from the heavens down.
The city was all of pure, shining gold,
Like gleaming crystal burnished bright,
With precious jewels set beneath,
With bantels twelve on the ready base,
The foundations twelve with joining rich;
Every plinth was a separate stone.
Thus excellently describes this very city,
In Apocalypse, the Apostle John.

84 As [John] þise stone3 in writ con nemme,
I knew þe name after his tale
Jasper hy3t þe fyrst gemme
Þat I on þe fyrst basse con wale—
He glente grene in þe lowest hemme;
Saffer helde þe secounde stale;
Þe calsydoyne þenne wythouten wemme
In þe þryd table con purly pale;
Þe emerade þe furþe so grene of scale;
Þe sardonyse þe fyfþe ston;
Þe sexte þe rybe—he con hit wale
In þe Apocalyppce, þe apostel John.

85 Ȝet joyned John þe crysolyt,
Þe seuenþe gemme in fundament;
Þe a3tþe þe beryl cler & quyt;
Þe topasye twynne-how þe nente endent;
Þe crysopase þe tenþe is ty3t;
Þe jacyngh þe enleuenþe gent;
Þe twelfþe—þe gentyleste in vch a plyt—
Þe amatyst purpre wyth ynde blente.
Þe wal abof þe bantels bent
O jasporye as glas þat glysnande schon;
I knew hit by his deuysement
In þe Apocalyppe3, þe apostel John.

86 As John deuysed, 3et sa3 I þare
Þise twelue degres wern brode & stayre;
Þe cyte stod abof ful sware,
As longe as brode, as hy3e ful fayre;
Þe strete3 of golde as glasse, al bare,
Þe wal of jasper þat glent as glayre.
Þe wone3 wythinne enurned ware
Wyth alle kynne3 perre þat mo3t repayre.
Þenne helde vch sware of þis manayre
Twelue forlonge space er euer hit fon
Of he3t, of brede, of lenþe, to cayre,
For meten hit sy3 þe apostel John.

84 Since John these stones in Scripture named,
I knew the name through his account
Jasper the first gem was called
Which I on the first foundation did discern—
On the lowest border it glistened green;
Sapphire held the second position;
The chalcedony then without a flaw
In the third table translucently paled;
The emerald the fourth, so green of scale;
The sardonyx the fifth stone;
The sixth the ruby—he singled it out
In the Apocalypse, the Apostle John.

85 Further added John the chrysolite,
The seventh gem in the foundation;
The eighth the beryl clear and white;
The topaz, twi-hued, marked the ninth;
The chrysoprase the tenth is set;
The jacinth the noble eleventh;
The twelfth—the noblest in every state—
The amethyst purple with deep blue blent.
Above the bantels extended the wall
Of jasper that glistening shone like glass;
I knew it by his description
In the Apocalypse, the Apostle John.

86 As John divined, I, too, envisioned there
These twelve tiers were broad and steep;
The city stood above foursquare,
As long as broad, full fair as high;
The streets—all bare—of gold like glass,
The wall of jasper that glistened like glaze.
Within, the dwellings were adorned
With all manner of gems that might be gathered.
Then each square of this city held
Twelve furlongs space ere ever it ceased
To reach in height, in breadth, in length,
For saw it measured the Apostle John.

XVIII

87 As John hym wryteȝ, ȝet more I syȝe:
Vch pane of þat place had þre ȝateȝ.
So twelue in pourseut I con asspye,
Þe portaleȝ pyked of rych plateȝ,
& vch ȝate of a margyrye,
A parfyt perle þat neuer fateȝ.
Vchon in scrypture a name con plye
Of Israel barneȝ, folewande her dateȝ,
Þat is to say, as her byrþ whateȝ;
Þe aldest ay fyrst þeron watȝ done.
Such lyȝt þer lemed in alle þe strateȝ,
Hem nedde nawþer sunne ne mone.

88 Of sunne ne mone had þay no nede;
Þe Self God watȝ her lombe lyȝt,
Þe Lombe her lantyrne wythouten drede;
Þurȝ Hym blysned þe borȝ al bryȝt.
Þurȝ woȝe & won my lokyng ȝede,
For, sotyle cler, noȝt lette no lyȝt.
Þe hyȝe trone þer moȝt ȝe hede,
Wyth alle þe apparaylmente vmbepyȝte,
As John þe appostel in termeȝ tyȝte;
Þe Hyȝe Godeȝ Self hit set vpone.
A reuer of þe trone þer ran outryȝte—
Watȝ bryȝter þen boþe þe sunne & mone.

89 Sunne ne mone schon neuer so swete!
A þat foysoun-flode out of þat flet;
Swyþe hit swange þurȝ vch a strete,
Wythouten fylþe oþer galle oþer glet.
Kyrk þerinne watȝ non ȝete—
Chapel ne temple þat euer watȝ set—
Þe Almyȝty watȝ her mynster mete,
Þe Lombe, þe Sakerfyse, þer to reget.
Þe ȝateȝ stoken watȝ neuer ȝet,
Bot euermore vpen at vche a lone;
Þer entreȝ non to take reset
Þat bereȝ any spot anvnde[r] mone.

XVIII

87 As John himself writes, yet more I saw:
Each side of that place had three gates.
Thus twelve in succession did I espy,
The gates adorned with precious metals,
And each portal of one pearl,
A perfect pearl which never fades.
Each one in writing did mark a name
Of the children of Israel, following their dates.
That is to say, according to their fortunes of birth;
The oldest thereon ever first was placed.
Such light there gleamed in all the streets,
They needed neither sun nor moon.

88 Of sun or moon they had no need;
God Himself was their lamplight,
The Lamb their lantern without dread;
Through Him the city shone all bright.
Through wall and dwelling my vision went,
For, subtly clear, nought stopped any light.
The high throne there you might perceive,
With all the hosts of Heaven ranged about,
As John the Apostle expounded clearly;
The High God Himself sat upon it.
From the throne straight forth there ran a river—
'Twas brighter than both the sun and moon.

89 Sun or moon never shone so bright!
Ever that copious flood flowed out from that,
Strongly it coursed through every street,
Free from filth or scum or slime.
Church therein there was none, moreover—
No chapel or temple that ever was built.
The Almighty was their minster meet,
The Lamb, the Sacrifice, there to redeem.
The gates were never fastened yet,
But evermore open at every lane;
There enters no one refuge to obtain
Who bears any stain under the moon.

90 The mone may þerof acroche no my3te;
To spotty ho is, of body to grym.
& also þer ne is neuer ny3t
What schulde þe mone þer compas clym?
& to euen wyth þat worþly ly3t
Þat schyne3 vpon þe broke3 brym,
Þe planete3 arn in to pouer a ply3t,
& þe self sunne ful fer to dym.
Aboute þat water arn tres ful schym,
Þat twelue fryte3 of lyf con bere ful sone;
Twelue syþe3 on 3er þay beren ful frym,
& renowle3 nwe in vche a mone.

91 Anvnder mone so gret merwayle
No fleschly hert ne my3t endeure
As quen I blusched vpon þat ba[y]l[e],
So ferly þerof wat3 þe fasure.
I stod as stylle as dased quayle
For ferly of þat freuch fygure,
Þat felde I nawþer reste ne trauayle
So wat3 I rauyste wyth glymme pure.
For I dar say wyth conciens sure,
Hade bodyly burne abiden þat bone,
Þa3 alle clerke3 hym hade in cure,
His lyf wer loste anvnder mone.

XIX

92 Ry3t as þe maynful mone con rys
Er þenne þe day-glem dryue al doun,
So sodanly on a wonder wyse,
I wat3 war of a prosessyoun.
Þis noble cite of ryche enpr[y]se
Wat3 sodanly ful wythouten sommoun
Of such vergyne3 in þe same gyse
Þat wat3 my blysful anvnder croun.
& coronde wern alle of þe same fasoun,
Depaynt in perle3 & wede3 qwyte;
In vchone3 breste wat3 bounden boun
Þe blysful perle wythouten delyt.

90 The moon may therefrom no power detract;
Too spotty it is, of substance too crude.
And besides, where it is never night
Why should the moon climb a circuit there?
And to be equal to that precious light
Which shines upon the river's brim,
The planets are in too poor a plight,
And the sun itself full far too dim.
All around that river are trees full bright,
Which twelve fruits of life can quickly bear;
Twelve times a year in full strength they yield,
And renew afresh at every moon.

91 Beneath the moon so great a marvel
No human heart might ever endure
As when I gazed upon that domain,
So amazing was the fashioning thereof.
I stood as still as dazèd quail
For wonder at that noble scene,
So that neither rest nor weariness I felt
So raptured was I with radiance pure.
For I dare say with conscience sure,
Had a person in body survived that boon,
Though all the learnèd men had him in care,
His life would be lost beneath the moon.

XIX

92 Just as the moon in full might doth rise
Before the day-gleam sinketh wholly down,
So, suddenly, in a wondrous way,
I was aware of a procession.
This noble city of great emprise
Was, without summoning, suddenly full
Of such virgins, in the same guise,
As was my blessèd crownèd one.
And in the same fashion all were crowned,
Arrayed in pearls and raiment white;
On each one's breast was fixed the destined,
The blessèd pearl beyond delight.

93 Wyth gret delyt þay glod in fere
On golden gateȝ þat glent as glasse.
Hundreth þowsandeȝ I wot þer were,
& alle in sute her liureȝ wasse.
Tor to knaw þe gladdest chere!
Þe Lombe byfore con proudly passe,
Wyth horneȝ seuen of red g[ol]de cler;
As praysed perleȝ His wedeȝ wasse.
Towarde þe throne þay trone a tras;
Þaȝ þay wern fele, no pres in plyt,
Bot mylde as maydeneȝ seme at Mas,
So droȝ þay forth wyth gret delyt.

94 Delyt þat Hys come encroched,
To much hit were of for to melle.
Þise aldermen, quen He aproched,
Grouelyng to His fete þay felle;
Legyounes of aungeleȝ togeder uoched
Þer kesten ensens of swete smelle;
Þen glory & gle watȝ nwe abroched—
Al songe to loue þat gay Juelle!
Þe steuen moȝt stryke þurȝ vrþe to helle,
Þat þe Vertues of Heuen of joye endyte,
To loue þe Lombe His meyny in melle.
Iwysse I laȝt a gret delyt!

95 Delit—þe Lombe for to deuise—
Wyth much meruayle in mynde went.
Best watȝ He, blyþest, & moste to pryse,
Þat euer I herde of speche spent,
So worþly whyt wern wedeȝ Hys,
His lokeȝ symple, Hymself so gent!
Bot a wounde ful wyde & weete con wyse
Anende Hys hert, þurȝ hyde torente;
Of Hys quyte syde His blod outsprent.
Alas, þoȝt I, who did þat spyt?
Ani breste for bale aȝt haf forbrent
Er he þerto hade had delyt.

93 With great delight, in company they glided
O'er golden streets which gleamed like glass.
A hundred thousand there were, I know,
And all alike was their apparel.
Difficult to know the happiest face!
The Lamb before did proudly pass,
With seven horns of clear red gold;
Like prizèd pearls His garments were.
Toward the throne they went in retinue;
Though many they were, no press in the plight,
But gentle as seemly maidens at Mass,
So they advanced with great delight.

94 The delight which His approach induced,
Too much 'twould be to speak about.
These ancients, when He drew near,
Prostrate at His feet they fell;
Legions of angels together called
There scattered incense of fragrance sweet;
Then were glory and joy poured forth anew—
All sang to praise that radiant Jewel!
Through earth to hell might strike the sound
Which the Virtues of Heaven with joy send forth
To praise the Lamb amidst His train.
In truth, I felt a great delight!

95 Delight—the Lamb to contemplate—
As well as much wonder entered my mind.
Best was He, most joyous, and most to prize
That ever I heard speech spent upon,
So fittingly white His garments were,
His expression artless, He Himself so noble!
But a wound full wide and wet did run
Close to His heart, through skin all rent;
From His white side His blood gushed forth.
Alas, thought I, who did that wrong?
Any breast ought to have been consumed with woe
Before therein it had had delight.

96 The Lombe delyt non lyste to wene!
Þaȝ He were hurt & wounde hade,
In His sembelaunt watȝ neuer sene,
So wern His glenteȝ gloryous glade.
I loked among His meyny schene
How þay wyth lyf wern laste & lade.
Þen saȝ I þer my lyttel quene
Þat I wende had standen by me in sclade.
Lorde, much of mirþe watȝ þat ho made
Among her fereȝ, þat watȝ so quyt!
Þat syȝt me gart to þenk to wade
For luf-longyng in gret delyt.

XX

97 Delyt me drof in yȝe & ere!
My maneȝ mynde to maddyng malte
Quen I seȝ my frely. I wolde be þere,
Byȝonde þe water, þaȝ ho were walte.
I þoȝt (þat noþyng myȝt me dere)
To fech me bur & take me halte,
& to start in þe strem—schulde non me stere—
To swymme þe remnaunt þaȝ I þer swalte.
Bot of þat munt I watȝ bitalt!
When I schulde start in þe strem astraye,
Out of þat caste I watȝ bycalt—
Hit watȝ not at my Prynceȝ paye.

98 Hit payed Hym not þat I so flonc
Ouer meruelous mereȝ, so mad arayde;
Of raas þaȝ I were rasch & ronk,
Ȝet rapely þerinne I watȝ restayed,
For, ryȝt as I sparred vnto þe bonc,
Þat brathe out of my drem me brayde.
Þen wakned I in þat erber wlonk;
My hede vpon þat hylle watȝ layde
Þer-as my perle to grounde strayd.
I raxled & fel in gret affray,
&, sykyng, to myself I sayd,
'Now al be to þat Pryncеȝ paye.'

96 The Lamb's delight let no one hope to imagine!
Though He was hurt and had a wound,
In His expression it was never seen,
His glances were so gloriously glad.
I beheld among His retinue bright
How they superabounded with life.
Then saw I there my little queen
Who I thought had been standing near me in the dale.
Lord, much merriment it was that she made
Among her companions, who was so white!
That sight caused me to think of crossing
For love-longing in great delight.

XX

97 Delight pursued me in eye and ear!
My mortal mind dissolved in madness
When I saw my beautiful one. I wanted to be there,
Beyond the water, though she were vexed.
I proposed (so that nothing might hinder me)
To work up speed for myself and to spring high,
And—should no one check me—to dive into the stream,
To swim the rest though I there died.
But I was shaken from that resolve!
When I was about to leap lawlessly into the stream,
Out of that venture I was called away—
It was not in accord with my Prince's will.

98 It pleased Him not that I thus plunged
Across miraculous boundaries, so madly inclined;
In the onrush though I was rash and proud,
Yet swiftly was I restrained therein,
For just as I charged up to the bank,
That violence wrenched me out of my dream.
Then wakened I in that garden fair;
My head upon that hill was laid
Where my pearl to ground had strayed.
I started up and fell into great confusion,
And, grieving, to myself I said,
'Now all be to that Prince's will!'

99 Me payed ful ille to be outfleme
So sodenly of þat fayre regioun,
Fro alle þo syȝteȝ so quyke & queme.
A longeyng heuy me strok in swone,
& rewfully þenne I con to reme:
'O perle,' quod I, 'of rych renoun,
So watȝ hit me dere þat þou con deme
In þys veray avysyoun!
If hit be ueray & soth sermoun
Þat þou so stykeȝ in garlande gay,
So wel is me in þys doel-doungoun
Þat þou art to þat Prynces paye.'

100 To þat Prynceȝ paye hade I ay bente,
& ȝerned no more þen watȝ me geuen,
& halden me þer in trwe entent
As þe perle me prayed, þat watȝ so þryuen,
As helde, drawen to Goddeȝ present,
To mo of His mysterys I hade ben dryuen.
Bot ay wolde man of happe more hente
Þen moȝten by ryȝt vpon hem clyuen.
Þerfore my ioye watȝ sone toriuen,
& I kaste of kyþeȝ þat lasteȝ aye.
Lorde, mad hit arn þat agayn þe stryuen,
Oþer proferen þe oȝt agayn þy paye.

101 To pay þe Prince oþer sete saȝte,
Hit is ful eþe to þe god Krystyin,
For I haf founden Hym boþe day & naȝte
A God, a Lorde, a Frende ful fyin.
Ouer þis hyul þis lote I laȝte,
For pyty of my perle enclyin.
& syþen to God I hit bytaȝte
In Krysteȝ dere blessyng & myn,
Þat in þe forme of bred & wyn
Þe preste vus scheweȝ vch a daye.
He gef vus to be His homly hyne
Ande precious perleȝ vnto His pay. Amen. Amen.

99 Full ill it pleased me to be expelled
So suddenly from that region fair,
From all those visions so vivid and dear.
An oppressive longing struck me into a swoon,
And afterward, repentantly, I cried aloud:
'O pearl,' said I, 'of rich renown,
It was so precious to me, what thou didst reveal
In this true vision!
If it be teaching real and true
That thou are thus set in garland gay,
Then happy am I in this prison of sorrow
That thou art to that Prince's pleasure.'

100 To that Prince's will had I always bowed,
And craved no more than to me was given,
And held me there in true intent
As the pearl me urged, who was so blessed,
Thus disposed, drawn to God's Presence,
To more of His mysteries I would have been led.
But ever would men seize more of good fortune
Than may by right belong to them.
Therefore my joy was shattered soon,
And I hurled from realms which ever endure.
Lord, mad are they who strive against Thee,
Or proffer Thee aught against Thy will.

101 To please the Prince or be reconciled,
It is quite easy for the good Christian,
For I have found Him both day and night
A God, a Lord, a Friend most noble.
Upon this hill this destiny I grasped,
Prostrate in sorrow for my pearl.
And afterward to God I gave it up
In the dear blessing and memory of Christ,
Whom, in the form of bread and wine,
The priest shows to us every day.
He gave us to be His servants dear
And unto His pleasure precious pearls. Amen. Amen.

Abbreviations

AN	Anglo-Norman
E.E.T.S.	Early English Text Society
EME	Early Middle English
G.[1]	Sir Israel Gollancz, *Pearl . . . with Modern Rendering,* ed. 1891
G.[2]	Sir Israel Gollancz, *Pearl . . . with Modern Rendering,* ed. 1921
GO.	E. V. Gordon, *Pearl,* ed. 1953
Gr.	Greek
L.	Latin
LG	Low German
M.	Richard Morris, *Early English Alliterative Poems,* ed. 1864
M.Du.	Middle Dutch
ME	Middle English
MHG	Middle High German
MLG	Middle Low German
MLN	*Modern Language Notes* (Baltimore, 1886 *et seq.*)
MLR	*Modern Language Review* (Cambridge, 1905 *et seq.*)
MnE	Modern English
MS	photographic facsimile (now at the College of Saint Elizabeth) of *The Pearl,* MS Cotton Nero A.x (f. 37*a*-55*b*), from the original manuscript in the Cotton collection in the British Museum
NED	see below, *OED*
NWM	North-West Midland
O.	Charles G. Osgood, *The Pearl,* ed. 1906
OE	Old English
OED	*The Oxford English Dictionary,* ed. James A. H. Murray and others (Oxford, 1888 *et seq.*). Until 1933, when it was reissued with a new title page as above, this work was entitled *A New English Dictionary on Historical Principles* (in brief, *NED*).
OF	Old French
O.Fris.	Old Frisian

ON	Old Norse
ONF	Old North French
PMLA	*Publications of the Modern Language Association* (Baltimore; Cambridge, Mass.; then New York, 1884 *et seq.*)
Scand.	Scandinavian
STR-BR	*A Middle English Dictionary*, ed. F. H. Stratmann; revised and enlarged by Henry Bradley (Oxford, 1891)
WM	West Midland

The usual dictionary abbreviations are used for parts of speech. Editions of *The Pearl* referred to above in brief are listed in detail in the Bibliography.

Textual Emendations

In the Explanatory Notes will be found the reasons for rejecting a number of emendations made in critical articles upon the poem and in the editions specified, particularly those of M., G., GO., and O.

MS Readings	Emendations
25. —t (*blurred, except final* t)	[mo]t, O.
26. runnen	runne, G.[1]
35. sprygande	spryg ande
49. spennd	spenn[e]d, M.
60. precos	prec[i]os, M.
95. gracos	grac[i]os, O.
103. feier	fei[r]er, G.[1]
106. bnkes	b[o]nkes, O.
115. A	A[s], G.[1]
192. precos	prec[i]os, M.
229. pyse	p[ec]e, Fick
235. pfered	p[ro]fered, M.
235. spyce	sp[e]ce, G.[1]
302. loueȝ (and 308)	l[e]ueȝ, G.[1]
309. īs	is, O.
363. rapely raue	rapely [I] raue, G.[1]
433. syde	s[a]yde, O.
436. bȳgyner	Bygynner, O.
441. heuenȝ	heuen[e]ȝ, O.
458. Ihū	Jesu
460. tyste	t[r]yste, M.
472. (*this line missing in* MS)	(*missing line is indicated*)
479. ho	h[e], O.
532. hen	he[m], O.
544. reprene	repren[y], G.[1]
596. p^{r}termynable	pretermynable, M.
635. ȝy– (*final letter blurred*)	ȝy[s]
649. out out	out, O.
675. fate	fa[c]e, O.

	MS Readings	Emendations
678.	hylleȝ	hylle, G.[1]
690.	onre	on[ou]re, cf. Bradley, [*on*]*oure*
691.	he	ho, Bradley
700.	sor	[f]or, O.
711.	ihc̄ (and 717)	Jesus
721.	Ihc̄	Jesus
733.	makelleȝ	makeleȝ (cf. 757)
739.	ryȝtywys (*second* y *corrected to* w, *but both letters blotted*)	ryȝtwys, M.
788.	john̄ (see also below, 996)	John, G.[1]
792.	jlrm̄ (and 793, 804, 805, 817, 828, 840, 841)	Jerusalem, O.
792.	u	o, G.[1]
802.	men	[n]e[m], G.[1]
816.	jrlm̄	Jerusalem
829.	ilrm̄	Jerusalem
860.	–n (*first letter blurred*)	[o]n, O.
861.	lonbe	lo[m]be, G.[1]
865.	talle (Line 865 with spelling *leste* and *tale*, as catchwords, is repeated below Stanza 72.)	tale (*as in catchwords*)
934.	gracous	grac[i]ous, O.
958.	fresth	f[l]es[c]h, O.
977.	wolde no	wolde [I] no, O.
984.	jhōn	John, G.[1]
985.	jhn̄ (and 1020)	John, G.[1]
996.	john̄ (and 1008, 1009, 1021, 1032, 1033, 1053)	John, G.[1]
997.	As þise, *etc.*	As [John] þise, *etc.*, G.[1]
1018.	O*f* jasporye	"Between O and *j* a later hand has inserted *f*." O.
1063.	mynyster	mynster
1064.	saker-fyse	Sakerfyse, O.
1068.	an vndeȝ	anvnder, O.
1083.	baly	ba[y]l[e], G.[1]
1097.	enpresse	enpr[y]se, G.[1]
1111.	glode	g[ol]de, O.
1179.	quykeȝ	quyke, G.[1]
1185.	īf	if, O.

Explanatory Notes

1. Perle. The actual pearl lost by the jeweler. In the first stanza the situation is clearly stated by the narrator—not to be identified with the author—namely, that he has lost a peerless pearl and has suffered exceedingly over the loss. The pearl may no doubt be representative in the sense that it stands for any *creature*—any person or thing which may draw the human heart from the Creator. But that it symbolizes a dead child, or a specific virtue, or the sensible sweetness of devotion, has not yet been proved, the very variety of view regarding its alleged symbolism constituting a forceful argument against symbolic interpretation. W. H. Schofield, "Symbolism, Allegory and Autobiography in *The Pearl*," *PMLA*, XXIV (1909), 611, points out that the opening stanza of the poem contains no mention whatever of the maiden 'Pearl.' Critics, he further observes, who themselves began with the wrong impression that such a maiden was mentioned, "have not only been led to seek out and emphasize unduly other possible personal references, but have lost sight of the author's artistic plan in the structure of the work."

prynces. Of a prince (any prince's). The line is simply the jeweler's exclamation in conventional phrasing over the quality of his lost pearl. It was "fit for a prince." Cf. 211, *sade for doc oþer erle*. Undoubtedly, of course, the poet is here preparing for the concluding idea, the lesson of the poem: *Christ, Our Lord, has brought it about that our souls are to Him as precious pearls to a prince* (1211-12).

O.'s note on *prynces* (printed in his text with a capital) in *Pearl* (ed. 1906), and his translation (1907), 'Pearl, delight of Christ the Prince,' cannot be justified, nor can G.'s use of a capital for 'prince' (ed. 1921). In refuting the assumptions of these two scholars, Schofield, *op. cit.*, pp. 589 ff., proved the general sense of *prynces* (genitive) in the opening line, and the special signification of the word, conveyed through accompanying pronouns, in 1164, 1176, 1188, and 1189. *Prince* (1201) is limited by the definite article.

2. To clanly clos. 'To set without flaw' or 'neatly.' This is one of many expressions clearly indicative of the jeweler's point of view, which has been assumed by the poet in order to convey the lesson of his poem. This jeweler is an expert. He is accustomed to appraise *gemmeȝ gaye,* and to recognize the best by their distinctive qualities (3-8). The thoughts of such a jeweler would naturally turn to the care which must be exercised in the setting of a perfect pearl. See G. F. Kunz and C. H. Stevenson, *The Book of the Pearl,* p. 389:

> The jeweler, in setting pearls, must use the greatest possible care, first in the cutting away of the settings as they are fastened to the pearl, not to scratch or mar it; and then when he files the setting, not to allow the file to touch the pearl, as both the steel tool and the file would injure it.

For *clanly,* 'neatly,' cf. *Purity* (ed. R. J. Menner) 310: *A cofer closed of tres, clanlych planed.*

3. Oute of Oryent. The jewel so prized by its owner was of the perfect type, found not in the waters of Britain, but imported from the Orient. Cf. Schofield, *op. cit.,* p. 594; O., p. 54; G., p. 115.

4. her. 'Its.' The feminine form of the pronoun here and in 8 and 9—*hyr*—indicating merely the grammatical gender of *perle,* is no doubt largely responsible for the elegy theory. G., e.g., renders *hyr* (8) 'my pearl,' though he admits in his note (p. 115) that "the feminine pronoun would not strike a mediaeval reader as in modern English." O. (ed. 1906), p. 54, affirms that the sudden change to *hit* (10) "indicates an imperfect identification of the symbol with the object"—the object being in his opinion a dead child. He is the more perplexed at the change because, as he points out—thereby furnishing an argument against the elegy theory—in *Purity* (1117-1128), "the fem. pron. only is used of the pearl, and that too without any evident personification." These lines from *Purity* (ed. Menner), with their consistent use of the feminine form of the pronoun, if placed beside the opening stanza of *Pearl* must for impartial minds effectually dispose of the notion that *her* (4) and *hyr* (8, 9) in that poem relate to the poet's little daughter:

> Perle praysed is prys þer perre is schewed,
> Þaȝ hym not derrest be demed to dele for penies.
> Quat may þe cause be called bot for hir clene hwes,
> Þat wynnes worschyp abof all whyte stones?
> For ho schynes so schyr þat is of schap rounde,
> Wythouten faut oþer fylþe, ȝif ho fyn were,
> And wax ever in þe worlde in werying so olde,
> Ȝet þe perle payres not whyle ho in pyese lasttes;
> And if hit cheve þe chaunce uncheryst ho worþe,
> Þat ho blyndes of ble in bour þer ho lygges,
> No-bot wasch hir wyth worchyp in wyn, as ho askes,
> Ho by kynde schal becom clerer þen are.

In *The Pearl,* as Schofield explains, *op. cit.,* p. 595, the indiscriminate use of the fem. and neut. forms of the pron. is due merely "to the fact that the word 'pearl' was feminine and *her* correctly used, yet *hit* was perhaps more natural as applied to an inanimate object. . . ." Cf. the masc. form of the pron., *he* (1001), ref. to 'jasper.'

5. **rounde.** Applicable to a pearl, but scarcely to an exquisitely beautiful child. See Schofield, *op. cit.,* p. 596, for a collection of inaccurate renderings of the adjectives (5-6) by translators who, in their determination to make the words describe the beauty of a little child, shirk their true meaning. G. is the exception. Evidently he saw no absurdity in praising a child for being 'round' and 'royal wherever ranged.'

reken. Schofield, *loc. cit.,* surmises 'radiant.' Cf. J. P. Oakden, *Alliterative Poetry in Middle English,* II, 186: " 'noble,'—a word of very lax application" found "chiefly in alliterative verse."

in vche araye. *Araye* has three usual meanings in ME: (1) dress, (2) condition, state, (3) arrangement, order; (3) fits the situation here. While the imperfect pearl must be set in such a way as to conceal flaws, the perfect pearl shows to advantage in any arrangement. This pearl, of course, had not yet been fixed in a setting; otherwise it would not have so easily been lost. O. glosses 'in all ways.'

6. **sydeȝ.** Another word applicable to a jewel. Cf. *Purity* 555-56 where the poet speaks of the burnished beryl

> Þat is sounde on uche a syde and no sem habes
> Wythouten maskle oþer mote as margerye-perle.

8. Among all the gems which the jeweler appraised—and naturally some must have been of great material value—he regarded this pearl with a very special liking. The phrase *in synglure* is surely synonymous with the frequently employed ME *in especial,* OF *en particulier.* The *ure* ending is a variant spelling of *ere,* as is *gingure* (43) for *ginger* (*gingivere*), *lere* (616) for *lure.* Fick, G.[1], and GO. emend *syngl*[*e*]*re;* O., *syng*[*u*]*l*[*e*]*re,* which G.[2] follows.

9. **erbere.** *OED,* 'a plot of ground covered with grass or turf; a garden lawn, or "green".' G., *op. cit.,* p. 115, affirms that "The poet is thinking of the graveyard as a garden." Only a communication from the poet himself would justify the assertion. All that he, or rather the person in the poem, *says* is that he lost a pearl in a garden, or *herbier.* Nor is it strange that he should lose it in such a place. The expert jeweler, indeed, would be aware that in the clear outdoor light the superior quality of his pearl could be more easily observed than in the indoor light. Cf. Kunz and Stevenson, *op. cit.,* p. 370:

> In absolutely pure daylight, more especially with an unclouded sky . . . it is possible to see the exact tint or color of pearls, that is,

> whether it is really a pure white with a tinge of pink or an orient tending to cream-white . . . Besides this, in pure light it is possible to see whether the pearl is brilliant; whether there are any cracks, scratches or mars on the surface; and lastly whether the form is entirely regular . . . .

A passage relative to this subject, quoted by Kunz and Stevenson, p. 371, from John and Andrew Rymsdyk, *Museum Brittanicum* (London, 1778), offers a further interest through its indiscriminate use of fem. and neut. pronouns in referring to the gem, in the manner of *Pearl,* Stanza I:

> To discover the hidden Defects and Faults of a Pearl and to know whether she is speckled or broken or has any other imperfections, the best way is to make trial of it by the Reverberations of the Sunbeams; for by this means your eye will penetrate into the very centre of the Pearl and discover the least defect it has; you will see then whether it be pure, and has any spots or not, and consequently you may better guess its value.

11. dewyne. For weak pret. without *-d,* see M. Day, *MLR,* XIV (1919), 413-15. The sense demands the pret. because, as the dreamer says (1185-88), his pining for the material pearl ceased after his great spiritual experience. For other examples of pret. without *-d,* see *hope,* 'guessed' (142) and *hope,* 'surmised' (185).

fordolked. *STR-BR* gives "*for-dolken,* v., ? 'wound severely'; *fordolked* (ppl.)," and refers to this line, relating the word to *dolc,* sb., 'ulcer, ? wound,' which is instanced as appearing in *Genesis and Exodus* 3027, *dolc sor and blein,* and in *Ancren Riwle,* p. 2, *wiþute knotte and dolke. OED,* quoting *Pearl* 11, emends *fordolled* from *fordull,* 'to make dull, to stupefy,' and adds: "Only in pa. ppl. Hence *fordulled* ppl. a." *STR-BR* would seem to offer the safer conjecture in view of (1) the MS reading, (2) the apparent derivation, and (3) the sense of the lines. Cf. for the last, OE *synnum for-wundod* in *Christ and Satan* (Junius MS, ed. Krapp) 130, and "deeply wounded with the affection of love," *Minor Works of Walter Hilton* (trans. Dorothy M. Jones), *op.* 2, ch. 8, p. 109.

luf-daungere. The dominion or mastery that the pearl exercised over the affections of the jeweler—in other words, his inordinate love for his earthly treasure. Cf. *daunger,* 'power,' in the companion poem, *Patience* (ed. H. Bateson) 109-10:

> Watȝ neuer so Joyful a Jue as Jonas watȝ thenne
> Þat þe daunger of þe dryȝtyn so derfly escaped.

'Power' also was the common meaning of OF *dangier.* See Godefroy, *Dictionnaire de L'Ancienne Langue Française,* for illustrations.

14-18. wele. The happiness incident to the jeweler's possession of the pearl. His absorption in his treasure had caused him to make light of his sin (*wrange*) of covetousness, one of the Seven Deadly Sins. Cf. the author's contemporary, Walter Hilton, *Scala Perfectionis* (reprint of ed. attrib. to Cressy), ch. 7, pp. 102-3:

> If thou have love and delight in the having and holding of anything thou hast, how mean soever it may be, with the which love thou feedest thy heart for a time, or if thou have a desire and yearning for to have something that thou hast not, with the which desire thy heart is disquieted and stumbled through unreasonable thinking of the thing, that the pure desire of virtue and of God cannot rest therein; this is a sign that there is covetousness in this image.

For **wrange,** 'sin, evil,' cf. *Pearl* 631, and *Purity* 76:

> More to wyte is her wrange þen any wylle gentyl . . . .

In the line from *Purity, wrange* refers to the fault of those who—as recorded in the Parable of the Wedding Feast—refused the invitation to come. Cf. also *Patience* 375-76, the passage descriptive of the repentance of the people of Nineveh who

> Dropped dust on her hede and dymly beȝaȝten
> Þat þat penaunce plesed him þat playnes on her wronge.

22. color. See n. 215.

26. 'Where such wealth to rot is run'—a phrasing which surely would not be used by a loving father in regard to the body of his dead child. G. glosses *rot,* 'decay,' but translates, "where such rich treasure wastes." The alleged parallels quoted by G. (p. 118) omit the "rot." In the parallel offered by O. (p. 55), the decay is also humanly and unrealistically ignored. Far from expressing a mere poetic fancy, however, the passage, *Pearl* 25-36, alludes with subtle art to the Christian teaching of the poem: "Unless the grain of wheat falling into the ground die, itself remaineth alone" (John 12:24). The jeweler well knows that the acid action of earth in contact with his pearl will soon result in the decomposition of its delicate organic layers, first destroying forever the fragile beauty of its outer scale. But the poet goes on to liken the lost pearl to a seed buried in the earth. The pearl, too, will produce fruit—spiritual fruit for the jeweler's own welfare, namely, a willingness to renounce that special earthly treasure which hinders his soul's salvation (1207).

28. schyneȝ. 'Will shine.' Present for future. Cf. *Patience* 88: *Be lyȝtly when lest, he letes me alone.*

39. hyȝ seysoun. The "high day" of August was and is the Feast of the Assumption. Possibly the 'season high' would be the time near that feast.

41. on huyle . . . trendeled; *huyle* is glossed by G. and O. 'mound.' This *huyle* covered with flowers (41-44) is the same as the *flory flaȝt* (57) under which the pearl is buriel, and the *balke* (62) where the dreamer's body remains prostrate while his spirit goes on its adventure in the vision-land. G., O., and others who hold the elegy theory, regard the *huyle* as the grave of the child.

GO. calls attention to a suggestion by G.[1] (p. 119) that *huyle* (41) and *hyul* (1205) "may represent the modern dialect *hile,* current in south-east Lancashire (Rochdale)," pointing out that *hile* "normally means 'a thick cluster of plants,' as in *whimberry-hile, rush-hile,* &c.; but the word is also used of a mound in *pisamoor-hile* 'ant-hill.' " GO. suggests that in line 1172, where *hylle* is used, "the word has probably been confused (possibly by the copyist) with 'hill'; so also in the glossary *Catholicum Anglicum* compiled in 1483 *hylle* appears for *hile* in *A Rysche hylle: cirpetum.*" If the forms *huyle* and *hyul* are indeed distinct from the forms *hyl, hylle, hil* (meaning 'hill' in this poem), it would seem to tell for the interpretation offered here, since the 'hillock' formed by thickly overgrown flowering plants (41-44) would be a likely place to drop and lose a small pearl, but hardly suggests the appearance of a well-kept grave-mound over the body of a beloved child.

43. gyngure. For form, see n. 8.

49-60. This stanza furnishes a key to the homiletic character of the poem. See Sister Mary Vincent Hillmann, "Some Debatable Words in *Pearl,* and Its Theme," *MLN,* LX (April, 1945), 241-48.

51. deuely. 'Devilish, diabolical, wicked.' The grief of the jeweler was wicked because it was contrary to reason (52) and Christian teaching (55), and because it was deliberately indulged (56). GO. equates the word with modern North and North-West dialect *deavely, davely,* used in the senses 'lonely' and 'desolate,' especially in Yorkshire and Cheshire, descended from late OE *deaflic* (and ultimately ON *daufligr*). Despite the plausibility of this suggestion—the cherishing of a 'wicked grief' would certainly create a sense of spiritual desolation, or "loneliness"—it would seem simpler and more direct to connect the word with ME *deuel* (OE *deofol, deoful,* 'devil'; cf. OE *deofollic,* 'diabolical, wicked'). G.[1] and M. read *denely;* O. amends *de[r]uely,* glossing '*adv. as adj.,* sudden'; G.[2], *deuly,* glossing 'deaf-like, dull.'

denned. 'Lodged.' Cf. "Þu was . . . dennet in a beastes cribbe," *OE Homilies and Homiletic Treatises of the Twelfth and Thirteenth Centuries* (ed. M.), E.E.T.S., Nos. 29, 32 (orig. ser.), p. 277. Cf. also Gordon and Onions, "Notes on the Text and Interpretation of *Pearl,*" *Medium Ævum,* I, No. 2, p. 127, who translate conjecturally 'to be hidden.'

54. fyrte. Possibly OF *fierté, firté,* 'wildness, violence, fierceness.' *Fyrte* must be governed by *wyth,* since *faȝt* to make sense must have an object, and the only available object is *skylleȝ.* O. glosses 'frightened, fearful,' with doubtful derivation from OE *fyrht.* G.[2], after Holthausen, emends *fyr[c]e,* translating, 'With wayward words that fiercely fought,' thus rather dislocating the text. GO. also emends *fyr[c]e,* glossing 'vehement.'

55. kynde of Kryst. The 'character' or 'nature' of Christ. The sense probably is that by the example of His life on earth Christ, the Divine Exemplar, taught fortitude in tribulation and patient acceptance of God's will.

61. in space. *Space* in ME usually signifies an interval of time.

65 ff. Though the scene of the vision includes the usual features of the mediaeval framework—the forest, the cliffs, the birds, the stream—it is to be noted that almost every detail in the picture is characterized by qualities of beauty which accord with that of the lost pearl. Psychology points here not to a human being, but to some precious glistening object as the inspiration for the dream.

77. onslydeȝ. 'Slip away.' The image suggested may be that of silver leaves moving or "slipping" in and out, or interlacing above and below each other, catching in their shimmering motion the light striking down on them through the many-leafed branches, as they quiver (78) and seem to 'slip away' as light and shade alternately strike them.

79. glodeȝ. *OED*, '? bright place in the sky; a flash of light.' Cf. MnE 'glade,' to which the word is perhaps, however obscurely, related. The translation 'glades' is chosen because the sense—to catch intermittent glimpses of a "bright place in the sky" or of "a flash of light" through the crowns of trees clustered into a 'glade'—fits the context.

86. garten. Pl. with sg. subject, a construction not unusual in ME. For further examples in this poem of disagreement in number of verb and subject, see lines 110 (*wern*), 124 (*fordidden*), 232 (*wore*), 1012 (*endent*), 1063, 1123 (*watȝ*), 1108, 1112 (*wasse*).

115. stroþe. Gordon and Onions, *op. cit.*, pp. 128-31, conjecture 'earth, growth-covered earth' (its meaning in Icelandic poetry as early as the tenth century). Hence *stroþe-men,* 'men of this green earth,' or 'men of earth, mortals.'

123. abated. 'Abolished.' A meaning which fits here since the related verbs in line 124 express the same idea: *fordidden,* 'dispelled'; *dystryed,* 'put an end to.' Cf. n. 617 ff. *abate.*

127. floty. O. and G. translate 'watery,' G. comparing OF *pré flotis.* E. Ekwall, *The Place-Names of Lancashire,* Intr. p. 11, derives it from ON *flot,* 'a level piece of land.' But these vales are not flat. They are diversified by hills (121, 976). *STR-BR* (quoting the line) gives, without etymology, 'waving,' which, if it signifies 'undulating,' is a reasonable conjecture. In lines 102-4, the jeweler finds 'No rise so great that it troubled me./The farther into the region, the fairer did rise/The plain. . . .' A possible etymology, then, would be OE *flot,* 'the sea,' and ME *-y* (*-ig*). Cf. OE *flotlic.*

129 ff. The mediaeval conviction that the gifts of Fortune, whether good or evil, are tests of character may account for the poet's use of the word *frayneȝ* ('makes trial, tries us'), 129. This idea, however, is subsidiary and may have been introduced by the poet for the sake of rhyme.

The main idea is carried by *fares*, 'continues' (129), meaning that Fortune, having chosen to bestow gifts upon a mortal, is likely to continue with the same sort of gift—good or evil. Thus, people still refer to "runs" of good or bad luck. The jeweler, accepting the fortune that has brought him to the wonderful land of his vision, expects his "good luck" to continue.

132. Hytteȝ. 'Is likely, runs the chance.' An ON meaning of the vb. (see Egilson, *Lexicon Poeticum*) is '*periculo se exponere.*' This meaning would seem more suitable here than that proposed by *OED* (quoting the line)—'aim, seek, strive'—since the recipient of *sore*, 'sorrow,' from Fortune would scarcely seek, strive for, or aim at *more.*

140. Radical emendation such as that of G.—'*Bytwene* [*mereȝ*] *by* [*Myrþe*] *made*'—is not necessary here. The key word is *mereȝ*, with the well-established meaning 'boundaries.' The jeweler has just said that he thinks himself in or close to Paradise (137-38). Like many mediaeval Christians, he apparently believed that Paradise consisted of a hierarchy of states of beatitude with boundaries fixed between them. The supreme example, of course, of the joys of Heaven constituted with definite boundaries is furnished by Dante. Cf. Piccarda's speech, *Il Paradiso* III, 70-87, particularly 82-85.

OED, defining 'mirth' as 'joy, happiness,' adds, "Often a religious joy," and illustrates from *Legend of St. Katherine* 2217: . . . *the murþes þæt neauer ne wonieþ.*

142. hope. For pret. without *-d*, see n. 11.

mote. *OED*, '(*poetic*) castle, fortress, city.'

merked. 'Reached.' Cf. "*The Wars of Alexander*," ed. Skeat, E.E.T.S., No. 31 (1878): *If I miȝt merke to Messedone.*

161. faunt. A word particularly responsible, no doubt, for the elegy theory. Though *faunt* may mean 'child,' it may also mean 'youthful being, youth.' Cf. *La Vie de Saint Eustace*, ed. Jessie Murray, p. 31: *E li dui enfant se herbergerent en la loge lor mere,* which in the Latin translation (XXVIII) is: *Illi ergo duo adolescentes hospitaverunt in tabernaculum matris suae.* Moreover, the phrase in apposition to *faunt* (*Pearl*), *a mayden of menske* ('a maiden of dignity'), and the non-parental attitude of the dreamer toward her certainly preclude the translation 'child' as in G.'s rendering. GO. also glosses 'child.'

163-68. The first thing that attracts the jeweler is the whiteness of the maiden's robe (163). There is no instantaneous reaction of fatherly love. He immediately identifies her with that which had engaged his thoughts just before he fell into the *slepyng-slaȝte*, namely, his lost pearl (164). He calls her not his daughter, not his child, but *þat schene* ('that bright one'), 165. Fatherly affection would have recorded itself in something other than a detailed description of the supposed child's appearance. But it is the pearl-like beauty of the maiden that attracts him—*Hyr* *vysayge whyt as playn yuore* (178)—and the lustrous whiteness of her dress (repeated in 220).

175-76. These lines definitely undermine the theory that *The Pearl* is a lament for a dead child. For, though the dreamer, knowing that his pearl had been lost in the ground, might indeed receive a shock at seeing it (as he fancies the maiden to be) in 'so strange a place' as *Paradyse* (137), he could not reasonably, as a Christian, be surprised at seeing his little dead daughter there. Cf. Sister M. Madeleva, *Pearl: A Study in Spiritual Dryness,* p. 131.

185. I hope . . . porpose. The jeweler surmises that the import of the vision is spiritual—as it turns out to be. For pret. without *-d,* see n. 11.

197. beaumys clearly in the MS. Probably *be-* (*bi-*) and *aumys,* OF *aumusse. Be-* (*bi-*), 'around, about,' occurs in composition (OE and ME) in words referring to clothing. Cf. ME vb. *bi-wimplen,* 'cover with a wimple.' *Beaumys,* therefore, would be the 'mantle or surcoat' (cf. MnE 'topcoat, overcoat,' and derivation of "amice" from *amictus*). O.'s difficulty (pp. 63 ff.) regarding the meaning of "amice" is solved by the article "*Amictus,*" *Catholic Encyclopedia* (by the Rev. Herbert Thurston, S.J.), in which it is shown that *amictus* was formerly identified with *anagolagium,* 'a sort of linen wrap used by women to throw over their shoulders. . . .' O. emends radically, *b*[*leaunt of biys*]. G. divides the word, *beau mys,* translating 'surcoat fine,' with deriv. of *mys* from OF *amis.* GO. emends *beau biys,* 'fair linen,' based on the *byssinum* of Apoc. 19:8.

209. werle. Possibly from a ME *whirl,* OE *hwyrfel* ? 'circlet or headband.' The line may simply reiterate 208, or refer to other ornaments, 'nets' or 'cauls' worn round the head by ladies in the fourteenth century.

210. lere leke clearly in the MS. 'Face-radiance, radiance of countenance.' *Lere,* ON *hleor* ('cheek,' with the ME meanings 'face, countenance'). *Leke,* as the writer has earlier suggested (see Hillmann, "*Pearl: lere leke,* 210, *MLN,* LIX [June, 1944], 417-18), is probably to be connected with OE *lacan* (ON sb. *leikr* related to the vb. *leika*), 'to flash, to flicker,' as in *Daniel* 475 (*lacende lig,* 'flickering flame'). OE *lacan* would seem in this meaning ('to move up and down, to leap,' etc.) to be a literal translation of the Latin *coruscare,* and probably in its derived meaning also to have followed the meaning of the Latin verb. 'Face-radiance, radiance of countenance' would therefore seem to follow the traditional meanings of both *lere* and *leke.*

The line has suffered several emendations and free translations: M. and G., [*h*]*ere* [*h*]*eke;* O., [*h*]*ere-leke;* Gordon and Onions (*op. cit.,* p. 165), [*h*]*ere leke;* and, most recently, GO., [*h*]*ere leke.* All refer the phrase to the maiden's hair (as does G. G. Coulton, trans. 1906). Despite the weight of editorial tradition in favor of reading *here* for *lere,* the fact remains that the maiden's hair (*fax*) is described below. Continuing in this stanza

(18) to describe the appearance of the 'youthful being,' the poet, having already mentioned the general appearance of her clothing, now pictures her crown (205-9), her facial expression (211), her complexion (212), her hair (213-14), her collar (215-16), her robe (217-20), and, finally, the priceless pearl on her breast (221-22). The words *lere leke,* appearing in line 210, immediately preceding the description of her expression (211), would seem naturally and logically, in this methodical accounting, to mean the 'radiance of her countenance,' her 'face-radiance.'

217. It is unnecessary to change the order of the words in this line as O. does (*'Pyȝt & poyned watȝ . . .'*). *Poyned* is a sb., OF *poignet,* 'cuff.' Cf. G. n., p. 131. See n. 811-15 for spelling.

233. nerre. 'Nearer,' not in relationship but in position, locality. She had come down to the very brink of the stream; therefore, the dreamer says, he is happier, his new measure of happiness arising from the facility with which he can now talk with her across the water. Note the force of *forþy* (234). If *nerre* is interpreted as referring to relationship (cf. O., ed. 1906, Intr. p. xxxi), then 233 and 234 are simply ludicrous. For, granting the existence of the stricken father, he would scarcely break down his narrative at this point solemnly to announce the undeniable fact that his daughter was more nearly related to him than his aunt or niece, and that therefore he was the happier.

aunte or nece. A phrase used in all probability as a rhyme-tag. Oakden, *op. cit.,* II, 391, says that the alliterative poets made use of these rhyme-tags, sometimes for metrical reasons, sometimes ostensibly to give assurance of the historicity of the details mentioned, but frequently for no apparent reason. Coulton says (*MLR,* II, 40): "It suited his [the poet's] rhyme." Other examples of "tags" in *Pearl* are: *I wot and wene,* 47, 201; *for doc oþer erle,* 211; *into Grece,* 231; *in sobre asente,* 391; *erly & late,* 392; *wyth syȝt,* 985.

245. aglyȝte. 'Glittered away'; (cf. *glyȝt,* 114). *Aglyȝte* is the poet's variant for *trendeled doun* in line 41, graphically reproducing the visual image present to the jeweler in the instant in which the pearl fell from his fingers and disappeared through the grass (10). Though both O. and G. rightly refer the word to ON *glia,* 'to shine'—and thus gloss *glyȝt* (114) —they inconsistently translate *aglyȝte* 'glide' (G.) and 'slip away' (O.) as if from *a-gliden.*

252. juelere. The dreamer is represented by the poet as an actual jeweler (cf. nn. 1, 2, 5, 9). Otherwise the word has no value. G. says (p. 132) that it indicates the "merchant" of the parable (Matt. 13:45-46). But the *homo negotiator* of the parable is not, because he buys pearls, necessarily a jeweler on that account any more than a man who purchases a painting is for that reason a painter. Nevertheless, the poet himself, who undoubtedly had the parable very much in mind, also refers to the "merchant" as a "jeweler" (730, 734), perhaps to strengthen his parallel at that point. That the actual jeweler of the poem is intended to represent the pearl-buyer of the parable is, however, denied by the fact that in lines 729-44 (wherein the dream-maiden refers to the other "jeweler"—the merchant), the jeweler of the poem is being told the story of a third person—certainly not himself. References to the owner of the lost pearl as an actual jeweler are plentiful: lines 252, 264, 265, 276, 288, 289, etc. It would be an unnecessary distortion of the poem to confuse him throughout with the "merchant."

253-64. In this stanza the poet subtly achieves the presentation of two points of view: that of the jeweler, who fancies that the maiden is his lost pearl (*juel,* 253) despite the fact that she has given no direct answer to his question (241-43); and that of the maiden (*perle,* 258), his soul —presented to him in vision as it might be were he a noble jeweler (264) —safely enclosed (259) in a true treasure chest (*forser,* 263), the garden of Heaven (260).

262. here in MS. G., GO., and O. emend [*n*]*ere,* their difficulty arising from their punctuation of the passage. The maiden's argument is: "Since neither loss nor mourning exists here in Heaven, here indeed would be your true treasure chest." (Cf. Matt. 6:19-20.) The second *here* is pleonastic.

265-76. The homiletic character of this stanza, its attack upon covetousness, and its language, parallel a passage in Ælfric's *Homily on the Assumption of St. John the Apostle,* ed. Thorpe, pp. 60 ff. The incident narrated is that of two young men who, under the influence of a philosopher, having converted their patrimony into precious stones, destroy them in proof of their contempt for earthly wealth. St. John points out the folly of this renunciation, motivated as it is by vanity alone, and miraculously restores the jewels to their original state. The two young men are converted, and once more, but this time through Christian motives, renounce earthly riches. Later, however, on seeing their former servants richly adorned while they themselves are garbed as poor men, they are tempted to regrets. Thereupon the saint, having by another miracle changed a green twig into gold and pebbles into precious stones (cf. *Pearl* 81-82), gives them to the young men, advising them to go and buy earthly goods since they have forfeited those of Heaven. "Bicgaþ eow," he continues, "pællene cyrtlas, þæt ge to lytelre hwile scinon swa swa rose [cf. *Pearl* 269] þæt ge hrædlice forweornion. Beoþ blowende and welige hwilwenlice, þæt ge ecelice wædlion."

For jewels symbolizing souls in Heaven, cf. Dante, *Divina Commedia, passim,* especially *Il Paradiso* (ed. G.) X, 70-72:

Nella corte del ciel, ond' io revegno
si trovan molte gioie care e belle
tanto che non si posson trar del regno.

269 ff. The missing material pearl, perishable by nature as a rose, is proved to be no pearl of price through the very character of the chest, i.e., the earth (cf. nn. 26, 253-64), in which it is enclosed. The jeweler's lot, i.e., the loss of his pearl, by inspiring this vision, will make clear to him the difference between the *noȝt* of earthly treasure and the *oȝt,* the something, the reality of heavenly treasure, i.e., the soul.

273-76. The jeweler's loss of his pearl will also, the dream-maiden assures him, act as the cure for his *wrange* (14-16). The same fate that removed his pearl has precipitated him, through the shock of that loss, into the dream-vision, wherein, with the symbol of his soul (the maiden) as guide, he will learn spiritual values.

no kynde jueler (276). Cf. Hilton, *op. cit.,* Bk. I, ch. 7, p. 102:

> . . . it is less mastery to forsake worldly goods than to forsake the love of them. Peradventure thou hast not forsaken thy covetousness, but only changed it from a great thing to a small; from a pound unto a penny, and from a silver dish unto a dish of a half-penny. This is but a simple change; thou art no good merchant.

282. 'I believed my pearl utterly gone.' Literally, "put out of days." The jeweler has missed the point of the maiden's instruction, impressed mainly with her statement that his pearl (to *him* the material pearl, to *her* the soul) is not *al awaye* (258).

283. ma feste. 'Rejoice, make merry.' (O. and G.)

286. broȝ. Gordon and Onions, *op. cit.,* 135-36, argue that this apparently incomplete form is really a phonetic spelling—*broȝt þys* probably having been pronounced *broȝ tis*—and, as a form of the past tense, quite as authentic as *hope* (142, 185). Their idea is that omission of the final *-d* (*-t*) occurs before an unaccented word beginning with *þ*. Hence, if *broȝ* is normalized as *broȝt* (cf. texts of GO., G., and O.), consistency, they say, would demand the addition of *-d* or *-t* to *hope* (142, 185), as in G. and GO. For omission of *-t* also, cf. *jacyngh þe* (1014).

289-300. A transitional stanza, a preparation for the maiden's discourse on faith (301 ff.) and on death and judgment (313-24).

307. west ernays. 'Empty pledge or covenant.' See Sister Mary Vincent Hillmann, "*The Pearl: west ernays* (307); *fasor* (431)," *MLN,* LVIII (Jan., 1943), 42-44. The two words are crowded in the MS so that they appear to form one, *westernays.* This fact M. had early recognized. His reading was *westerne ays;* his translation, 'western ways.' A possible reading here is *west* (OE *weste*) and *ernays* for *ernes,* a fourteenth-century form of 'earnest, pledge' (see *OED,* 'earnest' sb.[2]).

The usual reading, *westernays,* has been explained as an error for OF *bestorneis,* 'wrongfully, perversely.' See *OED, STR-BR,* O., and G., all drawing inferences from this line only. "To make words or a covenant void," however, is an expression occurring frequently in the Old Testament. Cf. Psalm 88:35: "Neither will I profane my covenant: and the words that proceed from my mouth I will not make void."

In *ernays,* the ending *-ays* is explainable—granting that the word is of French origin—by comparison with *cortayse* (433) and *corteȝ* (754). See Mildred K. Pope, *From Latin to Modern French,* p. 444, on the subject of indiscriminate use of *ai* and *e* in AN. If of Eng. origin, *ernays* may merely illustrate one of the poet's artificial rhymes. (Cf. *wace,* 65, *streny,* 551.)

320. keue. 'Sink,' from Scand. *kefja.* See Erik Björkman, *Scandinavian Loan Words in Middle English,* p. 246. *OED* finds Björkman's idea unsatisfactory for 981. But see n. on that line.

331-32. What serueȝ tresor. . . . *Tresor* here certainly refers not to a child, but to a material possession—the lost pearl—still identified (330) by the jeweler with the maiden.

339-40. lureȝ lesse. G. courageously translates 'losses small,' although the application is to the supposed father's bereavement. The supposed daughter appears hardhearted and un-Christian in her lack of compassion for the sufferer. If, however, 'minor losses' or 'losses small' refer to material objects, the severity of the maiden is understandable, and the lines definitely support the theme of the poem in its presentation of the evils of covetousness. See nn. 14-18, 265-76, 273-76. Through immoderate grief for material treasure a man may forego eternal happiness. Cf. Dante, *Il Paradiso* XV, 10-12:

> Ben è che senza termine si doglia
> chi, per amor di cosa che non duri,
> eternalmente quell' amor si spoglia.

349 ff. Cf. Hilton, *Minor Works,* trans. Dorothy Jones, ch. 5, pp. 186-87: "Thy privy dooms, Lord, are to be dreaded with love and reverence, not for to be disputed by man's reason." For similar ideas, cf. also, "Aȝen god to grucche is gret trespas," *Minor Poems of the Vernon MS, II,* ed. Furnivall, E.E.T.S., No. 117, p. 690.

351. mendeȝ. 'Opinions, thoughts.' For form, cf. Hilton, *Scala Perfectionis,* ch. 1, p. 46: *bi travuaille of þi mende,* quoted by Helen L. Gardner in "Walter Hilton and the Mystical Tradition in England," *Essays and Studies by Members of the English Association,* XXII, 116. O., G., and GO. derive *mendeȝ* from OF *amende,* O. glossing 'reparation,' G., 'amends,' GO., 'recompense.'

But to interpret the line in the sense that amends are valueless before God is to impute to the heavenly visitant a doctrine un-Christian and cruel. To say, on the other hand, that human thought in comparison with God's decrees is of no account is reasonable and consistent with Christian teaching. Thus, says the maiden, any thoughts or opinions the jeweler may hold as to the justice of his loss will alter God's judgment *not a myte.*

She is teaching him the lesson of humility and submission to God's will —that "man proposes, but God disposes."

357. O. F. Emerson, "More Notes on *The Pearl,*" *PMLA,* XLII (1927), 819, translates: 'And comfort may easily shine out from thy losses.' In the text *comforte* is modified by *Hys.* The meaning evidently is that material loss may be the occasion of consolation from God. Cf. n. 26.

371-72. 'Of care and me. . . .' Alluding to the jeweler's happiness in the possession of his jewel and his present oneness, or *acorde* with care and sorrow. See n. 14-18.

376. I wyste . . . gon. This could be said of a lost jewel, but certainly not by a Christian father of his dead child. Cf. Sister Madeleva, *op. cit.,* p. 131.

380. by stok oþer ston. Possibly a mild oath, or 'anywhere,' as O. glosses it, or perhaps only a rhyme-tag. The combination *stok and ston* is listed by Oakden, *op. cit.,* II, 247, as occurring frequently among alliterative phrases in ME poetry.

382. mare reȝ. 'Onrush, eloquence.' The letters are crowded together by the copyist, appearing to be *marereȝ.* ME *reȝ, res, rese, ræs,* like OE *ræs,* in its literal significance is 'rush, onset, rapid vigorous movement,' and is often applied to the rapid onward rush of a stream or river.

Two versions of a Middle English poem, "A Prayer of Penitence to God" (*English Lyrics of the Thirteenth Century,* ed. Carleton Brown), use the word *rese* evidently of speech. Both versions tell us (36-40) that at sight of the wounds of Our Redeemer on doomsday, we shall be speechless with fear:

> to speke thenne we bueþ vnbolde. (Harley MS)
>
> þere to speke y am vnbolde (Pratt MS)

The idea is reiterated in lines 41-42:

> Vnbold icham to bidde þe bote,
> swyþe vnreken ys my réés. (Harley MS)
>
> Vnbolde y am to byd bote,
> & al unredy of my rese. (Pratt MS)

Power of speech, readiness of language, fail the repentant sinner in the presence of God, his Judge. A similar state of inarticulateness besets the *jueler* of *The Pearl* at the 'onrush' of the vision-maiden's reproaches. With that 'onrush,' that 'eloquence,' he, poor mortal, cannot compete.

An interesting parallel to the situation and language occurs in Dante, *Il Purgatorio* XXXI, 7-9. Beatrice, on one side of the sacred stream, reproaches Dante on the other for his deflection from the high course of conduct with which she had formerly inspired him. He is speechless with shame (*vertù* is evidently 'power of speech').

Era la mia vertù tanto confusa,
  che la voce si mosse e pria si spensa
  che dagli organi suoi fosse dischiusa.

O., *marereȝ*, but admits that his interpretation, 'botcher's blunder' is farfetched. Moreover, application of the term 'botcher' to God, the Creator, would constitute a blasphemy on the part of the *jueler* completely discordant with the faith and reverence of his character as depicted in the poem. Holthausen's emendation *ma*[*n*]*ereȝ*, suggested in his review (*Athenæum*, 1891), is accepted by G.[2] and GO.

385-96. A transitional stanza, in which the jeweler expresses interest in the maiden's estate. It is the justified soul's estate which the poet is now ready to present, and which forms the most important section of the poem.

401. hyȝe pryde. The first of the Seven Deadly Sins.

411-12. Þow wost wel. . . . These lines at first glance would seem to support the elegy theory. Indeed, G. writes *perle* (411) with an initial capital for both text and translation. Since "Scribe D," the supposed copyist of the author's manuscript, used initial capitals sparingly (see, e.g., MS line 383: *bot chrystes mersy & mary & jon*), this would be permissible if the sense dictated it for modern reading. However, giving *schede* (OE *sceadan*) its normal meaning, 'shed, separate, fall' (see O., gloss.), and noting the maiden's use of *I* (412)—where one would expect *hit* or *ho*, if she were identifying herself with *perle* (411)—one finds in the lines another meaning: the *gostly . . . porpose* (185) anticipated by the dreamer.

This important "gostly porpose" is ever present to the poet. If as an artist he must make the vision-maiden express herself in such a way as to sustain the dreamer's delusion that she is his lost pearl, as a teacher he is careful to keep before his readers, or listeners, the important lesson of the poem, namely, that attachment to earthly treasure is a hindrance to eternal salvation. Hence, the maiden reminds the dreamer that when his pearl fell to the ground, his soul—which she here symbolizes—was spiritually immature. Cf. Ephes. 4:13-15: "That henceforth we be no more children tossed to and fro, and carried about with every wind of doctrine. . ." (v. 14).

The dream psychology is skillfully maintained here and through the rest of the poem in the subtle shifting of impressions—the maiden speaking now as the symbol of the dreamer's soul, now as symbol of any justified soul, the dreamer addressing her as his lost pearl until he begins to realize her supernatural character (745-54).

412 ff. Sister Madeleva, *op. cit.*, pp. 152-54, would restrict the application of these lines to religious. However, while it is quite true that in Apoc. 14:4, virgins (not necessarily religious) are mentioned as receiving the special reward of following the Lamb "whithersoever He goeth," it is the teaching of Catholic mysticism that Christ is the destined spiritual

Bridegroom of all souls of good will. (See Dom Louismet, *The Mystical Life*, pp. 65-66.) Moreover, the quotation adduced by Sister Madeleva, *ibid.*, p. 153, from the *Ancren Riwle*, in support of her argument, speaks not of the soul of the religious but of the "soul" as the spouse of Christ. St. Paul, it should be noted (II Cor. 11:2), addressing people of varied states of life, and, according to this and his first Epistle to the Corinthians, in need of much reformation, writes: "I have espoused you to one husband that I might present you a chaste virgin to Christ." Cf. also the second verse of a hymn sung at Mass in numerous Catholic churches by the saintly and the repentant of various states in life, at the time of Holy Communion: "And humbly I'll receive Thee,/The Bridegroom of my soul. . . ."

425. þat Grace of grewe. 'From whom sprang Grace,' i.e., Jesus Christ, God and Man, was the Son of Mary. Cf. Hilton, *op. cit.*, Bk. III, ch. xii, p. 294: "Jesus is love, Jesus is grace, Jesus is God." O.'s note (p. 71) on this line contains an incorrect statement, namely, that it is "a point of Catholic doctrine that the Virgin as well as the Godhead, is a source of grace." The Source of Grace, according to Catholic doctrine, is God alone. The phrase "Channel of Grace" is sometimes applied to Mary.

429-32. The point of this quatrain hinges on 431: *Þat freles fleȝe of hyr Fasor*. *Fasor* represents a form of OF *faiseor, faisour*, 'Maker, Creator.' Cf. illustrations listed by Godefroy, *Dictionnaire de L'Ancienne Langue Française.*

This meaning for *fasor* is supported by—and is probably traceable to—two passages in the "Phoenix Homily" (*Early English Homilies from the Twelfth Century*, ed. Rubie D-N. Warner, E.E.T.S., No. 152, pp. 147-48), which emphasize the fact of the creation of the marvelous bird by God:

> Þair wuneþ on an fugel fæȝer Fenix gehaten, he is mycel and mære swa se Mihtiȝe ȝesceop. . . .
>
> Þas halge fugel is Fenix ȝehaten, wlitiȝ and wynsum, swa hine God ȝesceop.

Compare also in the poem *Phoenix* a similar emphasis upon the idea that the bird is a beautiful work of the Creator. For further comment on *fasor*, see the article by this writer in *MLN*, cited in n. 307.

433-36. The maiden falls to her knees in an instant reaction of horror at the jeweler's ignorant but blasphemous question as to whether she means that she herself is *þe quene of heueneȝ blwe* (423), covering her face with her hands as she calls upon Mary, *Blessed Bygynner of vch a grace*, before rising to rebuke him.

For *Bygyn[n]er* (436), see n. 425.

457-68. These lines follow St. Paul's analogy in I Cor. 12:12-31.

462. myste. 'Might, power.' *OED*, quoting this line, explains the word as an obsolete form of 'mystical.' But cf. *miste,* 'might,' in "A Light is come to the World," *Lyrics of the Thirteenth Century,* ed. Brown, 11. 71-74, and *ibid.,* 1. 96. The phrase "Master of power" occurs in Wisdom 12:18—*dominator virtutis.*

472. A line, possibly overlooked by the scribe, is missing here. G. invents *Me þynk þou spekeȝ now ful wronge.*

481. **That cortayse.** Adj. as substantive. See other examples in *Pearl* (279, 368, 433, 469, 480, etc.).

484. **Þou lyfed not . . . þede.** The jeweler, in his extraordinary dream state, still holding the confused conviction that his lost material pearl is somehow personified in the pearl-maiden (his *anima*), now compounds his confusion by carrying that personification into the past. As is common in dreams, he sees nothing incongruous in reminding his "pearl" of her (its) total ignorance of elementary Christian practice while in his possession. He fails to understand why she (it) has been granted such high spiritual joys when, as he knew, she (it) had been imported into a Christian country (England) from the *Oryent* only two years before its (her) disappearance. He was certain, too, that his pearl had not learned even the rudiments of Christianity—*nawþer Pater ne Crede* (see below, n. 485). The principal cause of the jeweler's continuing confusion is his worldly concern for his material pearl. He has not yet concerned himself with his soul; he has not yet given up *noȝt* for *oȝt.*

485. **nawþer Pater ne Crede.** Not indicating childhood, as O. (p. 73) and G. (pp. 141-42) imply, but typifying the simple vocal prayers recommended for the early stages of conversion. Cf. Hilton, *op. cit.,* Bk. I, Pt. II, ch. 1, p. 37:

> This kind of prayer is commonly most profitable for every man in the beginning of his conversion . . . And therefore I hope . . . it is most speedful to use this manner of prayer, as to say his *Pater noster* and his *Ave,* and to read upon his Psalter and such other.

The Pater Noster and the Creed appear as the prayers of the unlearned in Lydgate, *Merita Missae,* E.E.T.S., No. 71, App. V:

> God of hewine, that sheop Erthe And helle,
> ȝyf me grace sume word to telle
> To the lewde that can not rede
> But the Pater Noster and the Crede.

492. **to dere a date.** 'A term too highly rated,' i.e., the reward is too high for the brief time (two years) spent upon earth.

497. **As Mathew . . . your messe.** The pronoun here may mean no more than "which you know well," or, in other words, "the Mass for Septuagesima Sunday, at which you have often heard this Gospel (Matt. 20:1-16) read." Or, *your* (if it means 'that of you mortals,' i.e., that re-

quired to be celebrated by man in perpetual commemoration of Christ's death and Sacrifice) implies the supernatural character of the maiden, that she herself is not of earth (see 413-20); there is no Mass in Heaven (cf. n. 1064).

Lines 501 ff. contain the poet's version of the Parable of the Laborers in the Vineyard; cf. verses from Matthew above cited.

505. þys hyne. 'These householders,' that is, householders in general, who know when to hire *werkmen* into the vineyards. G. changes the MS *þys* to *hys*, but proves (p. 143) that *hyne* signifies 'those of the household,' citing OE renderings of the Vulgate *paterfamilias* in this Gospel, namely, *hina fæder* (Rushworth gloss) and *higna fæder* (Lindisfarne gloss). O. argues for 'these hirelings.' GO. translates 'the labourers.'

516. In other words: "Don't you know what time it is?"

518. soȝt. 'Murmured, sighed.' OE *swogan*. This is O.'s understanding of the form. G. derives it from OE *secan*, glossing 'sought, given,' accepted by GO. The form *souȝed* (ME *swoȝen*, OE *swogan*) occurs in *Patience* 140.

523-24. pray clearly in MS (524). Retained by M.; O., G., and GO. emend *pay*, placing a period after *toȝt*, and understanding 523 as part of the speech of the *lorde*.

in dede & þoȝt (524): both by right of contract (522-23) and by reason of good intentions, i.e., both legally and morally bound.

549. pleny, an artificial form to rhyme with *peny*, 546. See Oakden, *op. cit.*, p. 84. Cf. *streny*, 551.

558. wanig clearly in the MS. 'Lacking.' Although to date the word has not been found elsewhere, there is little reason for rejecting it in this meaning, which does not strain the context. See n. 127 (*floty*). Cf. ME *witige, witi*, OE *witig*. O., G., and GO. emend *wa[n]ig*, but G. translates 'wrong.' M. emends *wrang*.

565. louyly. 'Lawful.' WM development of OE *lahlic*. For phonetic changes, see Oakden, *op. cit.*, p. 22, who points out that, though the usual ME development of OE *ag, ah*, is *aw* or *ow* (*aȝ* or *oȝ*), the "W. Midl. texts have *ou*, except *The Chester Plays* which have *au*." The first *y* in *louyly* I understand as representing *e* as in the ME adv. *lageliche*, OE *lahlice*. Emendations by G.[2]—*l[e]uyly*, ON *leyfiligr*, 'permitted, allowed'—and by O.—*l[awe]ly*—although conveying a similar meaning to that of the word in the MS, would seem unnecessary. G.[1] retains MS *louyly*, as do also M. and GO.

572. mykeȝ. 'Friends, chosen ones.' Defined by *OED* (without etymology) as 'friends.' The idea of the line is that though many are called to fellowship with Christ, few attain it, few are chosen to the Company. (Cf. lines 889-900.) The word may be related to OE *mæcca*, ME *mæcche, meche*, 'companion, equal, comrade.' Cf. *Crist to meche*, 'Christ for Companion,' illustr. in *STR-BR* from *Reliquiae Antiquae*, ed. T. Wright and J. O. Halliwell, I (1841-43), 225. The *k* for *ch* frequently occurs in NM and NWM, under the Scandinavian influence (cf. *mechel, michel, mikel,* 'much'). The difficulty lies in the first vowel: in *The Pearl* short *e* and *i* (*y*) are interchangeable, but in *mykeȝ* we have the long *i*.

GO. glosses 'the elect' (deriving from OF *amike,* 'friend,' L. *amicus,* noting that "*mykeȝ* is an aphetic form of *amike*" and that in context here it "must have the extended sense 'chosen companions of the Lord' " because of the line it so closely parallels in Matthew (20:16). Cf. also Matt. 22:14.

588. toȝere. 'This year.' Cf. Layamon *Brut* 8039. Those who still await their 'wages' (585-88) are presumably those who must first endure a term in Purgatory. (See note 617 ff.)

593. Cf. Psalm 61:13, the *verce ouerte* paraphrased in lines 595-96.

596. Pretermynable (MS, *P^r^termynable*). 'Before the terminable (that which can be limited)'; hence, without limits of any kind, not contingent; therefore, 'Eternal, Infinite.' See Gen. 1:2; also Psalm 73:12: *Deus rex noster ante saecula . . .* ; Psalm 89:2: *Priusquam montes fierent, aut formaretur terra, et orbis: a saeculo et usque in saeculum Tu es Deus.* With *Tu es Deus* as an expression of the Infinity of God, cf. Exodus 3:14: *Dixit Deus ad Moysen: EGO SUM QUI SUM.* For a modern presentation of the scholastic position, see Etienne Gilson, *The Spirit of Mediaeval Philosophy,* trans. A. H. C. Downes, p. 55: "The perfection of being [God] not only calls for all realizations, it also excludes all limits, generating thereby a positive infinity which refuses all determination."

Pretermynable has not thus far been found elsewhere. Possibly it is a coinage by the author, who was forced to find a rhyme for *determynable* (594). *OED* conjectures that it may translate a scholastic '**praeterminabilis,* predetermining.' G., rejecting the conjecture, says the word is "evidently for 'predeterminable,' for the purpose of euphony and rhyme," *predeterminable* meaning, he says, 'fixed beforehand, preordained.' O. (p. 75) relates the word (in the sense of "pre-ordaining") to a phrase employed by Albertus Magnus in commenting on Psalm 61: *divinae voluntatis ordinatio aeterna et perfecta.*

597-600. The parable retold by the maiden in reply to the dreamer's questioning (cf. Stanza 41) does not satisfy his conception of God's justice—'forever fixed,' according to Holy Writ (591-92). If the maiden is put ahead of him who *stod þe long day stable* (597) insofar as 'wages' are concerned, it seems to the jeweler that "the less work one accomplishes in the 'vineyard,' the more pay one is able to get; also, that the longer the space of time during which one does less work than the others, the more additional pay he will receive."

603-6. inlyche. 'Fully, in full' (603 as 546), corresponding to *al & sum* (584). The lines simply mean that everyone—whether his reward is little or much—receives what is his due from God, Who is both merciful and just. Carleton Brown ("The Author of *The Pearl* Considered in the Light of His Theological Opinions," *PMLA,* XIX [1904], 115-53) holds the false view that the poet (whom he attempts to enlist among the forerunners of sixteenth-century Protestantism) deviates here from the teaching of Catholicism. But he interprets the lines as meaning that grace alone without merit confers equal reward upon all after death. For discussions of the lines, which successfully dispose of Brown's thesis, cf. James Sledd, "Three Textual Notes on Fourteenth Century Poetry," *MLN*, LV (May, 1940), 381; Sister Mary Vincent Hillmann, "*Pearl: Inlyche* and *Rewarde*," *MLN*, LVI (June, 1941), 457-58; Marie P. Hamilton, "The Orthodoxy of *Pearl* 603-4," *MLN*, LVIII (May, 1943), 370-72. Miss Hamilton argues very interestingly for *inlych* (603) as 'completely' and *payed* (603) as 'satisfied.' However, *inlyche* (546) she would translate 'alike.' GO. argues for 'alike' in both lines (deriving from an alternation of *ilyche*, OE *gelice*), and translates 'what is due as recognition of merit' for *rewarde* (604), rejecting the simpler reading 'reward,' supported by this writer (cf. *op. cit.*) and by Sledd (cf. *op. cit.*).

But Walter Hilton, *op. cit.*, pp. 84-86, agrees with his contemporary, the author of *The Pearl:*

> Thou shalt understand that there be two rewards in the bliss of heaven, which Our Lord giveth to chosen souls. The one is *Sovereign* and *Principal*, and is called *Essential Reward*, and that is the knowing and loving God according to the measure of charity given by God to the soul while she lived here in mortal body. This reward is best and *Sovereign*, for it is God Himself, and is common to all the souls that shall be saved, in what state or degree soever they live in holy Church, more or less, according to the quantity and the muchness of their charity in this life, what degree soever they live in . . .
>
> Another reward there is that is *Secondary*, or *Accidental*, which our Lord giveth for special good deeds, which a man doth voluntarily, over that he is bound to do.

609-10. dard/To Hym. . . . 'Reverence paid to Him.' (*OED*, Dare . . . 'to be hid, lie hid, lurk.') This translation is offered because it seems to present a logical solution to the vexing problem of the prep. *to* (610), and because it fits the sense of the whole stanza (51). A clue is found in line 839 (see note), containing the infin. form *dare*, in which the sense, drawn from a scene in Apoc. 5, indicates that in the dialect of the poet *dare* ('lie hid') had developed the further meaning 'stand in awe of,' 'show reverence or respect to.' This probably grew out of the fact that mediaeval feelings of awe, respect, and reverence were commonly expressed in such ways as hiding the face (433-36), falling face downward, or prostrate (1120), or in some such manner demonstrating the human instinct of fearfulness, the need to "lie hid" from or before one inspiring fear and awe, as would God. By extension, this would include such acts of worship as kneeling, glorifying God in song, and so forth. 'Paid reverence to,' then, would be a suitable reading here for *dard to*, since reverence is, as Coleridge has said, "the synthesis of love and fear." GO. glosses 'shrank in fear before' or, alternatively, 'lay hidden, was inscrutable,' depending, he explains in a full note, on the reference of the pron. *hys* (*Hys*), opening line 609.

fraunchyse. 'Heritage, patrimony.' The man who always paid to God the reverence which is His due would certainly, by that token, be a good and faithful Christian. The *fraunchyse* of such a man, as granted him by the *gentyle Cheuentayn,* his Heavenly Father, would surely be *large:* that is, his spiritual inheritance, his *rewarde,* would be ample—abundant (cf. 607-8, 611). Cf. Walter Hilton, *loc. cit.,* as quoted at the end of n. 603-6, *supra.*

611. hem. 'Them,' where in context one might expect 'him' since it refers to *þat* (he who *euer dard to Hym*). It is possible that the poet intended to convey the sense "such men as this," "such a man." Reading the pron. 'such' keeps the meaning in translation. Cf. nn. 621, 685-88.

616. lere. Clearly *lere* in MS, a variant form of *lure* (cf. n. 8 for other variant forms of words of French origin used in this poem). In context, *lere* for 'lure, compensation, recompense' has the meaning 'something held forth or given equivalent to something suffered or done.' In this passage it refers to the *peny* promised to the laborers in the vineyard for their toil and pains (509-12). The maiden, restating the jeweler's dissatisfaction (see n. 597-600), first says that he thinks she has taken her *peny* unjustly (613-14). She then reminds him of his feelings that since she 'came too late'—after the others had toiled the long day through—she is not worthy *of so gret lere,* 'so large a recompense' (615-16), the *al & sum* (584) to which the jeweler has objected.

For *lure* in the sense 'estate, condition,' a possible alternative, see E. Fenimore, "A Monetary Question in *Gaulier D'Aupais?*" *MLN,* IV (1940), 338-42. O. and G. emend [*h*]*ere* (for *hire*), 'wages.' GO. emends [*f*]*ere,* glossing 'fortune, rank, dignity,' deriving from *fere,* an aphetic form, ultimately from OF *afeire.* He suggests the alternative *fere,* 'company' (OE *gefere*), referring to "the company of Heavenly queens."

617 ff. abate (617). In its usual significance: 'abate, slacken, lose zeal.' (For *abated,* 'abolished,' see n. 123.) The meaning of the passage is that the man who gradually loses his zeal for God, i.e., the intensity and fervor of his devotion and desire to please Him, will also gradually lose his watchfulness of soul. His mind and interest will be turned to earthly things. Eventually he will yield to worldly temptations and, 'in some kind of way' (619), fall into sin and forfeit the reward of Heaven—immediate beatitude—which will be delayed by Purgatory. Such a man may at the same time be *euer so holy in hys prayere* (618)—as was the "devout" Pharisee of the parable (Luke 18:10-14)—going through his devotions and religious duties with all outward appearance of holiness, while withering away spiritually for lack of zeal. Cf. Thomas à Kempis, *De Imitatione Christi,* Bk. II, chap. ix, 7-8:

I never found any so religious and devout, that he had not sometimes a withdrawing of grace, or felt not some decrease of zeal. . . . There followeth also temptation, lest he should wax proud of any good. The devil sleepeth not. . . .

The older such men grow while continuing to lose zeal, the more often they will depart from righteousness. Then only the mercy and grace of God (which is great enough to do so) will be able to guide him back to godliness (621-24). Cf. Thomas à Kempis, *op. cit.*, Bk. I, chap. xi, 5:

But now oftentimes we perceive . . . that we were better and purer at the beginning of our conversion, than after many years of our profession. Our fervor and profiting should increase daily: but now it is accounted a great matter, if a man can retain but some part of his first zeal.

G., O., and GO. translate *abate* as an artificial form of *abyde*, 'remain, endure.' Emerson proposes the past part. of *abaten* as meaning 'cast down, humbled.' But these scholars thus make the poet say—contrary to Christian teaching—that no matter how prayerful a man's life may be, he will at some time fall into sin. The reading 'lose zeal' provides an explanation and corrects this interpretation.

621. þay. 'They,' where 'he' might be expected for continuity of idea. It is obvious that unless *þay* relates back, through *he* (619), to its logical antecedent *bourne* (617), there ensues a confusing disruption of thought in the stanza. Again—as with *hem* in line 611—if the use of the plural pron. here is not simply colloquial, the intention may be to express the meaning "men like that one," "such men" (referring to *any bourne*). Assuming this, the pron. 'such' may be read for *þay* and the sense of the passage will be kept. Cf. nn. 611, 685-88.

647-48. O.'s punctuation, a semicolon after *plyt* (647), obscures the significance of these two lines. A semicolon after *water* (G.'s punctuation, 647) undoubtedly preserves the meaning, namely, that at the moment of Our Lord's death on the cross grace from God increased for mankind.

652. þe deth secounde. The condemnation of souls at the Last Judgment—*mors secunda* (Apoc. 2:11; 20:6, 14-15). O. calls attention also to Apoc. 21:8.

654. glayue. 'Lance.' See John 19:34.

657-60. G. capitalizes *he* (658). O. also makes the pronoun refer to God, explaining the meaning as: 'Now there is no obstacle between us and bliss that He has not withdrawn, and no means of approach that He has not restored. . . .' GO. translates similarly: 'Now there is nothing in the round world between us and bliss but what He has withdrawn, and that (the bliss) is restored in a blessed hour.'

But the logical and grammatical antecedent of *he* is surely *Adam* (656). It was Adam, through his transgression of God's command, who took away our bliss, i.e., the life of sanctifying grace. And that bliss is restored to us in a precious moment, the moment of Baptism, through the merits of Christ's passion and death. Cf. Hilton, *op. cit.*, Bk. I, ch. 3, p. 65: "Now are we restored again in hope by the passion of our Lord, to the dignity and bliss which we had lost by Adam's sin." For *wythdroȝ*, 'took away,' cf. Richard Rolle, "Tretys off the Ten Commandementys" in *English Prose Treatises of Richard Rolle de Hampole*, ed. G. G. Perry, E.E.T.S., No. 20, p. 12: "In the whylke [the Seventh Commandment] es forboden all manere of withdraweynge of oþer men thynges wrangwysely agaynes þaire wyll. . . ."

672. At inoscente. 'With the innocent.' O., p. 72, thinks *at* may be a scribal error for *þat*. G. retains *at*, but substitutes *by* for *&* and emends *inosen*[*c*]*e*, translating: 'according to (his) innocence. . . .' Gordon and Onions, *op. cit.*, p. 179, emend *a*[*s*], as does Holthausen. Later, GO. emends *and*, translating: 'And (he that is) innocent is redeemed and sanctified by divine grace.' He adds: "Or MS *At* may be emended to *As*: 'being innocent, &c.' " *At*, however, has a variety of meanings which would prohibit its change; *inoscente* is adj. for noun, as elsewhere (cf. 625, 666, 684, 696, 720).

673-74. The MS *god* must mean 'God'; otherwise, *hys* (675) and *hym* (676) lack an antecedent. Cf. n. 657-60. O., G., and GO. understand *god* as 'good.'

677-82. For probable source, cf. Psalm 23:3-4; also Psalm 14:1-2.

683. Cf. Psalm 14:5; also Psalm 120:3.

685-88. See Matt. 25:46 for Christ's promise that the just shall go into eternal life, from which source lines 685-86 may be drawn. For lines 687-88, cf. Psalm 23:4.

þat (687). 'That which.' Since *þat* here relates apparently to *the ryȝtwys man* (685), but is followed by the plural pron. *her* ('their'), repeated in 688, the question again arises (see n. 611) whether this use of the plural pron. is a colloquialism, an error, or written by intent to broaden its reference. As with *hem* in 611 and *þay* in 621 (see note), it seems logical to assume intent and the probable sense "such men as he" (i.e., the 'just man'), and to translate 'such as,' thus preventing distortion of context and unnecessary emendation.

689-94. þys ryȝtwys (689). 'This just man.' In the light of Wisdom 10:10, which Henry Bradley (*Academy* XXXVIII, 201) discovered, through the mention of Solomon in 689, to be the source of this passage, it may be assumed that this particular *ryȝtwys* (not the *ryȝtwys man*, in general, of 685) is Jacob. Although, like the other patriarchs described in Wisdom 10, he is not named, he has been traditionally identified as

Jacob through the phrase *profugum irae fratris iustum,* drawn from Gen. 27:41-44.

saȝ (689). 'Saw.' Solomon perceived how fittingly Jacob received honor; thus, he singled him out in Wisdom 10 as one guided and helped by the power of Wisdom, the handmaiden of God. GO. glosses 'says,' pointing out that 'says how' is good OE idiom and that "Solomon did not claim to see the righteous man's reception by Wisdom."

kyntly (690). 'Fittingly.' *Kyntly,* with this meaning, occurs in *Purity* 1. See *infra, ho* (691), for emendations.

on[ou]re (690). 'Honor.' For 'honour,' fourteenth century, *OED* gives 'onur, honour(e), onour(e).' Emending the word as here agrees in final form with Bradley's [*on*]*oure.* The word as written in MS, however, is *onre,* not *oure* as in texts of G. and O., and as assumed in the emendation suggested by Bradley (*op. cit.*), *How* [*Koyntyse on*]*oure,* accepted by GO. There is no lacuna in MS and the line is metrically sound; hence it was, no doubt, written as it stands. Bradley's suggestion, *onoure,* would seem to throw light on the subject: *onre* of the MS reflects *honestavit illum* in *laboribus* (Wisdom 10:10). "He" has been added in translation to provide the pronoun necessary in MnE clearly to relate *ryȝtwys* (689) to *con aquyle* (690).

ho (691). 'She.' This emendation of MS *he* was suggested by Bradley (*ibid.*) for agreement with his emendation of *kyntly* in 690, *Koyntise* (*Sapientia,* 'Wisdom'), GO. adopting both changes. The poet himself, however, does not mention Wisdom by name. Since lines 691-92 are almost exact renditions of parallel clauses in Wisdom 10:10 (*deduxit per vias rectas, et ostendit illi regnum Dei*), they may have been familiar enough to the author's mediaeval readers to quote out of context, trusting to the pronoun to carry an elliptical reference to Wisdom (cf. *haec* in Wisdom 10:10). *He,* then, must be a scribal error for *ho,* as was *ho* for *he* in line 492 (*q.v.*). G. and O. keep *he,* as fitting the antecedent *Kyng hym* (interpolated by G.[1] between *How kyntly oure* and *con aquyle*), and the later, emended interpolation by G.[2], *Koyntyse hym,* adopted from Bradley. According to G., *oure Koyntyse,* 'our Wisdom,' was a mediaeval, symbolic name for Christ.

See Gen. 28:10-15 for the account of Jacob's dream, in which he was shown *þe rengne of God,* as noted by Solomon in the Book of Wisdom (10:10).

698-700. Cf. Psalm 142:2.

703. The interpretation adopted here is based on the suggestion by Dorothy Everett and Naomi D. Hurnard, "Legal Phraseology in a Passage in *Pearl,*" *MÆ,* XVI (1947), 9, that *alegge* be taken as a conditional subjunctive rather than the imperative, the usual reading. G. has 'Renounce your claim,' O., 'Urge your privilege.' GO. supports Miss Everett and Miss Hurnard, who offer: 'If you plead right (or righteousness) you may be trapped (or refuted in argument). . . .'

714. touch. 'Touch.' Careful inspection of this word in MS makes it clear that the two final letters are actually *ch,* not the *th* M. believed it necessary to emend *ch.* Although inscribed in a smaller, cramped style, this *ch* when compared with the *ch* in *chylder,* one word away, agrees with it in form. It would seem, therefore, that emendation is not necessary.

721. mylde. 'Tender (or meek) ones.' Adj. as noun. For source, see Luke 18:15-17, espec. v. 16: *Jesus autem convocans illos. . . .* The poet's choice of *mylde* indicates that he was familiar with the Greek version of this story of Christ blessing the children, there being no ambiguity of pronoun there as in the Latin and English renderings (*illos,* them). Context, too, would signify that *mylde* for the disciples in this instance would be out of drawing, since Christ is rebuking them for their over-anxiety on His behalf and their consequent harshness toward *Hys mylde.* GO., in glossing 'gentle ones,' parenthetically identifies *mylde* as "Christ's disciples." The Greek, however, is clear: cf. *βρεφη . . . αυτα.* For other Gospel versions of this episode, see Matt. 19:13-15; Mark 10:13-16, both of which go beyond the implication of Luke's *convocans illos* in that one states that Christ laid His hands on the children in blessing, the other that He put his arms about them and blessed them. Cf. also Matt. 18:2: *Et advocans Jesus parvulum.*

729-32. Lines emphasizing the theme of the poem. Cf. Matt. 13:45-46, the parable of the merchant, termed by the poet a *jueler* (730, 734 *joueler*). Cf. n. 252.

733-44. O.'s comment, p. 82, on these lines, namely, that "the poet's interpretation of the pearl of great price (Matt. 13:45-46) is somewhat confused," is surely to be rejected. The poet definitely states that the pearl of great price, *þat boȝt is dere* (733) and for which the *joueler* gave all his goods (734), symbolizes the Kingdom of Heaven (735), the destiny of all the saved—their common reward (739). Cf. 221 and n. 603-6. The jeweler is therefore counseled by the maiden to buy *his* 'spotless pearl' (744); that is, to secure the Kingdom of Heaven for himself through renunciation of the world (743), the world in his case represented by his inordinate attachment to an earthly treasure.

749. Þy beaute . . . nature. The soul's beauty is supernatural; the beauty of the lost pearl was from nature (269-70). Cf. Hilton, *op. cit.,* Bk. I, ch. 3, p. 66:

> . . . whosoever once hath an inward sight, but a little of that dignity and that spiritual fairness which a soul hath by creation, and shall have again by grace, he will loathe in his heart all the bliss, the liking and the fairness of this world.

Cf. also a passage, *ibid.*, Bk. III, ch. 9, pp. 267-68, which probably contains the key to the meaning of *The Pearl* as a whole:

> Covetousness also is slain in a soul by the working of love, for it maketh the soul so covetous of spiritual good and so inflamed to heavenly riches that it setteth right nought by all earthly things. It hath no more joy in the having of a precious stone than a chalkstone . . . for he knows well that all these earthly things which worldly men set so great price by and love so dearly must pass away and turn to nothing, both the thing itself and the love of it. And therefore he worketh his thoughts betimes into that judgment and esteem of them which they must come to hereafter, and so accounteth them as nought.

759 ff. The soul is called to union with God, although in its sojourn upon earth that union sometimes seems too high a destiny.

761. wete. 'Woe.' OE *wite*. For vowel change, see Jordan, *Handbuch* . . ., p. 46, par. 26, M., G., O., and GO. gloss 'wet,' which seems forced here.

762. bonerte. 'Blessedness.' OF *boneurté*. This derivation is suggested by Gordon and Onions, *op. cit.*, p. 187, instead of the traditional *bonerte*, 'courtesy.'

766. on dese. 'At the dais' or, as O. translates, 'in a place of honor.'

768. & pyȝt me in perleȝ maskelleȝ. The soul is represented in Scripture as a bride adorned with jewels. Cf. Isaias 61:10. Lines 763-68 of the poem, a mosaic of various verses from the Bible, would be sufficient to disprove—were not the entire work composed after the same method—Carleton Brown's affirmation, *op. cit.*, p. 120 (in support of his view regarding the poet's alleged evangelicalism) that his handling of scriptural material is exceptionally accurate in detail. Cf. O., p. xix, n. 2, who takes issue with Brown on this question. (For lines 763-66, cf. Cant. 4:7-8; Apoc. 7:14.)

775. onvnder cambe. A conventional phrase, complimentary to ladies. O., p. 85, lists several similar expressions in other ME works.

786. A hondred & forty þowsande. Another instance (see n. 768) of the poet's freedom in handling scriptural detail (if it is not a scribal error). "One hundred forty-four thousand" is the number given in Apoc. 14:1 and 3. G. and GO. interpolate *fowre*. (Cf. lines 869-70, where the poet is specific.)

791. hyl coppe. 'Hilltop.' Emerson, "Some Notes on *The Pearl*," *PMLA*, XXXVII (1922), 77, emends *hyl-cot*, 'hill-dwelling,' in compliment to the poet's sense of rhyme. But since *cot* (OE and ME) is generally used of dwellings of a less dignified character than would befit the New Jerusalem, if any were to be found there (see n. 1027), the accepted MS reading of *coppe*—a word badly cramped, perhaps corrected—should probably be retained.

802. in lande [n]e[m]. MS, *in lande men.* 'Seizes on heath.' This is M.'s emendation, followed by G. and O. O. notes that Fick and Köbling would retain MS *men,* 'maim,' OF *mahaigner* (F., *in bonde men,* K., *in honde men*). There would be no serious objection to the imperfect rhyme; however, to this writer the MS is clearly *lande.* GO. states that "the second stroke of the *h*" appears to him to have been "joined to the first upright stroke of the *a*," thus providing the reading *in hande nem* (accepting M.'s emendation of *men*). Holthausen emends *in* [*h*]*onde* [*con*] [*n*]*e*[*m*].

For discussion of meaning, see n. 803.

803. query. 'Questioning, interrogation.' Perhaps from L. *quaere,* sg. imperative, *quaerere.* G. gives etymology, L., *quaerere,* def., 'query, question,' emending quer[e], for the sake of rhyme. *OED* and O. define 'complaint,' L. *queri,* which GO. adopts. Emerson, *op. cit.,* p. 79, criticizes *OED*'s assumption of a noun from the Latin as failing to account for the accent or the rhyme.

The meaning of this line is closely associated with that of lines 801-2, all three being drawn from Isaias 53:7:

> *Oblatus est quia ipse voluit, et non aperuit*
> *os suum: sicut ovis ad occisionem ducetur,*
> *et quasi agnus coram tendente se obmutescet,*
> *et non aperiet os suum.*

> He was offered because it was his own will, and
> he opened not his mouth: he shall be led as a
> sheep to the slaughter, and shall be dumb as
> a lamb before his shearer, and he shall not
> open his mouth.

The poet's addition *fro ych query/Quen Juez Hym iugged in Jerusalem* (803-4) refers the reader to the Gospel verses telling of the many questionings of Christ: by the high priest (Mark 14:60-61; Matt. 26:62-63); by the chief priests and the elders (Matt. 27:12); by Herod (Luke 23:9); and by Pilate (Mark 15:4-5; Matt. 27:13-14; John 19:9). Before all these questioners, we are told, "he did not say a single word."

806. wyth boyeȝ bolde. 'With malefactors.' Literally, 'with rogues bold,' in the sense "bold or shameless in wickedness." The poet here recalls the Good Friday scene: Christ *rent on rode* and, hanging on either side of Him, the *boyeȝ bolde.* These are the "two others" of John 19:18, the "two robbers" of Mark 15:27 and Matt. 27:38—the "malefactors" of Luke 23:32-33.

811-15. Cf. Isaias 53:2-9; also II Cor. 5:21. For retention of MS *lomp* (and *Lompe*, 945), see Gordon and Onions, *op. cit.*, pp. 182 ff., who have found these forms elsewhere, as, e.g., in the stanzaic *Life of Christ*, ed. Forster (E.E.T.S.), probably written in Chester. *Lombe* for *lompe* (1046), Gordon and Onions also argue, must be retained as another instance of "Western reverse spelling," parallel to *poyned* (217), *coumforde* (369), *marked* (513). GO., later, carries similar comments in his App. II, p. 93, App. III, p. 95.

For *bostwys*, 'rude' (814), see n. 911.

817-18. GO. notes: "There is no record of John the Baptist having baptised elsewhere than in Jordan. . . . doubtless the poet's ideas of the geography of Palestine were vague."

819. Cf. Isaias 40:3; also John 1:23; Matt. 3:3; Luke 3:4.

820 ff. Cf. John 1:29. Drawing accurately from this verse for St. John the Baptist's own words (820-24), the poet then has him continue with words found in Isaias (53:4-9).

823. dryȝe. 'Dry, blot'; hence, to remove or take away (by absorption). Perhaps a deliberate choice of word, since by His death and Sacrifice Christ absorbed into Himself the sins of the world. Note the use of *clem* in line 826 (see note). A verb, *dryȝe* is regarded as adj. by G. ('endless') and by O. and GO. ('heavy').

826. clem. 'Smear' (M.). Cf. *Purity* 312: *cleme*, 'daub.' An appropriate word—contrary to the opinions of G. and O.—as expressing the loathsomeness of sin, which is likened by Isaias (63:4) to leprosy (*et nos putavimus eum quasi leprosum*).

830-34. 'Twice as a Lamb was accounted. . . .' First by Isaias (53:7), then by St. John the Baptist (cf. n. 820 ff.); the third time (833-34), by St. John the Apostle (Apoc. 5:6).

837. boke with leueȝ sware. This was the "scroll" of Apoc. 5:1, which Christ, the Lamb, opened, as seen by the Apostle (Apoc. 5:6-8). Having the books of his own time in mind, the poet has imagined the scroll as a mediaeval book, having *leueȝ sware*.

839-40. douth (839). 'Creature, being.' The primary meaning of the word was 'manhood, man (collectively),' with the extended meaning 'being, creature.' Archaic in the fourteenth century; see Oakden, *op. cit.*, II, 178.

con dare (839). 'Worshipped (Him).' For etymology and explanation of meaning, see n. 609-10. 'Worshipped' (v.t. or v.i.) fits the sense here since during the scene portrayed in Apoc. 5—after the Lamb opened the Book—several immediate manifestations of worship and adoration took place: The *fowre besteȝ* and *þe aldermen* fell down before Him (v. 8); a new canticle was sung (v. 9); thousands of thousands of voices cried out in worship (vv. 11-12). Most relevant to line 839 is its source, verse 13. These creatures did not conceal themselves—hide—from the awesome presence of the Lamb. They 'worshipped Him.'

853-64. creste. The 'top, acme,' i.e., the best of pearls, the *wonder perle* (221) symbolizing the Kingdom of Heaven. Those who possess it —accounting all else negligible (*mote,* 'speck, trifle,' 855)—can not be tempted by any inferior (earthly) joy (*Lasse of blysse,* 853).

In accordance with the suggestion of Ten Brink (*History of English Literature,* I, 349, n. 2), O., Intr. xlvi, n. 1, believes that one stanza of Group XV (which contains six instead of the usual five) may be superfluous, and that No. 72 (853-64) is the stanza. G., without mentioning O., expresses the same conviction. O. argues that No. 72 contains nothing essential to the progress of the poem, and nothing which is not implied in the preceding stanza. Also, he believes the last six lines to be inferior in metrical quality to the rest of the poem.

GO. (App. I, p. 88) thinks Stanza 76 more likely to be the otiose one, "since all it says is 'Excuse me if after all I ask a question,' and the question is asked in 77." Only the first two lines of Stanza 76, he feels, are really necessary, whereas the explanation in line 859 (Stanza 77) is important.

860. 'Hope of one death,' i.e., the hope that the death of their earthly bodies has released their souls into eternal life; that they will avoid the *mors secunda* (see n. 652). The maiden rejoices because the company of the predestined (the 144,000) have been assured of this, since they bear the names of the Father and of the Lamb on their foreheads (871-72); cf. Apoc. 14:1.

867-88. These stanzas (73-75) retell the Apostle's vision of the Lamb standing on Mount Sion. Cf. Apoc. 14:1-5.

886-87. For *þe fowre bestez* and *þe aldermen,* see Apoc. 4:4, 6-8. The 'ancients' are the "four-and-twenty elders," identified by scriptural scholars as the holy ones of the Old and New Testaments; the beasts represent animated nature—man, birds, cattle, wild animals.

909. sympelnesse . . . enclose. 'Simplicity . . . enshrine.' In other words: "Thou who art the personification of simplicity." St. Paul commended as a virtue "the simplicity that is in Christ"; see II Cor. 8:2, 9:11, 9:13, and especially 11:3.

911. bustwys (*bostwys,* 814). 'Rude, rough, coarse.' Perhaps connected with the verb *bosten,* 'to boast, bluster.' Cf. ME *boistous,* 'boisterous' (derivation uncertain; cf. Welch *bwystus,* 'ferocious'). GO. gives OF *boisteus,* 'rough,' glossing 'roughly massive,' 814; 'rough, crude,' 911.

blose. 'Dolt, clod.' From OF *blos,* 'denué, privé (de bon sens),' suggested by G.[1] and followed by Emerson. Editors agree that this word is unknown in ME. M. glosses 'blaze, flame,' ON *blossi;* O., p. 89, expresses the opinion that "probably rime determined the choice of the word." G.[2] emends [*w*]*ose,* 'wild man,' OE [*wudu*]*wasa.* 'Churl' has been suggested by E. M. Wright, GO. notes, as noun from the French adj. *blos,* offered by G.[1] GO. believes *blose* may be an error for ME *bose* (*bosse*), 'a leather bottle,' a phrase applied in those days to crude persons. In *Richard the Redeless* III, 98, he finds the word *bosse* applied to a bear. He glosses '? rough, uncouth person.' Since in line 905, the dreamer has reached humility (*I am bot mokke & mul among*), some such expression of self-abasement is suitable here.

929. See n. 265-76.

931. gele. Said by Oakden, *op. cit.*, II, 188, to be the "most striking" of the "numerous archaic words in *The Pearl.*"

944. theme. The learned *th* instead of *t*, but with the sound of *t*, hence alliterating with *take*. See Jordan, *op. cit.*, p. 288, anm. 2. O., p. 89, notes *throne*, 1113, alliterating with *trone* and *tras*, and the spelling *trone*, 835, 920, 1051, 1055.

945. For **Lompe,** see n. 811-15.

947-48. flake. 'Spot, blemish.' Probably related to ON *flekkr*. The Lamb is without spot (945); His flock is without spot (947); therefore, His city is without spot, *moote* (948). The dwellings, 924 says, should be *wythouten mote*. And cf. *flok . . . wythouten flake* (947) with *meyny . . . wythouten mote* (960). G. and O. derive *flake* from ON *flaki*. G. glosses 'hurdle,' O., 'pinfold.' Both understand *moote* (948) to mean 'moat.'

981. keued. 'Sunken, low-placed.' Cf. n. 320. G., p. 161, explains the appropriateness of the poet's word, since the dreamer, from his position on the hill (979) sees, beyond the brook, the New Jerusalem (as the Apostle described it in Apoc. 21:2, 10-11) "descended, sunk down from heaven." (Cf. line 988.)

989 ff. Cf. Apoc. 21:11-27; 22:1-5 for the Apostle's vision of the celestial city, source for these stanzas.

992-93. Context makes it clear that, in the poet's mind, the *bantele3* were identical with the tiers of the foundation, the *fundamenta duodecim* of Apoc. 21:14.

1007. G. changes MS *rybe* to *sarde*, to accord with Scripture (Apoc. 21:20, *sardius*) and for the sake of alliteration with *sexte*.

1015. gentyleste. The superlative nobility of the amethyst. The jacinth is merely noble in the positive degree. G., [*try*]*este*.

1027. wone3. No dwellings are mentioned in the Apocalypse. Another departure from scriptural accuracy.

1039-41. Vchon in scrypture. . . . Literally: "A name in writing creased (i.e., wrought into, engraved) into each one." Apoc. 21:12 says that the names of the twelve tribes of the children of Israel were written on the twelve gates in the wall of the New Jerusalem. (Cf. Ezech. 48:31-34.) That these names were written 'according to their fortunes of birth' (1041)—that of the eldest first—comes from God's directions to Moses for the making of priestly attire for Aaron and his sons. The names of the twelve tribes were to be engraved on the two onyx stones (six on each) to be set into the ephod (cf. Exodus 28:9-12). It was specified that the names were to be *iuxta ordinem nativitas* (v. 10). The names were also to be engraved separately, one on each of twelve precious stones to be set into the rational of judgment (vv. 15-21). The poet may very well, as GO. suggests, have found the two passages (Apoc. and Exodus) juxtaposed in a scriptural commentary.

1046. lombe. See n. 811-15.

1050. lette no lyȝt. The transparent walls, obstructing no light, rendered the interior visible. G. emends [*s*]*yȝt*.

1051-54. Cf. Apoc. 4:2-3, 7:9-11. Most of the other passages following have their principal source in Apoc. 21 or 22, although here and there the poet interpolates a line or two drawn from other parts of the same book.

1058. flet here is probably the verb, with the nominal compound *foysoun-flode* as subject. The antecedent of *þat* would then be *trone* (1055). This construction is justified by the source of the lines (1055-60), Apoc. 22:1: "And he showed me a river of the water of life, clear as crystal, proceeding from the throne of God and of the Lamb." The traditional understanding of *flet* (M., F., O.) is 'floor, apartment,' OE *flett*. O. glosses 'ground,' GO., 'floor, ground (of a city).' *A* is emended *A*[*s*] by G., O., and GO.

1063. mynster. 'Church, minster.' MS *mynyster* is probably a scribal error. Cf. source, Apoc. 21:22.

1064. reget. 'Get again, redeem' (G.). *OED*, 'of obscure origin and meaning.' G. refers to Rev. v:6 (Apoc. 5:6), which includes the phrase "a Lamb standing, as if slain." Adding a reference to verse 9 of the same chapter would further support the reading 'redeem.'

O.'s glossing 'to reproduce,' and his note (p. 92), "the celebration of the mass in heaven," must be rejected. His interpretation is based upon a misunderstanding of the passage he quotes from Albertus Magnus, *De Eucharistica*, Dist. 3, Tract 4, cap. 5, *Opera*, ed. Borgnet, 38:

> Haec [eucharistia] enim erit coena nuptiarum Agni (Apoc. 19:9) . . . In deliciis paradisi Dei nostri sumitur corpus Domini. Ibi enim cum Patre aeterno nos honorante per suum consensum ad mensam sedemus. Ibi Filius praecinctus decore et lumine se nobis ministrat.

The passage (cf. Albertus' reference, Apoc. 19:9) concerns the "marriage supper of the Lamb." The consuming of the Body of the Lord —*sumitur corpus Domini*—means Holy Communion, *Eucharistia*. The Mass is something different, requiring the offering and the mystical slaying of the Divine Victum. There is no Mass in Heaven. For a complete exposition of this subject, see Dom Anscar Vonier, O.S.B., *A Key to the Doctrine of the Eucharist*, pp. 251 ff. One pertinent extract must suffice here:

> The Eucharistic sacrifice shares the transitoriness of the whole sacramental system; its sacramental character postulates this. There will be no Eucharistic sacrifice in heaven, as there will be no Baptism, as there will be no anointing with chrism.

GO., emending *refet,* rejects the sense 'redeem' as "unsuitable in the context." Adopting E. M. Wright's suggestion of *refet,* 'refection, nourishment,' OF *refait,* he suggests: 'the Lamb, the sacrifice, was there as refreshment,' explaining in a full note. But see *supra* for strong reasons to retain *reget,* 'redeem.'

Sakerfyse (MS *saker-fyse*) is in apposition with *Lombe,* meaning that He *has been* slain. Cf. Apoc. 5:9 and 5:12, in both of which the past tense (*slain*) is used.

1067-68. Cf. Apoc. 21:27.

1077-80. Cf. Apoc. 22:2.

1086. freuch. 'Noble.' Cf. *Rauf Coilyear,* ed. Herrtage, E.E.T.S., No. 39, p. 525: *Oft fair foullis ar foundin faynt, and als freuch. Frelich,* 'noble,' was suggested by M. (OE *freolic*).

1111. Cf. Apoc. 5:6.

1119-24. Cf. Apoc. 5:5-10.

1126. þe Vertues of Heuen. One of the nine orders of celestial beings. (See Dante, *Il Paradiso* XXVIII.)

1141. An ordinary meaning of *wene* is 'imagine.' For the subjunctive *lyste,* cf. *forbede* (379) and *loke* (710). The sense of the line is: "It is impossible to imagine the Lamb's delight." *Lombe,* as a title, genitive without inflectional ending. O. translates, "(Yet) it would please none to doubt the Lamb's joy"; G., "To no one was there desire to question the delight of the Lamb"; Emerson, "The Lamb's delight (pleasure) none list to think of . . ."; Coulton, "Yet His delight none doubted then."

1153-55. These lines are surely misinterpreted by Sister Madeleva, *op. cit.,* pp. 46-47, as indicating the desire, which all mystics share, "to die and leave the world" in order to enjoy eternal happiness with God. The fact is that many mystics, as, e.g., St. Thérèse (the Little Flower), have expressed a desire to live and suffer in order to save souls. The words of the text, moreover, fail to support Sister Madeleva's interpretation. The *luf-longyng* (1152) of the dreamer was aroused not by God, but by the beauty of the vision-maiden. When he sees *her* (1147) in the *meyny* of the Lamb (1145), *þat syȝt* (1151) causes him to *þenk to wade. My maneȝ mynde to maddyng malte* (1154) records not ecstasy (cf. Sister Madeleva, *op. cit.,* p. 4) but the folly of the jeweler's uncontrolled passion for beauty. He emphasizes especially the 'whiteness' (1150) associated in his mind with his lost pearl (see n. 163-68).

1156. walte. 'Vexed.' The maiden would be vexed at the jeweler's crossing, because she had earlier (318-24) set forth the serious reasons prohibiting it. Derivation here is from OE *-wælan*. For *a* from OE *æ* in *Pearl*, cf. *clanly* (2), *laste* (956), *lasteȝ* (1198), *strateȝ* (1043).

1157-60. To fech me bur. 'To work up speed for myself.' Literally: "To go and get for myself speed," i.e., to walk or run back, then turn and run forward with all the speed thus gathered or "worked up."

take me halte. 'Spring high.' Literally: "betake me, or take myself high." In ME, as in MnE, *take* ('take') has a variety of meanings; cf. *STR-BR* illustration: 'Þat Adam god forlet & toc him to þe deofel,' *Ormulum* 356. For *halte, OED* gives 'haut, a. and sb. (OF *halt,* fourteenth to sixteenth centuries).'

O. and G. place a semicolon after *halte,* O. translating adj., 'lame,' G. glossing n., 'hold, support, "take-off" ' but translating freely. But *to fech,* (*to*) *take,* and *to start* would seem to be in parallel construction, infinitives after *þoȝt*—all preliminary to the final infin., *to swymme* (1160). The picture is of one who works up his speed, stops to spring high for the dive, then plunges far enough out into the stream to permit the space he must cover by swimming to be called *þe remnaunt.*

1174. raxled. *OED* '(*poetic*) To rax up, to start up or waken from a swoon.'

1175. syking. This form of the pres. part. (which in NWM normally ends in *-ande*) is not scribal, says Oakden, *op. cit.,* p. 81, and "at any rate would not be dialectically impossible in this area."

1177. outfleme. 'Expelled,' past part. In OE the word was either verb, noun, or adjective. Here, according to *OED,* O., and G., it is a noun; according to Miss Day (*MLR,* XIV, 413-15) and to Oakden (*op. cit.,* p. 82), it is a past part., the *-d* lost; to GO., an adj., 'driven out.'

1181. rewfully. 'Repentantly.' The jeweler, remembering the Heavenly bliss he has seen in his vision, is filled with grief and remorse that he attempted to cross the stream in spite of the maiden's warning (299-300; cf. also n. 1156 and lines noted). Because of his disobedience and wilfulness in following his own wishes, he has displeased the Prince (1164-66), and is now deprived of the wonderful vision. His spiritual awakening and repentance are expressed in the words he cries out to the dream-maiden (1182-88).

1183. For **deme,** 'say, tell (reveal),' cf. Oakden, *op. cit.,* II, 186.

1186. stykeȝ in garlande. . . . 'Stickest (art set) in garland.' The soul is a jewel set in a *garlande* of souls. For similar use of the word garland, cf. Dante, *Il Paradiso* X, 91-93, who pictures the souls circling round Beatrice, making of themselves a crown:

> Tu vuoi saper di quai piante s'infiora
> questa ghirlanda, che intorno vagheggia
> la bella donna ch' al ciel t'avvalora.

Cf. also *ibid.* XII, 19-20, still relating to the encircling souls:

cosi di quelle sempiterne rose
volgeansi circa noi le due ghirlande. . . .

O., n. on *Pearl* 735-43, quotes from the "Hymn of St. Ephrem," *Select Hymns and Homilies*, trans. H. Burgess, p. 14: "Like pearls in diadems children are inserted in the kingdom. . . ." Both the figure and the verb (*inserted*) elucidate *Pearl* 1186; yet O., like G., emends *st[r]ykeȝ* and understands, as G. does, *garlande* to be the crown described in 205-8. See Sister Mary Vincent Hillmann, "Some Debatable Words in *Pearl* and its Theme," *MLN*, LX (April, 1945), 241-48.

1193. helde, past part. of *helden*, 'disposed.' *Helde* is the regular preterite form of the verb, though *heldet* (*-ed*) and *heldit* occur. In *Pearl*, the absence of the final *-d* is not unusual; see n. 11. The suggestion made by G. that *helde* is the equivalent of the modern dialect word *helt*, 'readily' (as comp. form, OE *held*) was adopted by O. and by Gordon and Onions, *op. cit.*—later by GO. The latter, however, refers the word ultimately to ON *heldr* (as a positive inferred from the comp. *helder*). G. translates 'belike.' GO. offers alternatives: (1) 'as likely as possible,' 'very likely' (with *as* intens.); (2) 'as likely as not,' 'quite probably' (with correl. *as*).

But all four scholars have difficulty with etymological proofs and with meaning. *Helde*, 'disposed,' fits context and also supports the orthodox teaching that humility wins grace from God.

1201. sete saȝte. 'Make peace, be reconciled,' through renunciation of whatever hinders friendship with God.

1205. lote I laȝte. The lot or destiny of the soul is friendship with God. This destiny the jeweler has at length grasped as being the lesson of the vision.

1207 ff. The concluding stanza shows the jeweler ready, through renunciation (*bytaȝte*, 1207), to enter upon the mystical life, the life tending to union with God, an objective which has been made possible for mankind through the Incarnation. It was Christ, says the jeweler, who by His death and Sacrifice secured for all who follow Him the privilege of belonging to His household—souls purchased at a great price, 'precious pearls,' pleasing to Him. For *homly hyne*, cf. Ephes. 2:18-19: "For by him we have access in one Spirit to the Father. Now, therefore, you are no more strangers and foreigners; but you are fellow citizens with the saints, and domestics of God." (Note also Apoc. 19:10.)

hit (1207). The material pearl, lost in the garden—now recognized by the penitent jeweler as truly *noȝt* (see n. 269 ff.).

in (1207). 'Through.' Cf. a similar expression, line 63.

The preterite *gef* (1211) is erroneously, I believe, pronounced a subjunctive by O. and G., and by Carleton Brown in his review of R. M. Garrett's "*The Pearl:* an Interpretation," *MLN*, XXXIV (1919), 42-45, all three scholars apparently expecting at the end of the poem the conventional mediaeval prayer. GO. also gives the subj., but points to the comma he inserts in text after *myn* (1208) as a sign of uncertainty; *Þat* in 1209, he says, may refer to *Krysteȝ* (1208), or it may introduce the expected prayer.

It is to be observed also that the thought of the Redemption through the passion and death of Our Lord quite naturally brings to the mind of the poet the thought of the Sacrifice of the Mass, which, identical with the Sacrifice of the Cross, perpetuates that sacrifice throughout the world and for all time.

Bibliography

Editions

Morris, Richard. *Early English Alliterative Poems in the West-Midland Dialect of the Fourteenth Century,* E.E.T.S., No. 1, London, 1864.

Gollancz, Sir Israel. *Pearl, An English Poem of the Fourteenth Century. Edited with Modern Rendering,* London, David Nutt, 1891.

Gordon, E. V. *Pearl* (Revised by Ida L. Gordon, 1952), Oxford, Clarendon Press, 1953.

Osgood, Charles G. *The Pearl. A Middle English Poem.* Edited with Introductory Notes and Glossary, Boston, D. C. Heath & Co., 1906.

Translations

Coulton, George G. *Pearl, a Fourteenth Century Poem. Rendered into Modern English,* London, David Nutt, 1906.

Gollancz, Sir Israel. *Pearl, An English Poem of the Fourteenth Century. Edited with Modern Rendering,* London, David Nutt, 1891.

——— *Pearl, an English Poem of the XIVth Century: Edited with Modern Rendering,* London, Chatto & Windus, 1921.

Osgood, Charles G. *The Pearl: an Anonymous English Poem of the 14th Century, rendered in Prose,* Princeton (privately printed), 1907.

Interpretation and Criticism

Brown, Carleton. "The Author of *The Pearl* Considered in the Light of His Theological Opinions," *PMLA,* XIX (1904), 115-53.

——— Review of "*The Pearl:* an Interpretation," by R. M. Garrett, *MLN,* XXXIV (1919), 42-45.

Chapman, C. O. "The Authorship of *The Pearl,*" *PMLA,* XLVII (1932), 346-53.

Coulton, George G. "In Defense of 'Pearl,'" *MLR,* II (1906), 39-43.

Fick, Wilhelm. *Zum mittelenglischen Gedicht von der Perle,* Kiel, Lipsius und Tischer, 1885.

Fletcher, Jefferson B. "The Allegory of *The Pearl*," *Journal of English and Germanic Philology*, XX (1921), 1-21.

Garrett, R. M. "*The Pearl*: an Interpretation," *Studies in English, University of Washington Publications*, IV (1918), 1-48.

Gordon, E. V., and C. T. Onions. "Notes on the Text and Interpretation of *Pearl*," *Medium Ævum*, I (1932), 126-36; II (1933), 165-88.

Greene, W. K. "*The Pearl*: a New Interpretation," *PMLA*, XL (1925), 814-27.

Holthausen, Ferdinand. Review of *The Pearl*, ed. Sir Israel Gollancz, 1891, *Athenæum* (1891), p. 184.

Hulbert, James R. "The 'West Midland' of the Romances," *Modern Philology*, XIX (1921), 1-16.

Madeleva, Sister Mary. *Pearl: a Study in Spiritual Dryness*, New York, D. Appleton & Co., 1925.

Menner, Robert J. "Four Notes on the West Midland Dialect," *MLN*, XLI (1926), 451-58.

——— Review of *Pearl: a Study in Spiritual Dryness*, by Sister M. Madeleva, *MLN*, XLI (1926), 411-14.

Northup, Clark S. "Recent Studies of *The Pearl*," *MLN*, XXII (1907), 21-22.

Oakden, J. P. *Alliterative Poetry in Middle English*, Manchester, 1931, 1935. 2 vols.

Schofield, William H. "The Nature and Fabric of *The Pearl*," *PMLA*, XIX (1904), 154-215.

——— "Symbolism, Allegory, and Autobiography in *The Pearl*," *PMLA*, XXIV (1909), 585-675.

Wellek, R. "*The Pearl*: an Interpretation of the Middle English Poem," *Studies in English*, IV, Prague, Charles University, 1933.

Language and Dialect

Ames, Sir Harry. *Domesday Book*, Southampton, 1861-1864. 33 vols.

Björkman, Erik. *Scandinavian Loan Words in Middle English*, Halle, 1900-1902.

Bone, Gavin. "A Note on *Pearl* and *The Buke of the Howlat*," *Medium Ævum*, VI (1937), 169-70.

Cook, Albert S. "*Pearl*, 212 ff.," *Modern Philology*, VI (1908-1909), 197-200.

Day, Mabel. "The Weak Verb in the Works of the Gawain Poet," *MLR*, XIV (1919), 413-15.

——— "Two Notes on 'Pearl,'" *Medium Ævum*, III (1934), 241-42.

Einarsson, Stefán. "Old and Middle English Notes," *Journal of English and Germanic Philology*, XXXVI (1937), 183-87.

Ekwall, Eilert. *The Place-Names of Lancashire*, Manchester, 1922.

Emerson, Oliver F. "Imperfect Lines in *Pearl* and in the Rimed Parts of *Sir Gawain and the Green Knight,*" *Modern Philology,* XIX (1921-1922), 131-41.
——— "Some Notes on *The Pearl,*" *PMLA,* XXXVII (1922), 52-93.
——— "More Notes on *The Pearl,*" *PMLA,* XLII (1927), 807-31.
Hillmann, Sister Mary Vincent. "*Pearl:* 382; *mare reȝ mysse?*" *MLN,* LXVIII (1953), 528-31.
——— "Some Debatable Words in *Pearl* and Its Theme," *MLN,* LX (1945), 241-48.
——— "*Pearl: lere leke,* 210," *MLN,* LIX (1944), 417-18.
——— "*The Pearl: west ernays* (307); *fasor* (431)," *MLN,* LVIII (1943), 42-44.
——— "*Pearl: Inlyche* and *Rewarde,*" *MLN,* LVI (1941), 457-58.
Jordan, Richard. *Handbuch der mittelenglischen Grammatik* (bearbeitet von H. Ch. Matthes), Heidelberg, Carl Winter, 1934.
Luick, Karl. *Historische Grammatik der englischen Sprache,* Leipzig, Tauchnitz, 1921.
Pope, Mildred K. *From Latin to Modern French,* Manchester, 1934.
Serjeantson, M. S. "The Dialects of the West-Midlands," *Review of English Studies,* III (1927), 54-67, 186-203, 319-31.

Texts

Bateson, H. (ed.) *Patience. A West Midland Poem of the Fourteenth Century,* ed. with Introduction, Bibliography, Notes, and Glossary, Manchester, 1912; 2d ed. rev., 1918.
Bright, J. W. (ed.) *The West Saxon Gospel of Saint Matthew,* Boston and London, D. C. Heath & Co., 1904.
——— *The West Saxon Psalms,* Boston and London, D. C. Heath & Co., 1907.
Brown, Carleton. *Religious Lyrics of the Fourteenth Century,* Oxford, Clarendon Press, 1924.
——— *Religious Lyrics of the Thirteenth Century,* Oxford, Clarendon Press, 1932.
——— *Religious Lyrics of the Fifteenth Century,* Oxford, Clarendon Press, 1939.
Furnivall, F. J. (ed.) *Political, Religious, and Love Poems,* London, E.E.T.S., No. 15, 1886.
Herrtage, S. J. H. (ed.) *Rauf Soilyear,* London, E.E.T.S., No. 39, 1882.
Horstmann, C., and F. J. Furnivall. *Minor Poems in the Vernon Manuscript,* London, E.E.T.S., No. 98, 1892; No. 117, 1901.
Menner, R. J. (ed.) *Purity, a Middle English Poem,* ed. with Introduction, Notes, and Glossary, *Yale Studies in English,* LXI, New Haven, Yale University Press, 1920.

Morris, Richard. (ed.) *Early English Alliterative Poems in the West-Midland Dialect of the Fourteenth Century,* London, E.E.T.S., No. 1, 1864. (Revised and reprinted, 1869, 1885, 1896, 1901.)

——— *An Old English Miscellany,* London, E.E.T.S., No. 49, 1872.

——— The *Cursor Mundi* in Four Texts, London, E.E.T.S., Nos. 57, 59, 62, 66, 68, 99, 1874-1893.

Savage, H. L. (ed.) *St. Erkenwald: a Middle English Poem, Yale Studies in English,* LXXII, New Haven, Yale University Press, 1926.

Skeat, W. W. (ed.) *Richard the Redeless,* London, E.E.T.S., No. 54, 1873.

Sweet, H. (ed.) *Oldest English Texts,* London, E.E.T.S., 1885.

Thorpe, B. (ed.) *Homilies of the Anglo-Saxon Church,* London, Ælfric Society, 1844-1846. 2 vols.

Tolkien, J. R. R., and E. V. Gordon. (eds.) *Sir Gawain and the Green Knight,* Oxford, Clarendon Press, 1925. (Rev. eds., 1930, 1946.)

Warner, Rubie D-N. (ed.) *Early English Homilies from the Twelfth Century,* London, E.E.T.S. (orig. ser.), No. 152, 1917 for 1915.

Way, Albertus. (ed.) *Promptorium Parvulorum,* London, Camden Society, 1843-1865.

General

Alighieri, Dante. *The Divine Comedy,* ed. Sir Israel Gollancz, London, J. M. Dent & Sons, 1933.

Bridgett, T. E. *Our Lady's Dowry,* London, Burns & Oates, 1875.

Calthrop, D. C. *English Costume,* Vol. II, *Middle Ages,* London, Black, 1906.

Compers, Frances. *The Life and Lyrics of Richard Rolle,* London and Toronto, J. M. Dent & Sons; New York, E. P. Dutton, 1929.

Eyre-Todd, G. (ed.) *Early Scottish Poetry,* Glasgow, Hodge & Co., 1891.

Gardner, Helen. "The Text of the *Scale of Perfection,*" *Medium Ævum,* V (1936).

Gilson, Etienne. *The Spirit of Mediaeval Philosophy,* trans. A. H. C. Downes, New York, Charles Scribner's Sons, 1936.

Garrigou-Lagrange, Réginald. *Christian Perfection and Contemplation according to St. Thomas Aquinas and St. John of the Cross,* trans. Sister M. Timothea Doyle, O.P., St. Louis and London, Herder, 1937.

Goodier, Alban. *An Introduction to the Study of Ascetical and Mystical Theology,* New York, Benziger Bros., 1938.

Hilton, Walter. *Scala Perfectionis,* ed. Cress (reprinted with intro. by J. B. Dalgairns), London, Art and Book Co., 1901.

Knowles, David, O.S.B. *The English Mystics,* New York, Benziger Bros., 1927.

Kunz, G. F., and C. H. Stevenson. *The Book of the Pearl,* New York, Century, 1908.

Louismet, Savinien, O.S.B. *The Mystical Life,* New York, P. J. Kenedy & Sons, 1917.
Vonier, D., O.S.B. *A Key to the Doctrine of the Eucharist,* New York, Benziger Bros., 1925.
Wells, John Edwin. *A Manual of the Writings in Middle English,* and *Supplements,* New Haven, Yale University Press, 1919-1938.

The Bible

The Holy Bible. Douay-Rheims version, Bishop Challoner, Baltimore, John Murphy Company. Accurate reprint of the Rheims and Douay edition with Dr. Challoner's notes. Approved by His Eminence James Cardinal Gibbons, 1899.
Biblia Sacra Vulgatae Editionis. Tornaci Nerviorum, Society of St. John the Baptist, 1901.

Glossary

The arrangement of the Glossary is as follows: (1) the letter ȝ in all its uses follows the letter g; (2) þ follows t; (3) u and v, having the same phonetic value in the MS, are treated as one letter, following t; (4) y, which in the MS is used alternatively with i, is given its modern place alphabetically, both as consonant and vowel.

A

a (1), an, *indef. art.*, A, AN, 19, 23, 34, etc.; ONE, 1037. OE an.
a (2), *adv.*, AYE, 144; EVER, 1058. OE a.
a (3), *prep.*, IN, 1113. OE an, on.
abate, *v., infin.*, ABATE, SLACKEN, LOSE ZEAL, 617; *pret. 3 sg.*, abated, PUT AN END TO, ABOLISHED, 123. OF abatre. (See nn. 123, 617 ff.)
able, *adj.*, ABLE, 599. OF able.
abof, *adv.*, ABOVE, 1023; *prep.*, 1017. OE a-bufan.
aboute, *adv.*, NEAR, ABOUT, 932; *prep.*, AROUND, ALL AROUND, 75, 1077; abowte, 149; CONCERNING, 268; NEAR, 513. OE a-butan.
abroched, *pp.*, POURED FORTH, 1123. OF abrochier.
abyde, *v., infin.*, AWAIT, 348; *pp.*, abiden, EXPERIENCED, 1090. OE abidan.
acheue, *v., infin.*, ACHIEVE, 475. OF achever.
acorde, *n.*, ACCORD, 371; AGREEMENT, 509. OF acord.
acorded, *v., pret. 3 pl.*, ACCORDED, 819. OF acorder.
acroche, *v., infin.*, DETRACT, 1069. OF acrocher.
Adam, *n.*, ADAM, 656.
adaunt, *v., infin.*, OVERPOWER, 157. OF adanter.
adoun, *adv.*, DOWN, 988. OE adune.
adubbement, *n.*, ADORNMENT, RESPLENDENCY, SPLENDOR, 84, 96, 108, 120; adubmente, 72; adubbemente, 85. OF adoubement.
adyte, *v., 2 sg., imv.*, INDICT, ACCUSE, 349. OF enditer.
affray, *n.*, ALARM, CONFUSION, 1174. OF esfrei.
after, *prep.*, ALONG, 125; AFTER, 256; ACCORDING TO, THROUGH, 998. OE æfter.
agayn, *adv.*, AGAIN, 326; *prep.*, AGAINST, 28, 1199, 1200; agaynȝ, 79. OE ongegn; ON i gegn.
age, *n.*, AGE, 412. OF aäge.

aglyȝte, *v., pret. 2 sg.,* GO GLITTERING, GLITTER AWAY, 245. Cf. ON glia. (See n. 245.)

agrete, *pp.,* AGREED, 560. OF agreer.

aȝt, *see* **oȝe.**

aȝtþe, *adj.,* EIGHTH, 1011. OE eahtoþa.

al, *adj.,* ALL, ENTIRE, 16, 86, 424, 441, etc.; *pron.,* EVERYTHING, 360; EVERYBODY, EACH ONE, 447; WHOLE, 584; alle, 73, 119, 292, 372, etc.; *adv.,* WHOLLY, FULLY, QUITE, etc., 97, 197, 204, 210, etc. OE eall.

alas, *interj.,* ALAS, 1138; allas, 9. OF a las.

alder, aldest, see **olde.**

aldermen, *n.,* ANCIENTS, ELDERS, 887, 1119. OE ealdormann.

alegge, *v., 2 sg., subj.,* ALLEGE, PLEAD, 703. OF esligier. (See n. 703.)

Almyȝty, *n.,* THE ALMIGHTY, 1068; Almyȝt, *adj.,* ALMIGHTY, 498. OE ælmihtig.

alone, *adj.,* ALONE, 933. OE eal an.

alow, *v., infin.,* ALLOW, CONCEDE, 634. OF alouer.

aloynte, *pp.* as *adj.,* REMOVED FAR OFF, AFAR, 893. OF aloigner.

also, *adv.,* TOO, ALSO, 685, 872; BESIDES, 1071; als, 765. OE eal swa.

alþaȝ, *conj.,* ALTHOUGH, THOUGH, 759, 857, 878. OE eal þeah.

alyue, *adj.,* LIVING, 445, OE on life.

am, see **be.**

amatyst, *n.,* AMETHYST, 1016. OF amatiste.

among, *prep.,* AMONG, 470, 848, 1145, 1150; *adv.,* MIXED or MINGLED WITH, 905. OE onmang.

an, see **a (1).**

and (&), *con.,* AND, 16, 18, 27, 44, 273, 777, etc.; ande, 35; IF, 378, 560, 598, etc.; ande, 1212; IF *in* & wele & wo, in sense, COME . . . OR, 342; WHEN, 538. OE and, an.

anende, *prep.,* CONCERNING, 697; CLOSE TO, 1136; anendeȝ, OPPOSITE, 975; onende, CONCERNING, 186. OE onefen, onemn.

angel-hauyng, *n.,* ANGEL-MANNER, 754. OF angele; ME hauing.

anger, *n.,* ANGER, 343. ON angr.

ani, see **any.**

anioynt, *pp.,* ASSIGNED, UNITED, 895. OF enjoindre.

anon, *adv.,* AT ONCE, FORTHWITH, STRAIGHTWAY, 584, 629. OE on-an.

anoþer, *adj.,* ANOTHER, 297. OE an, oþer.

answar, *n.,* ANSWER, 518. OE andswaru.

anunder, *prep.,* AT THE FOOT OF, BENEATH, UNDER, 166, 1081, 1092, 1100; anvnder, 1068; onvunder, 775; *adv.,* anvnder, BENEATH, 991. OE onunder.

any, *adj.* or *pron.,* ANY, 345, 463, 617, 800, 1068; ani, 1139. OE ænig.

apere, *v., infin.,* APPEAR, 405. OF apareir.

apert, *adv.,* FRANKLY, 589. OF apert.

Apocalyppeȝ, *n.*, APOCALYPSE, 787, 996, 1020; Apokalypeȝ, 834; Apokalypce, 983; Apocalyppce, 944, 1008; Appocalyppece, 866.

apostel, *n.*, APOSTLE, 790, 836, 944, 984, 985, 996, 1008, 1020, 1032; appostel, 1053. OE apostol.

apparaylmente, *n.*, APPARELMENT, EQUIPMENT, RETINUE, in sense, HOSTS OF HEAVEN, 1052. OF apareillement.

apple, *n.*, APPLE, 640. OE æppel.

appose, *v.*, *pres. 1 sg.*, POSE, PUT QUESTIONS, 902. OF aposer.

aproche, *v.*, *infin.*, APPROACH, 686; *pret. 3 sg.*, aproched, 1119. OF aprochier.

aquyle, *v.*, *infin.*, RECEIVE, 690; *pp.*, aquylde, ACQUIRED (PERMISSION), 967. OF acuillir.

araye, *n.*, ORDER, ARRANGEMENT, 5; array, 191; aray, DEGREE, 491. OF arrei. (See n. 5.)

arayed, *pp.*, PREPARED, 719; ARRAYED, 791; arayde, DISPOSED, 1166. OF arreier.

areþede, *n.*, A NATION OF A FORMER TIME, ANCIENT LAND, 711. OE ær, þeod.

arme, *n.*, ARM, 459, 466. OE earm.

aros, *v.*, *pret. 3 sg.*, AROSE, ROSE, 181. OE arisan.

Arraby, *n.*, ARABY, 430.

aryȝt, *adv.*, STRAIGHT ON, 112. OE on riht.

Arystotel, *n.*, ARISTOTLE, 751.

aryue, *v.*, *infin.*, ARRIVE, 447. OF ariver.

as, *adv.*, AS, 20, 76, 815, 822, etc.; THUS, 97, 984, 1193, etc.; *conj.*, 787, 915, etc.; SINCE, 997; *with adjectives, expressing the superlative degree,* 645, 836. OE eal swa.

asent, *n.*, HARMONY, 94; asente, ACCORD, 391. OF as(s)ent.

aske, *v.*, *infin.*, ASK, 316, 910; *gerundive,* 580; ask, 564. OE ascian.

assemble, *n.*, UNION, 760. OF as(s)emblee.

asspye, *v.*, *infin.*, ESPY, DISCOVER, DISCERN, 1035; *pret. 1 sg.*, asspyed, 704, 979. OF espier.

astate, *n.*, ESTATE, 393; asstate, 490. OF estat.

astraye, *adv.*, LAWLESSLY, 1162. OF estraie.

asyse, *n.*, FASHION, MANNER, 97. OF asise.

at, *prep.*, AT, 161, 198, 218, 291, 529, 547, 635, 647, 839, 862, 1066, 1115; IN, 199, 321; BY, 188, 953; WITH, 287, 672; IN ACCORD WITH, 1164; þat a., THAT WHICH, 536. OE at, æt.

atount, *pp.*, STUNNED, 179. OF estoner.

atslykeȝ, *v.*, *pres. 3 sg.*, GLIDES AWAY, GLIDES OFF, 575. Cf. MLG sliken (with ME at).

atteny, *v.*, *2 sg.*, *subj.*, ARRIVE, 548. OF ataindre.

auenture, *n.*, ADVENTURE, 64. OF aventure.

Augoste, *n.*, AUGUST, 39.

aungele3, *n.*, ANGELS, 1121. OF angele.
aunte, *n.*, AUNT, 233. OF ante.
avysyoun, *n.*, VISION, 1184. OF avision.
away, *adv.*, AWAY, 488, 655, 823; awaye, 258. OE on weg.
awayed, *pp.*, INFORMED, 710. OF aveier.
awhyle, *adv.*, AWHILE, BRIEFLY, 692. OE ane hwile.
ay, *adv.*, EVER, ALWAYS, 33, 44, 56, 101, 366, 1189, 1195; aye, 1198. ON ei.
ayþer, *adj. pron.*, EACH (of two), 831. OE ægþer.

B

bale, *n.*, GRIEF, SUFFERING, WOE, 18, 373, 478, 651, 1139; *pl.*, 123, 807. OE balu.
balke, *n.*, BANK, 62. OE balca.
bantele3, *n.*, BANTELS, 992; bantels, 1017. OF bandel, bandele. (See n. 992-93.)
baptem, *n.*, BAPTISM, 653; babtem, 627. OF baptême.
baptysed, *v.*, *pret. 3 sg.*, BAPTIZED, 818. OF baptiser.
bare, *adj.*, EMPTY, BARE, 1025; PLAIN *in* as b., AS PLAINLY (AS POSSIBLE), i.e., MOST PLAINLY, 836. OE bær.
Barne, *n.*, CHILD, 426; barne3, CHILDREN, 712, 1040. OE bearn.
basse, *n.*, BASE, FOUNDATION, 1000. OF base.
basyng, *n.*, BASE, 992.
bayle, see **bayly.**
bayly, *n.*, DOMINION, 315; JURISDICTION, SWAY, 442; bayle, DOMAIN, 1083. OF baillie.
bayn, *adj.*, READY, 807. ON beinn.
baysment, *n.*, AMAZEMENT, 174. OF abaissement.
be, *v.*, *infin.*, BE, 29, 281, etc.; *pres. 1 sg.*, am, 246, 335, etc.; *pres. 2 sg.*, art, 242, 276; arte, 707; *pres. 3 sg.*, bet3, 611; is, 26, 33; nis (ne-is), 100; nys, 951; *pres. 3 pl.*, arn, 384, 402; ar, 923; be, 470; bene, 785; ben, 572; *1 pl.*, *subj.*, be, 379; *2 sg.*, *imv.*, 344, 406; *pret. 3 sg.*, wat3, 45, 133, 1065, etc.; wace, 65; wore, 232, 1170; wasse, 1108, 1112; *3 pl.*, wore, 154; *pret. 2 sg.*, *subj.*, wer, 972, 1092; were, 264, 1167, etc.; wore, 142; *pl.*, wern, 451; wore, 574; *pp.*, ben, 252, 373, OE beon.
be, *prep.*, see **by.**
beaumys, *n.*, MANTLE, SURCOAT, 197. (See n. 197.)
beaute, *n.*, BEAUTY, 749; bewte, 765. OF beauté.
bede, see **bydde3.**
bele, *v.*, *infin.*, BURN, 18. ON bæla.
bem, *n.*, CROSS, 814. OE beam.
bene, *adj.*, BEAUTIFUL, 110; *adv.*, BEAUTIFULLY, 198. Etymology uncertain; cf. OF bien.

bent, *pp.*, BOUND, 664; bente, BENT, BOWED, 1189; EXTENDED, 1017. OE bendan.

bere, *v.*, *infin.*, BEAR, 807, 1078; *pres. 2 sg.*, bereȝ, 746; *pres. 3 sg.*, 1068; HAS, 100; HOLDS, 756; *pl.*, beren, 854, 856; YIELD, 1079; *2 sg.*, *subj.*, ber, WEAR, 466; *pret. 1 sg.*, bere, BORE, TURNED, 67; *3 sg.*, ber, BORE, 426; *pp.*, bore, BORN, 239; borne, 626. OE beran.

bereste, see **breste**.

beryl, *n.*, BERYL, 110, 1011. OF beryl.

best(e), *adj.*, see **god**.

besteȝ, *n.*, BEASTS, 886. OF beste.

bete, *v.*, *pret. 3 pl.*, BEAT, 93; VANQUISH, 757. OE beatan.

better, *adv.*, see **wel**.

bewte, see **beaute**.

beyng, *n.*, BEING, NATURE, 446. Cf. *v.* **be**.

bifore, see **byfore**.

bitalt, *pp.*, SHAKEN, 1161. OE -tealtian.

blaȝt, *pp.*, 'BLEACHED,' WHITE, 212. OE blæcan.

blake, *adj.*, BLACK, 945. OE blæc.

blame, *v.*, *infin.*, BLAME, REPROACH, 303; *pres. 2 sg.*, blameȝ, 275; *n.*, blame, REPROACH, 715. OF blasmer; blâmer.

blayke, *adj.*, PALE, 27. ON bleikr.

ble, *n.*, COLOR, 76; COMPLEXION, 212. OE bleo.

bleaunt, *n.*, A TUNIC-LIKE GARMENT, A GARMENT OF RICH MATERIAL, 163. OF bliaut.

blent, *pp.*, BLENT, ASSOCIATED, BLENDED, 385; blente, 1016. ON [ge]-blendan.

blesse, *v.*, *infin.*, BLESS (make the Sign of the Cross), 341; *pres. 3 sg.*, *subj.*, BLESS, 850; *pp.*, BLESSED, 436. OE bletsian.

blessyng, *n.*, BLESSING, GRACE, 1208.

blo, *adj.*, DARK, 83; LEADEN or BLUE-BLACK, 875. ON blar.

blod, *n.*, BLOOD, 646, 650, 1137, etc. OE blod.

blody, *adj.*, BLOODY, 705. OE blodig.

blom, *n.*, BLOOM, 578; *pl.*, blomeȝ, FLOWERS, BLOOMS, 27. ON blom.

blose, *n.*, (?) DOLT, CLOD, 911. Etymology unknown. (See n. 911.)

blot, *n.*, BLOT, 782. Cf. OF blotte.

blunt, *adj.*, BLUNT; make b., BENUMB, 176. EME. Etymology unknown.

blusched, *v.*, *pret. 1 sg.*, LOOKED, GAZED, 980, 1083. OE blyscan.

blwe, *adj.*, BLUE, 27, 76; *n.*, 423. OF bleu.

blynde, *adj.*, DIM, 83. OE blind.

blynne, *v.*, *infin.*, CEASE, 729. OE blinnan.

blys, *n.*, BLISS, BLESSEDNESS, HAPPINESS, 123, 126, etc.; blysse, 372, 373, 384, 385, 396, etc. OE blis.

blysful, *adj.*, BLISSFUL, HAPPY, 907, 964; blysfol, 279; BLESSED, 1100, 1104; as *n.*, BLESSED (ONE), 421.

blysned, *pp.,* SHONE, 1048.

blyþe, *adj.,* GLAD, 352; JOYOUS, BRIGHT, 738; *superl.,* 1131; *n.,* MERCY, FAVOR. OE bliþe.

blyþely, *adv.,* BLITHELY, JOYOUSLY, 385.

bod, see **byde.**

body, *n.,* BODY, 62, 460; SUBSTANCE, 1070. OE bodig.

bodyly, *adj.,* BODILY, 478; *adv.,* 1090.

boffeteȝ, *n.,* BUFFETS, 809. OF bufet.

boȝ, *v., pres. impers.,* IT BEHOOVES; b. vch ma, EACH MAN MUST, 323; *pret.,* byhod *in* yow b., YOU OUGHT, 928. OE bihofian.

boȝe, *v., infin.,* TO BEND ONE'S STEPS, TO COME, 196; boȝ, PASS, 323; *2 sg., imv.,* bow, BOW, 974; *pret. 1 sg.,* bowed, WENT, 126. OE bugan.

boȝt, see **bye.**

bok, *n.,* BOOK, 710; boke, 837. OE boc.

bolde, *adj.,* BOLD, SHAMELESS, 806. OE bald.

bolleȝ, *n.,* BOLES, 76. ON bolr.

bolne, *v., infin.,* SWELL, 18. ON bolgna.

bon, *n.,* BONE, 212. OE ban.

bone, *n.,* PRAYER, 912, 916; BOON, 1090. ON bon.

bonerte, *n.,* BLESSEDNESS, 762. OF boneurté. (See n. 762.)

bonk, *n.,* RIDGE, RISE, 102; bonc, BANK OF A STREAM, 907, 1169; bonke, 196; bonkeȝ, 110, 138, 931; bonkes, 106. O. Fris. bank.

bor, *n.,* ABODE, 964. OE bur.

borde, *v., pres. 2 pl.,* JEST, MOCK, 290. OF bourder.

borȝ, *n.,* CITY, 957, 989, 1048; burghe, 980. OE burh.

borneȝ, *n., gen. sg.,* STREAM, RIVER, 974. OE burna.

bornyst, *pp.,* BURNISHED, 77; burnist, 990; as *adj.,* bornyste, LUSTROUS, 220. OF burnir.

boroȝt, see **bryng.**

bostwys, *adj.,* (?) BOISTEROUS, RUDE, ROUGH, 814; bustwys, 911. (See n. 911.)

bot, BUT, ONLY, SAVE, HOWEVER; *adv.,* 17, 18, 83, 269, 382, 551, 592, 905; *conj.,* 66, 91, 265, 308, 428, 723, 972; *prep.,* 331, 336, 337, 496, 658, 842, 892, 922, 952, 955. OE butan.

bote, *n.,* REMEDY, CURE, 275, 645. OE bot.

boþe, *adj.,* BOTH, 373, 731, 950, 1056; *conj.,* 90, 329, 682, 1203. ON baþir.

boun, *adj.,* PREPARED, 534; READY, 992; DESTINED, 1103. ON buinn.

bounden, *pp.,* FASTENED, FIXED, 198, 1103. OE bindan.

bourne, see **burne.**

bow, bowed, see **boȝe.**

boyeȝ, *n., pl.,* MEN, ROGUES, KNAVES; *in* b. bolde, SHAMELESS ROGUES, hence, MALEFACTORS, 806. Cf. OF boie. (See n. 806.)

boȝ, *v.*, *pres. impers.*, IT BEHOOVES, i.e., MUST, 323; *pret.*, byhod, 928. OE bihofian.
brade, see **brode.**
brathe, *n.*, VIOLENCE, 1170; *pl.*, braþeȝ, FURIES, 346. ME braþ; ON braþr.
braþ(eȝ), see **brathe.**
braundysch, *v.*, *pres. 2 sg.*, *subj.*, THREATEN, 346. OF brandir.
bray, *v.*, *pres. 2 sg.*, *subj.*, SHOUT, 346. OF braire.
brayde, *v.*, *pret. 3 sg.*, WRENCHED, 1170; *3 pl.*, THRUST, DREW QUICKLY, 712. OE bregdan.
brayneȝ, *n.*, THOUGHTS, BRAIN, 126. OE brægn.
bred, *n.*, BREAD, 1209. OE bread.
brede (1), *n.*, BREADTH, 1031. OE brædu.
brede (2), *v.*, *infin.*, FLOURISH, EXTEND, 814. OE brædan.
bredful, *adj.*, BRIMFUL, 126. OE bred, ful.
bref, *adj.*, BRIEF, EPHEMERAL, TRANSIENT, 268. OF bref.
breme, *adj.*, WILD, 346; GLORIOUS, 863. OE breme.
brent, *v.*, *pret. 3 pl.*, BURNED, GLOWED, 106; *pp.*, brende, REFINED, PURE, 989. OE bernan; ON brenna.
breste, *n.*, BREAST, 18, 222, 740, 1103, 1139; bereste, 854. OE breost.
breue, *v.*, *2 sg.*, *imv.*, TELL, 755. ON brefa.
brode, *adj.*, WIDE, BROAD, 650, 1022, 1024; brade, 138. OE brad.
broȝ, broȝte, see **bryng.**
broke, *n.*, STREAM, BROOK, RIVER, 141, 146; brok, 981; *gen. sg.*, brokeȝ, 1074. OE broc.
broun, *adj.*, BROWN, DUSKY, DARK, 537; POLISHED (made brown), i.e., BRIGHT, 990. OE brun.
brunt, *n.*, BRUNT, BLOW, JOLT, 174. Etymology uncertain; cf. ON bruna ('to advance at fire-speed').
bryd, *n.*, BRIDE, 769. OE bryd.
bryddeȝ, *n.*, BIRDS, 93. OE brid.
bryȝt, *adj.*, BRIGHT, SHINING, RADIANT, 75, 110, 755, 769, 989, 1048; bryȝter, 1056. OE beorht.
brym, *n.*, BRIM, EDGE, 1074; brymme, BRINK, 232. OE brymm.
bryng, *v.*, *infin.*, BRING, RECALL, 853; *2 sg.*, *imv.*, 963; *pret. 3 sg.*, broȝte, 527; *pp.*, broȝ, 286; boroȝt, 628. OE bringan. (See n. 286.)
bur, *n.*, SPEED, 1158; burre, SHOCK, 176. ON byrr.
burde, *v.*, *pret. impers.*, BEHOOVED, 316. OE [ge]byrian.
burghe, see **borȝ.**
burne, *n.*, MAN, 1090; MAN OF NOBLE QUALITIES, hence, NOBLE SIR, 397; bourne, 617; *pl.*, burneȝ, PEOPLE, 712. OE beorn.
burnist, see **bornyst.**
burre, see **bur.**
bustwys, see **bostwys.**

busyeȝ, *v.*, *pres. 2 sg.*, BUSY *in* b. þe, BUSY THEE (THYSELF), 268. OE bisgian.

by, *prep.*, BY, OVER, NEAR, ALONG, THROUGH, IN ACCORD WITH, etc., 107, 141, 152, 380, 704, 907, 921, 1019, etc.; be, 523. OE bi.

bycalle, *v.*, *pres. 1 sg.*, CALL UPON, 913; *pp.*, bycalt, CALLED AWAY, 1163. OE -ceallian; ON kalla.

bycawse, *conj.*, BECAUSE, 296.

bycom, *v.*, *pret. 3 sg.*, BECAME, 537. OE becuman.

byddeȝ, *v.*, *pres. 3 sg.*, BIDS, 520; *pret. 3 pl.*, bede, 715. OE biddan.

byde, *v.*, *infin.*, BIDE, ABIDE, 399; DELAY, 977; ENDURE, 664; *pres. 2 sg.*, 907; *3 pl.*, STAND, 75; *pret. 3 sg.*, bod, REMAINED, STAYED, 62, OE bidan.

bydene, *adv.*, STRAIGHTWAY, FORTHWITH, 196. Etymology uncertain.

bye, *v.*, *infin.*, BUY, PURCHASE, 732; byye, 478; *pret. 3 sg.*, boȝt, 651; *pp.*, 733, 893. OE bycgan.

byfalle, *v.*, *infin.*, BEFALL, 186. OE befeallan.

byfore, *adv.*, GONE BY, AGO, 172; BEFORE, 1110; *conj.*, 530; *prep.*, 885; AHEAD OF, 294, 598; bifore, BEFORE, 49. OE beforan.

byg, *adj.*, BIG, GREAT, 102; *comp.*, bygger, GREATER, 374. Etymology unknown.

bygly, *adj.*, PLEASANT, 963. ON byggiligr.

bygonne, see **bygynne.**

bygyng, *n.*, DWELLING, 932. ON bygging.

bygynne, *v.*, *infin.*, BEGIN, 581; *pres. 2 sg.*, bygynneȝ, 561; *2 sg.*, *imv.*, 547; *pret. 3 pl.*, bygonne, 549; *pp.*, 33. OE beginnan.

Bygynner, *n.*, BEGINNER, 436.

byȝe, *n.*, RING, 466. OE beah, beag.

byȝonde, *prep.*, BEYOND, 141, 146, 158, 287, 981, 1156. OE begeondan.

byhod, see **boȝ.**

byholde, *v.*, *infin.*, BEHOLD, LOOK UPON, 810. OE behealdan.

bylde, *n.*, HOUSE, DWELLING, 727, 963. Cf. OE byldan.

bylde, *v.*, *pret. 3 sg.*, CAUSED, AROUSED, 123. OE byldan.

byrþ whateȝ, *n.*, FORTUNES OF BIRTH, ORDER OF BIRTH, 1041. ME byrþ (prob. Scand.; cf. Icel. burþr); OE hwatu.

bysech, *v.*, *infin.*, BESEECH, 390. OE besecan.

byseme, *v.*, *infin.*, BEFIT, 310. OE by- ; cf. ON soema.

byswykeȝ, *v.*, *pres. 1 sg.*, DECEIVE, 568. OE beswican.

bytaȝte, *v.*, *pret. 1 sg.*, GAVE UP, 1207. OE betæcan.

byte, *v.*, *infin.*, BITE, 640; SECURE, 355. OE bitan.

bytwene, *adv.*, BETWEEN; ay b., EVERYWHERE, 44; *prep.*, 140, 658. OE betweonan.

bytwyste, *prep.*, AMONG, 464. OE betweox.

bytyde, *v.*, *infin.*, BETIDE, BEFALL, 397. OE be, tidan.

byye, see **bye.**

C

caggen, *v.*, *pres. 3 pl.*, BIND, 512. Etymology uncertain; cf. OF cagier.

caȝt, *v.*, *pret. 3 sg.*, SEIZED, 50; caȝte, CAUGHT, 237. OF cachier.

calder, see **colde.**

calle, *v.*, *infin.*, CALL, 173, 182, 721; *pres. 1 pl.*, 430; *pret. 3 sg.*, called, 542; calde, 762; *pp.*, called, 273, 572. OE ceallian.

calsydoyne, *n.*, CHALCEDONY, 1003. OF calcedoine.

cambe, *n.*, COMB, 775. OE camb.

can, see **con.**

care, *n.*, CARE, BURDEN, 50, 371, 861; *pl.*, careȝ, 808. OE caru.

carpe, *v.*, *infin.*, SPEAK, 949; carp, 381; *pret. 3 sg.*, 752; *n.*, UTTERANCE, 883. ON karpa.

cas, *n.*, CASE, INSTANCE, 673. OF cas.

caste, *n.*, HAZARD, VENTURE, 1163. ON kasta.

castel-walle, *n.*, CASTLE WALL, 917. OF castel, OE weall.

causeȝ, *n.*, CAUSES, 702. OF cause.

cayre, *v.*, *infin.*, GO, REACH, 1031. ? ON keyra.

cete, see **cyte.**

ceur, *v.*, *infin.*, COVER, REMIT, GIVE UP, 319. OF covrir.

chace, *v.*, *infin.*, DRIVE, 443. OF chacier.

chambre, *n.*, CHAMBER, 904. OF chambre.

chapel, *n.*, CHAPEL, 1062. OF chapel.

charde, *v.*, *pret. 3 sg.*, TURNED ASIDE, SWERVED, 608. ME *pret.*, scheren; OE sceran.

charyte, *n.*, CHARITY, 470. OF charité.

chayere, *n.*, THRONE, 885. OF chaiere.

chere, *n.*, DEMEANOR, MIEN, 407, 887; FACE, 1109. OF chiere.

ches, chese, see **chos.**

Cheuentayn, *n.*, CHIEFTAIN, 605. OF chevetain.

chos, *v.*, *pret. 1 sg.*, DISCERNED, 187; *3 sg.*, ches, CHOSE, 759; chese, 954; *pp.*, ichose, 904. OE ceosan.

chyche, *n.*, NIGGARD, 605. OF chiche, *adj.*

chyde, *v.*, *infin.*, CHIDE, 403. OE cidan.

chylde, *n.*, CHILD, 723; *pl.*, chylder, 714, 718. OE cíld.

cite, see **cyte.**

clad, *pp.*, CLAD, COVERED, 22. Cf. OE claþian.

clambe, see **clym.**

clanly, *adv.*, NEATLY, WITHOUT FLAW, 2. OE clænlice. (See n. 2.)

clem, *v.*, *infin.*, SMEAR, 826. OE clæman.

clene, *adj.*, PURE, CLEAN, 289, 682, 737, 767, 969; FLAWLESS, 227; STAINLESS, 972; *adv.*, ALL, COMPLETELY, 754; PRECISELY, 949. OE clæne.

clente, *pp.*, SECURED, 259. OE [be]clencan.

cler, *adj.*, CLEAR, 74, 207, 227, 1011, 1050, 1111; clere, 2, 737; *adv.*, 882, 913; cler, 274; *n.*, clere, BRIGHTNESS, 620, 735. OF cler.

clerkeȝ, *n.*, LEARNED MEN, 1091. OF clerc.

cleuen, *v.*, *pret. 3 pl.*, CLEAVED (THE AIR), 66. OE cleofan.

clos, *v.*, *infin.*, SET, 2; close, ENCLOSE, 271; *pret. 3 sg.*, closed, CLOSED, 803; *adj.*, clos, CLOSED, 183; close, COMPACT, 512. OF clos.

clot, *n.*, CLAY, 22, 320; MASS (OF LAND), MOUNT, 789; clotteȝ, CLODS, 857. OE clott.

cloystor, *n.*, ENCLOSURE, 969. OF cloistre.

clyffe, *n.*, CLIFF, 159; *pl.*, klyfeȝ, 66; klyffeȝ, 74. OE clif.

clym, *v.*, *infin.*, CLIMB, ASCENT, 1072; klymbe, 678; *pret. 2 sg.*, clambe, 773. OE climban.

clynge, *v.*, *pres. 3 pl.*, DECAY, 857. OE clingan.

clypper, *n.*, SHEARER, 802. Cf. ON klippa.

clyuen, *v.*, *infin.*, BELONG, 1196. OE clifian.

cnawyng, *n.*, CONSCIOUSNESS, 859. Cf. OE cnawan.

cnoken, *v.*, *pres. 3 pl.*, KNOCK, 727. OE cnucian.

cofer, *n.*, COFFER, 259. OF cofre.

colde, *adj.*, COLD, 50, 808; *comp.*, calder, 320. OE cald.

colour (1), *n.*, COLLAR, 215. OF colier.

colour (2), *n.*, COLOR, 753; color, 22. OF colo(u)r.

com, *v.*, *infin.*, COME, 676, 701; *pres. 3 sg.*, 262; commeȝ, 848; *2 sg.*, *imv.*, cum, 763; *pret. 1 sg.*, come, 582; com, 615; *2 sg.*, 598; *3 sg.*, 155, 230, 645, 749; *pres. 3 pl.*, *subj.*, 574; *pret. 3 sg.*, 723, 724. OE cuman.

come, *n.*, COMING, APPROACH, 1117.

comfort, *n.*, COMFORT, SOLACE, CONSOLATION, HELP, 55; comforte, 357; coumforde, 369. OF confort. (See n. 811-15.)

comly, *adj.*, BEAUTIFUL, 259, 775; cumly, 929. OE cymlic.

commune, *adj.*, COMMON, 739. OF comun.

compas, *n.*, COMPASS, CIRCUIT, 1072. OF compas.

compayny, *n.*, COMPANY, 851. OF compaignie.

con (1), *v.*, CAN, (*aux.*) DO; *pres. 1 sg.*, 931; *2 sg.*, 769; *3 sg.*, 165; coneȝ, 482, 909, 925; *3 sg.*, 294, 495, etc.; can, 499; *2 pl.*, 381, 914; conne, 521; *3 pl.*, 509, 1078; *pret. 1 sg.*, cowþe, 134; *2 sg.*, cowþeȝ, 484; *3 sg.*, couþe, 95; *3 pl.*, 855. OE cunnan.

con (2), *v.*, DID, *1 sg.*, 147, 148, etc.; *2 sg.*, 313, 777, 1183; *3 sg.*, 81, 111, 165, 171, 173; *3 pl.*, 78, 551, 690. OE gan, *pret.* of ginnan (*infl. by* con).

consciens, *n.*, CONSCIENCE, 1089. OF conscience.

contryssyoun, *n.*, CONTRITION, 669. OF contricion.

coppe, *n.*, TOP, 791. OE coppe. See **hylle.**

corne, *n.*, CORN, 40. OE corn.

coroun, *n.*, CROWN, 237, 255; coroune, 205; croune, 427; croun, 1100; *pl.*, corouneȝ, 451. OF corone.

corounde, *v.*, *pret. 3 sg.*, CROWNED, 415; *pp.*, 480, 1101; *pret. 3 sg.*, coronde, 767. OF coroner.

corse, *n.*, CORPSE, 320; *pl.*, corses, 857. OF cors.

cortayse, *adj.*, COURTEOUS, 433; corteȝ, 754; as *n.*, cortayse, 469, 480, 481. OF corteis, curteis, courtois.

cortaysly, *adv.*, COURTEOUSLY, URBANELY, hence, WITH COURTEOUS WIT, 381.

cortaysye, *n.*, COURTESY, 432, 444, 456, 468; courtaysye, 457. OF cortesie, courtoisie, curtesie.

corte, see **court.**

cortel, *n.*, KIRTLE, 203. OE cyrtel.

corteȝ, see **cortayse.**

coruen, see **keruen.**

couenaunt, *n.*, AGREEMENT, 562; couenaunde, 563. OF covenant.

coumforde, see **comfort.**

counsayl, *n.*, DESIGN, PLAN, 319. OF co(u)nseil.

counterfete, *v.*, *infin.*, LIKEN, EQUAL, 556. OF contrefet, *pp.*, of contrefaire.

countes, *n.*, COUNTESS, 489. OF contesse.

countre, *n.*, COUNTRY, 297. OF contrée.

court, *n.*, COURT, 445; corte, 701. OF cort, court.

couþe, cowþe, see **con (1).**

crafteȝ, *n.*, POWERS, 356; ARTS, 890. OE cræft.

craue, *v.*, *infin.*, IMPLORE, 663. OE crafian.

crede, *n.*, THE CREED, 485. OE creda.

cresse, *n.*, CRESS, 343. OE cresse.

creste, *n.*, CREST, TOP, ACME, i.e., THE BEST, 856. OF creste.

crokeȝ, *n.*, SICKLES, 40. ON krokr.

crysolyt, *n.*, CHRYSOLITE, 1009. OF crisolite.

crysopase, *n.*, CHRYSOPRASE, 1013. OF crisopace.

crystal, *adj.*, CRYSTAL, 74, 159. OF cristal.

Crystes, see **Kryst.**

cum, see **com.**

cumly, see **comly.**

cure, *n.*, CARE, 1091. OF cure.

cyte, *n.*, CITY, 792, 939, 1023; cete, 927, 952; cite, 1097; cyty, 986. OF cité.

D

daleȝ, *n.*, *pl.*, DALES, 121. OE dæl.

dam, *n.*, STREAM, 324. M.Du. dam; ON damr.

dampned, *pp.*, CONDEMNED, 641. OF dampner.

damysel, *n.*, DAMSEL, DEMOISELLE, 489; damyselle, 361. OF damisele.

dar, *v.*, *pres. 1 sg.*, DARE, 1089; *pret. 1 sg.*, DURST, 143; dorste, 182. OE durran.

dard, see **dare.**

dare, *v.*, *infin.*, LIE HID; *in* con d., WORSHIPPED (HIM), 839; *pret. 3 sg.*, dard, *in* d. to Hym, PAID REVERENCE TO HIM, 609. OE darian. (See n. 609-10.)

dased, *pp.*, DAZED, 1085. ON dasast.

date, *n.*, SEASON, TIME, DATE, LIMIT, HOUR, TERM, TERMINATION, 492, 493, 504, 505, 516, 528, 529, 540, 541; *in* d. of day, BREAK OF DAY, 517; *pl.*, dateȝ, 1040. OF date.

Dauid, *n.*, DAVID, 920.

daweȝ, see **day.**

daunce, *v.*, *pres. 2 sg.*, *subj.*, DANCE, LEAP ABOUT, 345. OF dancier.

daunger, *n.*, POWER, DANGER, DURESS, 250; cf. **luf-daungere.** OF dangier. (See n. 11 *luf-daungere.*)

day, *n.*, DAY, 486, 510, 516, etc.; daye, 517, 541, 1210; *gen. sg.*, dayeȝ, 533, 554; *pl.*, TIME, 416; daweȝ, DAYS, 282. OE dæg.

day-glem, *n.*, DAY-GLEAM, DAYLIGHT, 1094.

dayly, *v.*, *infin.*, DALLY, SPEAK LIGHTLY, 313. OF dalier.

debate, *n.*, DEBATE, 390. OF debat.

debonere, *adj.*, DEBONAIRE; *in* ful d., OF HIGH ESTATE, 162. OF de bon aire.

debonerte, *n.*, GENTLENESS, MEEKNESS, 798. OF debonaireté.

declyne, *v.*, WASTE AWAY, 333; SUBMIT, 509. OF decliner.

dede (1), *adj.*, DEAD, 31. OE dead.

dede (2), *n.*, DEED, 481; BOND, CONTRACT, 524. OE dæd.

degres, *n.*, *pl.*, DEGREES, TIERS, 1022. OF degre.

del, dele, see **doel.**

dele, *v.*, *pres. 3 sg.*, *subj.*, DEAL, 606. OE dælan.

delfully, *adv.*, GRIEVOUSLY, 706.

delyt, *n.*, BLISS, DELIGHT, 642, 1104, 1105, 1116, etc.; delit, 1129. OF delit.

delyuered, *v.*, *pret. 3 sg.*, DELIVERED, 652. OF delivrer.

deme, *v.*, *infin.*, EXPECT, 336; DECREE, 348; JUDGE, 360; TELL, REVEAL, 1183; dem, 312; *pret. 1 sg.*, demed, SAID, 361; *2 sg.*, *imv.*, JUDGE, 313, 349; *pres. 3 sg.*, *subj.*, JUDGE, 324, OE deman. (See n. 1183.)

demme, *v.*, *infin.*, BE CHECKED, STOP, 223. OE -demman.

dene, *n.*, VALE, 295. OE denu.

denned, *v.*, *pret. 3 sg.*, LODGED, 51. OE *dennian; ME dennien. (See n. 51.)

dep, see **depe.**

departed, *v.*, *pret. 1 pl.*, PARTED, 378. OF departir.

depaynt, *pp.*, DEPICTED, ARRAYED, 1102. OF depeint.

depe, *adj.*, DEEP, 143, 215; as *n.*, *pl.*, DEPTHS, 109; *adv.*, DEEPLY, 406. OE deop.

depres, *v.*, *infin.*, PUSH DOWN, 778. OF depresser.

depryue, *v.*, *infin.*, DEPRIVE, DISPOSSESS, 449. OF depriver.

dere (1), *v., infin.*, TROUBLE, HINDER, 1157; *n., pl.*, dereȝ, TROUBLES *in* did me d., CAUSED ME TROUBLES, i.e., TROUBLED ME, 102. OE derian.

dere (2), *adj.*, COSTLY, PRICELESS, PRECIOUS, HIGHLY RATED, DEAR, BELOVED, 72, 108, 229, 368, 492, 504, etc.; as *adv.*, DEARLY, 733; derely, EXCELLENTLY, 995. OE deore.

dereȝ, see **dere (1)**.

derely, see **dere (2)**.

derk, *n.*, DARKNESS, 629. OE deorc.

derþe, *n.*, BEAUTY, GLORY, 99. ON dyrþ.

derworth, *adj.*, PRECIOUS, 109. OE deorwurþe.

dese, *n.*, DAIS, 766. OF deis.

desserte, *n.*, DESERT, 595. OF desserte.

dessypeleȝ, *n.*, DISCIPLES, 715. OF disciple.

Destyne, *n.*, DESTINY, 758. OF destinee.

determynable, *adj.*, DETERMINABLE, 594. OF determinable.

deth, *n.*, DEATH, 323, 630, 652, 656; *dethe*, 860. OE deaþ.

deuely, *adj.*, DEVILISH, DIABOLICAL, WICKED, 51. (See n. 51.)

deuise, *v., infin.*, OBSERVE CAREFULLY, CONTEMPLATE, 1129; *pres. 3 sg.*, deuyseȝ, DESCRIBE, 984, 995; *pret. 3 sg.*, deuysed, DIVINED, 1021. OF deviser.

deuote, *adj.*, DEVOUT, REVERENT, 406. OF devot.

deuoyde, *v., infin.*, ANNIHILATE, MAKE NOUGHT OF, 15. OF desvoidier.

deuyse, *n.*, DIVISION, 139; OPINION, JUDGMENT, 199. OF devise.

deuysed, deuyseȝ, see **deuise**.

deuysement, *n.*, DESCRIPTION, 1019. OF devisement.

dewyne, *v., pres. 1 sg.* (for *pret.*), DROOP, PINE AWAY, 11; dowyne, 326. OE dwinan. (See n. 11.)

did, see **do (2)**.

do (1), *n.*, DOE, 345. OE da.

do (2), *v., infin.*, DO, 424, 496, etc.; *pres. 1 sg.*, PLACE, PUT, 366; *2* and *3 sg.*, dotȝ, DO, DOES, 17, 293, 338, etc.; MAKE, 556; *3 pl.*, don, ENDURE, 511; *pret. 3 sg.*, did, CAUSED, 102; DID, 1138; dyd, CAUSED, 306; dyt, DID, 681; *3 pl.*, dyden, 633; *imv.*, do, PUT *in* d. way, PUT AWAY, FORBEAR, 718; *pp.*, don, PUT, 250; d. out of daweȝ, PUT OUT OF DAYS (i.e., LIFE), hence, UTTERLY GONE, 282; DONE, 930; MADE, 942; done *in* to d., FULFILLED, 914; PLACED, 1042. OE don.

doc, *n.*, DUKE, 211. OF duc.

doel, *n.*, GRIEF, SORROW, 336, 339, 642; del, 250; dele, 51; dol, 326. OF doel.

doel-dystresse, *n.*, DISTRESS OF GRIEF, GRIEF'S DISTRESS, 337. OF doel, destresse.

doel-doungoun, *n.*, DOLE-DUNGEON, PRISON or DUNGEON OF SORROW, 1187. OF donjon.

dole, *n.*, PART, 136. OE dal.

dom, *n.*, MIND, JUDGMENT, 157, 223; SENTENCE, JUDGMENT, 667; dome, 580, 699. OE dom.

don, done, see **do (2).**

dorst, dorste, see **dar.**

dotȝ, see **do (2).**

double, *adj.*, DOUBLE, TWOFOLD, 202. OF double.

doun, *adv.*, DOWN, 30, 41, etc.; d. after, FOLLOWING, 125; *prep.*, DOWN, 196, etc. OE adun.

doun, *n.*, HILL, DOWN, 121; *possess.*, douneȝ, 73; *pl.*, 85. OE dun.

doungoun, see **doel-doungoun.**

dousour, *n.*, SWEETNESS, 429. OF doucor.

doute, *n.*, DOUBT, 928. OF doute.

douth, *n.*, CREATURE, BEING, 839. OE duguþ. (See n. 839-40.)

dowyne, see **dewyne.**

draȝ, *v.*, *2 sg.*, *imv.*, DRAW, 699; *pret. 3 pl.*, droȝ, MOVED, 1116; *pp.*, drawen, 1193. OE dragan.

dred, *v.*, *pret. 1 sg.*, FEARED, 186. OE [on]drædan.

drede, *n.*, FEAR, APPREHENSION, DREAD, 181, 1047. Cf. OE [on]drædan.

drem, *n.*, DREAM, 790, 1170. OE dream.

dresse, *v.*, *infin.*, ESTABLISH, DIRECT, 495; *pp.*, drest, 860. OF dresser.

dreue, *v.*, *infin.*, GO, PASS, 323; *pret. 1 sg.*, PRESSED, PUSHED, 980. OE dræfan.

drof, see **dryue.**

drounde, *v.*, *pret. 3 sg.*, DROWNED, 656. OE druncnian.

drwry, *adj.*, DREARY, 323. OE dreorig.

dryȝe, *v.*, *infin.*, DRY, BLOT, TAKE AWAY, REMOVE, 823. OE dryg[e]an; cf. LG dröge. (See n. 823.)

dryȝly, *adv.*, AT GREAT LENGTH, UNCEASINGLY, 125; IN EXHAUSTION, EXHAUSTEDLY, 223. ON driugliga.

Dryȝtyn, *n.*, GOD, 324, 349. OE Dryhten.

dryue, *v.*, *pres. 3 sg.*, *subj.*, SINKS, 1094; *pret. 3 sg.*, drof, FLED, HURRIED, 30; PURSUED, 1153; *pp.*, dryuen, LED, 1194. OE drifan.

dubbed, *pp.*, ADORNED, DECKED, 73, 202; dubbet, 97. OF adouber.

dubbement, *n.*, ADORNMENT, 121; dubbemente, 109. OF adoubement.

due, *adj.*, DUE, 894. OF deu.

dunne, *adj.*, DARK, 30. OE dunn.

durande, *part. adj.*, LASTING, ENDLESS, 336. OF durer.

dyche, *n.*, DIKE, CHANNEL, 607. OE dic.

dyd, dyden, see **do.**

dyȝe, *v.*, *infin.*, DIE, 306, 642; *pret. 3 sg.*, dyȝed, 828; dyed, 705. ON deyja.

dyȝt, *v.*, *infin.*, ORDER, DISPOSE, 360; *pp.*, ESTABLISHED, SET, 920; ADORNED, 987; dyȝte, ORNAMENTED, 202. OE dihtan.

dylle, *adj.*, SLOW, 680. Cf. OE dol.
dym, *adj.*, DIM, 1076. OE dim.
dyne, *n.*, CLAMOR, 339. OE dyne.
dyscreuen, *v.*, *infin.*, DESCRY, 68. OF descrivre.
dysplese3, *v.*, *pres. 3 sg.*, DISPLEASES, 455; *2 sg.*, *imv.*, BE DISPLEASED, 422. OF desplaisir.
dyssente, *v.*, *pres. 3 pl.*, DESCEND, 627. OF descendre.
dystresse, *n.*, DISTRESS, 280, 337; dysstresse, 898. OF destresse.
dystryed, *v.*, *pret. 3 pl.*, PUT AN END TO, 124. OF destruire.
dyd, dyde, dyt, see **do (2).**

E

efte, *adv.*, AGAIN, 328, 332. OE eft.
elle3, *adv.*, ELSE, 32, 130, 491, 567, 724. OE elles.
emerad, *n.*, EMERALD, 118; emerade, 1005. OF esmeraude.
emperise, *n.*, EMPRESS, 441. OF emperesse.
empyre, *n.*, EMPIRE, DOMINION, 454. OF empire.
enchace, *v.*, *infin.*, PURSUE, IMPEL, 173. OF enchacier.
enclose, *v.*, *infin.*, ENCLOSE, ENSHRINE, 909. Cf. OF enclos (*pp.* of enclore).
enclyin, *adj.*, PROSTRATE, 1206. OF enclin.
enclyne, *v.*, *infin.*, BOW, 630; *pres. part.*, enclynande, 236. OF encliner.
encres, *v.*, *infin.*, INCREASE, 959. OF encreistre.
encroched, *v.*, *pret. 3 sg.*, INDUCED, 1117. OF encrochier.
endele3, *adj.* as *adv.*, WITHOUT END, 738. OE endeleas.
endent, *v.*, *pret. 3 sg.*, MARKED, 1012; *pp.*, endente, 629. OF endenter.
endorde, *pp.* as *n.*, ADORED, 368. OF adorer.
endure, *v.*, *infin.*, ENDURE, LAST, 225; endeure, 1082; *pp.*, endured, 476. OF endurer.
endyte, *v.*, *pres. 3 pl.*, INDITE, PROCLAIM, SEND FORTH, 1126. OF enditer.
ene, *adv.*, ONCE; *in* at e., AT ONE TIME, FORMERLY, 291, 953. OE æne.
enle, *adv.*, SEVERALLY, SINGLY, 849. OE ænlice.
enleuenþe, *adj.*, ELEVENTH, 1014. OE endleofan.
enpryse, *n.*, EMPRISE, 1097. OF enprise.
ensens, *n.*, INCENSE, 1122. OF encens.
entent, *n.*, INTENT, ENDEAVOR, 1191. OF entent.
enter, *v.*, *infin.*, ENTER, 966; *pres. 3 sg.*, entre3, 1067; *pret. 1 sg.*, entred, 38. OF entrer.
enurned, *pp.*, ADORNED, 1027. OF aorner.
er, *conj.*, BEFORE, ERE, 188, 224, etc.; er-þenne, 1094; *prep.*, 49, 517; *adv.*, FIRST, 319; ONCE, 372; ERE, 164. OE ær.
erber, *n.*, GARDEN, 38, 1171; erbere, 9. OF herbier. (See n. 9.)
erde, *n.*, LAND, 248. OE eard.
ere (1), see **er.**

ere (2), *n.*, EAR, 1153. OE eare.
erle, *n.*, EARL, 211. OE eorl.
erly, *adv.*, EARLY, 392, 506. OE ærlice.
ernays, *n.*, PLEDGE, COVENANT, 307. (See n. 307.)
errour, *n.*, ERROR, 422. OF error, errour.
erþe, *n.*, EARTH, 840; vrþe, 442, 893, 1125; *adj.*, vrþely, EARTHLY, 135. OE eorþe; eorþlic.
erytage, see **herytage.**
eschaped, *v. pret. 3 sg., subj.*, EVADE, ESCAPE, 187. OF eschaper.
etente, *pp.*, HEEDED, CONSIDERED, 257. OF atendre.
eþe, *adj.*, EASY, 1202. OE eaþe.
euel, *adv.*, ILL, 310, 930. OE yfele.
euen (1), *adv.*, EXACTLY, 740. OE efne.
euen (2), *v., infin.*, TO BE EQUAL, 1073. OE efnan.
euensonge, *n.*, EVENSONG, 529. OE æfensang.
euentyde, *n.*, EVENTIDE, 582. OE æfentid.
euer, *adv.*, EVER, 144, 153, 180, 200, etc.; *intens.* with *v.*, watȝ bore, 239. OE æfre.
euermore, *adv.*, FOREVER, EVERMORE, 591, 666, 1066.
excused, *pp.*, PARDONED, 281. OF excuser.
expoun, *v., pres. 1 sg.*, SET FORTH, DESCRIBE, 37. OF espondre.
expresse, *adj.*, EXPRESS, DEFINITE, 910. OF expres.

F

fable, *n.*, FABLE, 592. OF fable.
face, *n.*, FACE, FEATURES, 169, 434, 675, 809. OF face.
fader, *n.*, FATHER, 639, 736; *gen.*, faderez, 872. OE fæder.
faȝt, *v., pret. 3 sg.*, FOUGHT, 54. OE feohtan.
fande, see **fynde.**
farande, *adj.*, BECOMING, FITTING, 865. ON farandi; cf. OE faran.
fare (1), *n.*, WAYS, 832. OE faru.
fare (2), *v., infin.*, GO, JOURNEY, 147; *pres. 3 sg.*, CONTINUES, 129; *pres. 1 pl.*, FARE, 467. OE faran.
Fasor, *n.*, MAKER, CREATOR, 431. (See n. 429-32.)
fasoun, *n.*, MANNER, 983; FASHION, 1101. OF façon.
faste, *adv.*, FAST, SWIFTLY, 54, 150. OE fæstan.
fasure, *n.*, FASHIONING, 1084. OF faisure.
fateȝ, *v., pres. 3 sg.*, FADE, GROW DIM, 1038. OF fader.
faunt, *n.*, YOUNG PERSON, YOUTHFUL BEING, 161. OF enfant; cf. OF faon, feon. (See n. 161.)
fauour, *n.*, FAVOR, GRACE, 428, 968. OF favour.
fax, *n.*, HAIR, 213. OE feax.
faye, *n.*, FAITH, 263; fay, 489. OF fei.

fayly, *v., infin.*, FAIL, COME TO NOUGHT, 34; fayle, 317; *pret. 3 sg.*, fayled, 270. OF faillir.

fayn, *adj.*, GLAD, 393, 450. OE fægen.

fayr, *adj.*, FAIR, BEAUTIFUL, BEAUTEOUS, 147, 810; FAIR, JUST, 490; fayre, 169, 177, 747, etc.; *comp.*, feirer, 103; *adv.*, fayr, GENTLY, COURTEOUSLY, 714; fayre, ACTUALLY, 88; EVENLY, 884; FAIR, 1024. OE fæger.

fech, *v., infin.*, FETCH, WORK UP, 1158; *3 sg., subj.*, feche, 847. OE feccan.

fede, *adj.* or *pp.*, WITHERED, 29. Cf. OF fade.

feirer, see **fayre.**

fel, *v., pret. 1 sg.*, FELL, 1174; felle, 57; *3 pl.*, 1120. OE feallan.

felde, *v., pret. 1 sg.*, FELT, 1087. OE felan.

fele, *adj.*, MANY, 21, 439, 716, 874, 927, etc. OE fela.

felle, *adj.*, FELL, CRUEL, 367; DEADLY, 655. OF fel.

felonye, *n.*, FELONY, 800. OF felonie.

fenyx, *n.*, PHOENIX, 430. OE fenix.

fer, *adv.*, FAR, 334, 1076; *comp.*, fyrre, 103, 127, 148, etc. OE feor.

fere (1), *n.*, COMPANY, 1105; *in* in f., IN FLOCKS, 89; IN UNISON, 884. OE [ge]fer.

fere (2), *n.*, COMPANION; pl., fereȝ, COMPANIONS, 1150. OE [ge]fera.

fereȝ (1), see **fere (2).**

fereȝ (2), *v., pres. 3 sg.*, CARRY, LEAD, 98; *pp.*, feryed, 946. OE ferian.

ferly, *adj.*, WONDERFUL, AMAZING, 1084; *n.*, WONDER, 1086. OE feorlic.

feryed, see **fereȝ (2).**

feste, *n.*, FEAST; *in* ma f., MAKE FEAST, i.e., REJOICE, 283. OF feste. (See n. 283.)

fete, see **fote.**

fewe, *adj.*, FEW, 572. OE feawe.

flaȝt, *n.*, SWARD, 57. Cf. LG flagge.

flake, *n.*, FLECK, SPOT, BLEMISH, 947. Cf. ON flekkr. (See n. 947-48.)

flambe, *v., infin.*, SHINE, 769; *pres. part.*, flaumbande, FLAMING, 90. OF flamber.

flauoreȝ, *n., pl.*, FRAGRANCES, 87. OF flaur.

flayn, see **flyȝe.**

fle, *v., infin.*, FLEE, 294. OE fleon.

fleȝe, *v., pret. 3 sg.*, FLEW, 431; *3 pl.*, flowen, 89. OE fleogan.

fleme, *v., pres. 3 pl., subj.*, DRIVE, BANISH, 334. OE fleman.

flesch, *n.*, FLESH, 306, 958. OE flæsc.

fleschly, *adj.*, FLESHLY, 1082. OE flæslic.

fleten, *v., pret. 3 pl.*, DRIFTED, 21; *3 sg.*, flot, FLOATED, 46; flet, 1058. OE fleotan. (See n. 1058.)

flode, *n.*, SEA, RIVER, 736, 1058; *gen. pl.*, flodeȝ, WATERS, 874. OE flod.

flok, *n.*, FLOCK, 947. OE flocc.

flonc, *v.*, *pret.* *1 sg.*, FLUNG (MYSELF), PLUNGED, 1165. Cf. ON flengja.
flor, *n.*, FLOWER, 29, 962; flowreȝ, 208; *adj.*, floury, FLOWERY, 57. OF flor, flour.
flor-de-lys, *n.*, FLEUR-DE-LIS, 195; flour-de-lys, 753. OF flour de lis.
flot (1), *n.*, FLOCK, COMPANY, RETINUE, 786; flote, 946. OF flote.
flot (2), see **fleten.**
floty, *adj.*, WAVING, UNDULATING, 127. (See n. 127.)
floury, see **flor.**
flowen, see **fleȝe.**
flowered, *v.*, *pret.* *3 sg.*, FLOWERED, 270. OF florir.
flowreȝ, see **flor.**
flurted, *pp.*, FIGURED, 208. OF fleureté.
flyȝe, *v.*, *infin.*, SCOURGE, 813; *pp.*, flayn, TORN, FLAYED, 809. OE flean.
flyte, *v.*, *infin.*, DISPUTE, 353. OE flitan.
fode, *n.*, FOOD, 88. OE foda.
folde (1), *n.*, LAND, EARTH, 334, 736. OE folde.
folde (2), *v.*, *infin.*, BEND, 813; *pp.*, COVERED *in* f. up, COVERED UP, CONCEALED, 434. OE fealdan.
folȝed, *v.*, *pret.* *1 sg.*, FOLLOWED, 127; *3 sg.*, 654; *pres. part.*, folewande, 1040. OE folgian.
fon, see **fyne (2).**
fonde (1), *v.*, *infin.*, TRY, 150; SEEK OUT, 939; EXAMINED, SCANNED, 170. OE fandian.
fonde (2), fonte, see **fynd.**
fonge, *v.*, *infin.*, ATTAIN, 479; *pres. 3 pl.*, fongeȝ, RECEIVE, 439; *pret. 3 pl.*, fonge, CAUGHT, 884. OE fon.
for (1), *conj.*, FOR, 31, 269, 321, etc.; BECAUSE OF, 898; OE for.
for (2), *prep.*, FOR, 50, 99, etc.; fore, 734. OE for.
forbede, *v.*, *pres. 3 sg.*, *subj.*, FORBID, 379. OE forbeodan.
forbrent, *pp.*, CONSUMED, 1139. OE forbeornan.
fordidden, *v.*, *pret. 3 pl.*, DISPELLED, 124. OE fordon.
fordolked, *pp.*, GRIEVOUSLY WOUNDED, SORE-WOUNDED, 11. Cf. ME dolc, dolke; OE dolgian. (See n. 11.)
foreste, *n.*, FOREST, 67. OF forest.
forfete, *v.*, *infin.*, FORFEIT, 639; *3 sg.*, *subj.*, forfeted, 619. OF forfaire.
forgarte, *pp.*, STRICKEN, 321. ON fyrirgöra.
forgo, *v.*, *infin.*, FOREGO, 328; *pres. 3 sg.*, forgos, 340. OE forgan.
forȝete, *v.*, *infin.*, FORGET, 86. OE forgietan.
forhedeȝ, *n.*, FOREHEADS, 871. OE forheafod.
forlete, *v.*, *pret. 1 sg.*, LOST, 327. OE forlætan.
forlonge, *n.*, *pl.*, FURLONGS, 1030. OE furlang.
forloyne, *v.*, *pres. 1 sg.*, *subj.*, ERR, BE IN ERROR, 368. OF forloignier.
forme (1), *adj.*, FIRST, 639. OE forma.
forme (2), *n.*, FORM, 1209. OF forme.

formed, *v., pret. 3 sg.,* FASHIONED, 747. OF former.
forpayned, *pp.,* TORMENTED, 246. OE for; OF peiner.
forsake, *v., infin.,* RENOUNCE, 743. OE forsaken.
forser, *n.,* TREASURE CHEST, JEWEL CASE, 263. OF forsier.
forsoþe, *adv.,* IN TRUTH, FORSOOTH, INDEED, 21, 292. OE for soþe.
forth, *adv.,* ON, FORWARD, ONWARD, 98, 101, 510, 980, 1116. OE forþ.
fortune, *n.,* FORTUNE, DESTINY, 129, 306; fortwne, 98. OF fortune.
forty, *num.,* FORTY, 786, 870. OE feowertig.
forþe, *n.,* FORD, 150. OE ford.
forþy, *adv.,* THEREFORE, 137, 234, 845; THUS, 701. OE for þy.
fote, *n.,* FOOT, 161, 350, 970; *pl.,* fete, 1120. OE fot.
founce, *n.,* BOTTOM, RIVER BED, 113. OF fonz, funz.
foundementeȝ, see **fundament.**
founden, see **fynde.**
fowleȝ, *n.,* BIRDS, 89. OE fugol.
fowre, *num.,* FOUR, 870, 886. OE feower.
foysoun, *n.* in *nominal-compound,* foysoun-flode (lit., PLENTY-RIVER), COPIOUS FLOOD, 1058. OF foisoun.
fraunchyse, *n.,* FRANCHISE, HERITAGE (spiritual), PATRIMONY, 609. OF franchise.
frayneȝ, *v.,* MAKES TRIAL, TRIES US, 129. OE fregnan.
frayste, *v., pret. 1 sg.,* QUERIED, 169. ON freista.
fre, *adj.,* LIBERAL, 481; NOBLE, 299, 796. OE freo.
frech, *adj.,* FRESH, 87, 195. OE fersc.
freles, *adj.,* FLAWLESS, 431. Cf. ON fryjulaus.
frely, *adj. as n.,* FAIR or BEAUTIFUL (ONE), 1155. OE freolic.
frende, *n.,* FRIEND, 558, 1204. OE freond.
freuch, *adj.,* NOBLE, 1086. Northern form, from OE fresh (froh). (See n. 1086.)
fro, *adv.,* FRO, 347; *conj.,* SINCE, 251, 375, 958; *prep.,* FROM, 10, 13, 33, etc.; AGAINST, 803. ON fra.
frount, *n.,* FOREHEAD, 177. OF front.
frym, *adv.,* IN STRENGTH, 1079. Etymology and meaning uncertain; cf. OE freme.
fryt, *n.,* FRUIT, 894; fryte, 29; *pl.,* fryteȝ, 87, 1078. OF fruit.
fryth, *n.,* WOODLAND, 89; WOODED DOWNS, 98; REGION, 103. OE fryhþ.
ful, *adj.,* FULL, 1098; *adv.,* QUITE, MOST, FULL, VERY, 28, 42, etc. OE full, *adj.;* ful, *adv.*
fundament, *n.,* FOUNDATION, 1010; *pl.,* foundementeȝ, 993. OF fo(u)n-dement.
furþe, *adj.,* FOURTH, 1005. OE feorþa.
fyf, *num.,* FIVE, 849; fyue, 451. OE fif.
fyfþe, *adj.,* FIFTH, 1006. OE fifta.
fygure, *n.,* FIGURE, 170; FORM, 747; IMAGE, SCENE, 1086. OF figure.

fyldor, *n.,* THREAD OF GOLD, 106. OF fil d'or.
fylþe, *n.,* FILTH, 1060. OE fylþ.
fyn, *adj.,* FINE, 106; SLENDER, 170; fyin, NOBLE, 1204. OF fin.
fynde, *v., infin.,* FIND, DISCOVER, 150; *pres. 3 sg.,* fyndeȝ, 508, 514; *pret. 1 sg.,* fande, 871; *pp.,* fonde, 283; fonte, 327; founden, 1203. OE findan.
fyne (1), *n.,* END (OF THE ROW), i.e., FURROW'S END, 635. OF fin.
fyne (2), *v., pres. 1 sg.,* DIE, 328; *2 sg., imv.,* CEASE, 353; *pret. 3 sg.,* fon, 1030. OF finer.
fynger, *n.,* FINGER, 466. OE finger.
fyrre, see **fer.**
fyrst, *adj.,* FIRST, 486, 549, 570, 571, 999, 1000; *adv.,* 316, 583, 1042; fyrste, 638. OE fyrst.
fyrte, *n.,* VIOLENCE, 54. OF fierte, firte. (See n. 54.)
fyue, see **fyf.**

G

Galalye, *n.,* GALILEE, 817.
galle, *n.,* GALL, BLEMISH, 189; SPITE, 915; gawle, RANCOR, 463; SCUM, 1060. OE gealla.
gardyn, *n.,* GARDEN, 260. ONF gardin.
gareȝ, *v., pres. 3 sg.,* CAUSES, 331; *pret. 3 sg.,* gart, 1151; *3 pl.,* garten, 86. ON göra. (See n. 86.)
garlande, *n.,* GARLAND, 1186. OF garlande.
garten, see **gareȝ.**
gate, *n.,* WAY, 526, 619; MANNER OF ACTING or DOING, i.e., WAY OF LIFE, STATE, 395; *pl.,* gateȝ, STREETS, 1106. ON gata.
gaue, see **gyue.**
gawle, see **galle.**
gay, *adj.,* GAY, BRIGHT, RADIANT, 1124, 1186; gaye, 7, 260; as *n.,* gay, BRIGHT (ONE), 189; gaye, 433. OF gai.
gayn, *prep.,* OPPOSITE, FACING, 138. OE gegn.
gayne, *v., pres. 3 sg.,* GAIN, 343. ON gegna.
gef, see **gyue.**
gele, *v., infin.,* DELAY, TARRY, 931. OE gælan. (See n. 931.)
gemme, *n.,* GEM, 118, 219, etc.; *pl.,* gemmeȝ, 7, 253, 991. OF gemme.
generacyoun, *n.,* GENERATION, 827. OF generacion.
gent, *adj.,* NOBLE, 1014, 1134; gente, 118, 253, 265. OF gent.
gentyl, *adj.,* NOBLE, GENTLE, 264, 278, 605, etc.; as *n.,* 602; gentyle, 632; *superl.,* gentyleste, 1015. OF gentil.
gesse, *v., infin.,* IMAGINE, INVENT, IMPROVISE, 499. Cf. ON gisse.
geste, *n.,* GUEST, VISITOR, 277. ON gestr.
gete, *v., infin.,* ATTAIN, 95. ON geta.
gilofre, *n.,* GILLYFLOWER, 43. OF girofre.

glace, *v.*, *infin.*, FLASH, 171. OF glacer.
glade, *adj.*, GLAD, HAPPY, BLISSFUL, 136, 1144; *comp.*, gladder, 231; *superl.*, gladdest, 1109. OE glæd.
gladeȝ, *v.*, *pres. 3 sg.*, GLADDENS, 861; *pres. part.*, gladande, 171. OE gladian.
gladneȝ, *n.*, GLADNESS, 136.
glas, *n.*, GLASS, CRYSTAL, 114, 990, 1018; glasse, 1025, 1106. OE glæs.
glauereȝ, *v.*, *pres. 3 pl.*, DECEIVE, 688. ? Welsh glafru.
glayre, *n.*, GLAIR, GLAZE, 1026. OF glaire.
glayue, *n.*, LANCE, 654. OF glaive.
gle, *n.*, JOY, 95, 1123. OE gleo.
glem, *n.*, GLEAM, 79. OE glæm.
glemande, *pp.*, GLEAMING, 70, 990.
glene, *v.*, *infin.*, GLEAN, 955. OF glener.
glent, *v.*, *pret. 3 sg.*, SHONE, 70; GLITTERED, 1026; glente, GLISTENED, 1001; GLANCED AT, 671; *pret. pl.*, glent, GLISTENED, 1106. Cf. Swedish glänta.
glente, *n.*, LIGHT, 114; *pl.*, glenteȝ, GLANCES, 1144.
glet, *n.*, MIRE, 1060. OF glette.
glod, see **glydeȝ.**
glodeȝ, *n.*, ? GLADES, 79. (See n. 79.)
glory, *n.*, GLORY, 70, 171, 934, 959, 1123. OF glorie.
gloryous, *adj.*, GLORIOUS, 799, 915; as *adv.*, 1144. OF glorios, glorious.
glowed, *pret. 3 pl.*, GLOWED, 114. OE glowan.
glydeȝ, *v.*, *pres. 3 sg.*, GLIDE, 79; *pret. 3 pl.*, glod, 1105. OE glidan.
glyȝt, *v.*, *pret. 3 pl.*, GLITTERED, GLEAMED, 114. Cf. ON glia.
glymme, *n.*, RADIANCE, 1088. Etymology obscure; cf. OE gleomu, glæm.
glysnande, *pres. part.*, GLISTENING, 165, 1018. OE glisnian.
go, see **gon.**
God, *n.*, GOD, 314, 342, 379, 674, etc.; *gen. sg.*, Godeȝ, 63, 601; Goddeȝ, 591, 1193. OE God.
god, *n.*, GOODS, POSSESSIONS, 734; goude, 731; GOOD THING, 33; goud, GOOD, 33. OE god.
god, *adj.*, GOOD, 310, 1202; goude, 568, 818; *superl.*, best, BEST, 1131; beste, 863; as *n.*, 279. OE god; best, fr. OE *adj.*, betst.
Godhede, *n.*, GODHEAD, 413.
godnesse, *n.*, GOODNESS, 493.
golde, *n.*, GOLD, 2, 165, 213, etc.; golde, 1111. OE gold.
golden, *adj.*, GOLDEN, 1106. OE gylden.
golf, *n.*, GULF, BAY, 608. OF golfe.
gome, *n.*, MAN, 231, 697. OE guma.
gon, *v.*, *infin.*, GO, 820; *pres. 3 sg.*, gotȝ, 365; *3 pl.*, 510; *pres. 3 sg.*, *subj.*, 530; *imv.*, 559; *pl.*, gos, 521; gotȝ, 535; *pret. 3 sg.*, ȝede, PURSUED, 526; WENT, 1049; *3 pl.*, WENT FORTH, 713; yot (var. of ȝede),

WENT, 10; *pp.*, gon, GONE *in* is g., i.e., GONE FORTH, 63; GONE, 376; MOVED HITHER AND THITHER, i.e., BEAMED, 210. OE gan.

gos, see **gon.**

gospel, *n.*, GOSPEL, 498. OE godspel.

goste, *n.*, SPIRIT, SOUL, 63, 86. OE gast.

gostly, *adj.*, SPIRITUAL, GHOSTLY, 185, 790. OE gastlic.

gote, *n.*, STREAM, 934; *pl.*, goteȝ, 608. Cf. OE geotan.

gotȝ, see **gon.**

goud, goude, see **god**, *n.*

grace, *n.*, GRACE, 63, 194, etc. OF grace.

gracios, *adj.*, GRACIOUS, BEAUTIFUL, PLEASING, 189; gracios, 95; gracious, 934; as *adv.*, CHARMINGLY, 260. OF gracios.

grauayl, *n.*, GRAVEL, 81. OF gravele.

graunt, *n.*, PERMISSION, 317. OF *v.* graanter.

graye, *adj.*, GRAY, 254. OE græg.

grayneȝ, *n.*, *pl.*, GRAINS, 31. OF grain.

grayþely, *adv.*, READILY, 499. ON greiþliga.

Grece, *n.*, GREECE, 231.

greffe, *n.*, GRIEF, 86. OF gref.

greme, *n.*, WRATH, 465. ON gremi.

grene, *adj.*, GREEN, 38, 1001, 1005. OE grene.

gresse, *n.*, GRASS, 10, 31, 245. OE græs.

gret, *adj.*, GREAT, MUCH, LARGE, 250, 330, 511, 612, 616, etc.; grete, 90, 237, 280, etc. OE great.

grete, *v.*, *infin.*, WEEP, 331. OE gretan.

greue (1), *n.*, GROVE; Paradys g., PARADISE-GROVE (Garden of Eden), 321. OE græf.

greue (2), *v.*, *pres. 3 sg.*, *subj.*, GRIEVE, 471. OF grever.

grewe, see **grow.**

gromylyoun, *n.*, GROMWELL, 43. Cf. OF gromil.

grounde (1), *n.*, GROUND, 10, 372, etc.; *in* on g., UNDERFOOT, 81. OE grund.

grounde (2), *v.*, see **grynde.**

grouelyng, *pp.*, GROVELING, PROSTRATE, 1120. ME grovelinge (gru, felinge); ON gru, OE feallan.

grow, *v.*, *infin.*, 31; *pret. 3 sg.*, grewe, SPRANG, 425. OE growan.

grym, *adj.*, CRUDE, 1070. OE grim.

grymly, *adv.*, CRUELLY, 654. OE grimlice.

grynde, *v.*, *infin.*, GRIND, 81; *pp.*, grounde, 654. OE grindan.

gryste, *n.*, ANNOY, IRRITATION, 465. OE grist.

gulte, *n.*, GUILT, SIN, 942; *pl.*, gylteȝ, SINS, 655. OE gylt.

gyfte, *n.*, PREROGATIVE, RIGHT TO BESTOW, 565; *pl.*, gyfteȝ, GIFTS, 607. OE gift.

gyle, *n.*, GUILE, 671, 688. OF guile.

gylteȝ, see **gulte.**
gyltleȝ, *adj.*, GUILTLESS, 799; as *n.*, GUILTLESS (ONE), 668. OE gyltleas.
gyltyf, *adj.*, GUILTY, 669. OE gyltig.
gyng, *n.*, COMPANY, 455. OE genge.
gyngure, *n.*, GINGER, 43. OF gengibre. (See n. 8.)
gyrle, *n.*, MAIDEN, 205. OE gyrl.
gyse, *n.*, GUISE, 1099. OF guise.
gyternere, *n.*, GITTERN PLAYER, 91. OF guiterner.
gyue, *v.*, *pres. 3 sg.*, *subj.*, GRANT, GIVE, ALLOT, 707; *2 sg.*, *imv.*, gyf, 543, 546; *pret. 3 sg.*, gef, 174, 270, 734, 765, 1211; gaue, 667; *pp.*, geuen, 1190. OE giefan; ON gefa. (See n. 1207 ff. *gef.*)

Ȝ

ȝare, *adv.*, CLEARLY, 834. OE gearwe.
ȝate, *n.*, GATE, PORTAL, 1037; *pl.*, ȝateȝ, 1034, 1065. OE geat.
ȝe, see **þou.**
ȝede, see **gon.**
ȝemen, *n.*, *pl.*, YEOMEN, 535. OE geongman.
ȝer, *n.*, YEAR, 1079; ȝere, 503, 505, 588; *pl.*, ȝer, 483. OE gear.
ȝerned, *pp.*, YEARNED, CRAVED, 1190. OE geornian.
ȝet, *adv.*, YET, MOREOVER, TOO, BESIDES, FURTHER, etc., 19, 46, 145, 205, 215, etc.; ȝete, 1061. OE giet.
ȝete, *v.*, *infin.*, CONCEDE, 558. OE geatan.
ȝif, see **if.**
ȝon, *adj.*, YON, 693. OE geon.
ȝong, *adj.*, YOUNG, 412; ȝonge, 474, 535. OE geong.
ȝore, *adv.*, IN THE PAST, 586. OE geara.
ȝore-fader, *n.*, FIRST FATHER (i.e., ADAM), 322.
ȝys, *adv.*, YES, 635. OE gese.

H

had, hade, haf, see **haue.**
hafyng, *n.*, HAVING, 450. See **haue.** Cf. OE hæfen.
halde, *v.*, *infin.*, HOLD, 490; *pres. 1 sg.*, 301; *3 sg.*, haldeȝ, 454; *pret. 3 sg.*, helde, 1002; OCCUPIED, FILLED, 1029; *pp.*, halden, 1191. OE haldan.
haleȝ, *v.*, *pres. 3 sg.*, FLOWS, 125. OF haler.
half (1), *n.*, SIDE, 230. OE healf.
half (2), *adv.*, HALF, 72. OE healf.
halle, *n.*, HALL, 184. OE heall.
halte, *adv.*, HIGH, 1158. OF halt. (See n. 1157-60.)
han, see **haue.**
happe, *n.*, GOOD FORTUNE, FORTUNE, 16, 1195; BLESSING, 713. ON happ.
harde, *adv.*, HARD, 606. OE hearde.

hardyly, *adv.*, BOLDLY, ASSUREDLY, CONFIDENTLY, 3, 695. OF hardi and suffix -ly.

harme, *n.*, HARM, 681; *pl.*, harmeȝ, WRONGS, 388. OE hearm.

harmleȝ, *adj.*, INNOCENT, SINLESS, 676, 725.

harpe, *n.*, HARP, 881. OE hearpe.

harpen, *v.*, *pres. 3 pl.*, HARP, 881. OE hearpian.

harporeȝ, *n.*, *pl.*, HARPERS, 881. OE hearpere.

hate (1), *adj.*, BURNING, 388. OE hat.

hate (2), *n.*, HATRED, HATE, 463. Cf. OE hete.

hated, *pp.*, HATED, 402. OE hatian.

hatȝ, see **haue.**

haþel, *n.*, WORTHY FELLOW, MAN, 676. Cf. OE æþele, hælep.

haue, *v.*, *infin.*, HAVE, 132, 661, 928; haf, 194, 1139; *pres. 1 sg.*, 14, 242, 244; *2 sg.*, hatȝ, 770, 935, 971; *3 sg.*, 446, 465, 625, etc.; *1 pl.*, hauen, 859; *2 pl.*, haf, 917; *pret. 3 sg.*, 1034; hade, 209, 502, etc.; *3 pl.*, 1045; *pret. 1 sg.*, *subj.*, hade, 134; *3 sg.*, 1142; *3 pl.*, 1091; *pp.*, had, 1140; as *aux.*, *pres. 1 sg.*, 704, 967; *2 sg.*, hatȝ, 291; *3 sg.*, hatȝ, 274; *1 pl.*, haf, 519, 553; han, 554; *2 pl.*, haf, 257; han, 373; *3 pl.*, han; *pret. 1 sg.*, had, 170; hade, 164; *3 sg.*, had, 1148; hade, 476; *3 pl.*, hade, 550; *1 sg.*, *subj.*, hade, 1189, 1194; *3 sg.*, 1090. OE habban.

hawk, *n.*, HAWK, 184. OE hafoc.

haylsed, *v.*, *pret. 3 sg.*, GREETED, 238. OE halsian; ON heilsa.

he, *pron.*, *pers.*, *masc.*, 302, 332, 475, etc.; *dat.* and *accus.*, hym, 324, 598, etc.; *fem.*, ho, 129, 130, 131, etc.; scho, 758; *accus.*, hir, 188, 428; *dat.* and *accus.*, hyr, 8, 9, 164, 167, etc.; *neut.*, hit, 10, 13, 30, etc.; as *pl.*, 895, 1199; hyt, 270, 271, 283, etc.; *pl.*, þay, 80, 94, etc.; *dat.*, hem, 717, 728; *accus.*, 69, 70, 75, etc.; hym, 635, 813. OE he, *masc.*; heo, *fem.*; hit, *neut.* (See nn. 611 *hem;* 621 *þay;* 689-94 *ho.*)

hed, hede, see **heued.**

hede, *v.*, *infin.*, OBSERVE, PERCEIVE, 1051. OE hedan.

heȝt, see **hyȝt (1).**

helde (1), *pp.*, DISPOSED, 1193. ME helden. OE heldan. (See n. 1193.)

helde (2), see **halde.**

hele, *n.*, WELL-BEING, 16; HEALING, 713. OE hælu.

helle, *n.*, HELL, 442, 643, 651, 840, 1125. OE helle.

hem, see **he.**

hemme, *n.*, HEM, 217; BORDER, 1001. OE hemm.

hende, *adj.*, READY TO HAND, ALERT, 184; as *n.*, hynde, GRACIOUS (ONE), 909. OE [ge]hende.

hente, *v.*, *infin.*, GRASP, 669; SEIZE, 1195; *pres. 1 sg.*, MEET WITH, 388. OE hentan.

her (1), *pron.*, *poss.*, HER, 4, 6, 131, etc.; in sense, ITS, 4; hir, 22, 191, 197; hyr, 163, 169, etc.; in sense, ITS, 8, 9. Cf. **he.** (See n. 4.)

her (2), *pron.*, *poss.*, THEIR, 92, 93, 96, etc. Cf. **he.**

here (1), *adv.*, HERE, 298, 389, 399, etc.; her, 263, 519. OE her.
here (2), *v.*, *infin.*, HEAR, 96; *pret. 1 sg.*, herde, 873, 879, 1132. OE heran.
here-inne, *adv.*, HEREIN, 261, 577. OE her, inne.
herneȝ, *n.*, BRAINS, SENSES, 58. ON hiarni.
hert, *n.*, HEART, 17, 51, 174, 179, 682, 1082, 1136; herte, 128, 135, 176, 364. OE heorte.
herytage, *n.*, HERITAGE, 417; erytage, 443. OF heritage.
heste, *n.*, BEHEST, 633. OE hæs.
hete (1), *n.*, HEAT, 554, 643. OE hætu.
hete (2), *v.*, *pres. 1 sg.*, ASSURE, PROMISE, 402; *pret. 3 sg.*, hyȝte, 305; hyȝt, WAS CALLED, 999; *pl.*, 950. OE hatan.
heterly, *adv.*, STRONGLY, 402. Cf. MLG hetter.
heþen, *adv.*, HENCE, FROM HERE, 231. ON heþan.
heue, *v.*, *infin.*, CAST, HURL, 314; *pres. 2 sg.*, LIFT, 473; *infin.*, heuen, EXALT, 16. OE hebban.
heued, *n.*, HEAD, 459, 465, 974; hed, 209; hede, 1172. OE heafod.
heuen, *n.*, HEAVEN, 473, 490, etc.; *pl.*, heueneȝ, 441; *gen. sg.*, 423, 620; heuenesse, 735. OE heofon.
heuen-ryche, *n.*, KINGDOM OF HEAVEN, 719. OE heofon-rice.
heuy, *adj.*, OPPRESSIVE, 1180. OE hefig.
hider, *adv.*, HITHER, 517; hyder, 249, 763. OE hider.
hiȝe, see **hyȝe.**
hil, see **hylle.**
hir, see **he, her** (1).
his, see **hys.**
hit (1), *pron.*, *pers.*, see **he.**
hit (2), *pron.*, *poss.*, ITS, 108, 120, 224; hyt, 446.
ho, see **he.**
hol, *adj.*, ENTIRE, ALL, 406. OE hal.
holte-wodeȝ, *n.*, FORESTS, 75. OE holtwudu.
holteȝ, *n.*, GROVES, 921. OE holt.
holy (1), *adj.*, HOLY, 592, 618, 679. OE halig.
holy (2), *adv.*, WHOLLY, 418. Cf. **hol.**
homly, *adj.*, OF THE HOUSEHOLD, hence, INTIMATE, DEAR, 1211. OE ham and suffix -ly.
honde, *n.*, HAND; *in* com on h., CAME TO HAND, i.e., CAME TO (MY) ATTENTION, 155; *pl.*, 49, 218; hondeȝ, 706. OE hand.
hondelyngeȝ, *adv.*, WITH HANDS, 681. OE handlinga.
hondred, see **hundreth.**
hone, *v.*, *infin.*, STAND, 921. Etymology uncertain; cf. OE han.
honour, *n.*, HONOR, 424, 475, 852, 864; onoure, 690. OF honour(e), onour(e), onur. (See n. 689-94.)
hope (1), *n.*, HOPE, 860. OE hopa.

hope (2), *v., pres. 1 sg.,* SUPPOSE, 225; *pret. 1 sg.,* GUESSED, 142; SURMISED, 185; hoped, SUPPOSED, 139. OE hopian. (See n. 11 *dewyne.*)
horneȝ, *n.,* HORNS, 1111. OE horn.
houreȝ, see **oure.**
how, *adv.,* HOW, 334, 690, 711, 1146. OE hu.
how, *n.,* see **hwe.**
hue, *n.,* CRY, 873. OF hu.
huee, see **hwe.**
hundreth, *num.,* HUNDRED, 1107; hundreþe, 869; hondred, 786. OE hundred. ON hundraþ.
hurt, *pp.,* HURT, 1142. OF hurter.
huyle, see **hylle.**
hwe, *n.,* HUE, COLOR, 896; huee, 842; how, 1012; *pl.,* hweȝ, 90. OE hiw.
hyde, *n.,* SKIN, 1136. OE hyd.
hyȝe, *adj.,* HIGH, 596, 1024, 1051, 1054; HAUGHTY, 401; EXALTED, 395; hyȝ, 39, 678; *adv.,* 473, 773; hyȝe, 454; hiȝe, 207. OE heah.
hyȝt (1), *n.,* HEIGHT, 1031; on hyȝt, ON HIGH, 501; heȝt, 1031. OE heahþo.
hyȝt (2), hyȝte, see **hete (2).**
hylle, *n.,* HILL, HILLOCK, 678, 1172; hyl, 789, 979; *in* h. coppe, HILLTOP, 791; hil, 976; huyle, 41; hyul, 1205. OE hyll. (See n. 41.)
hym, see **he.**
hymself, *pron., refl.,* 808, 811, 826; *intens.,* 680, 812, 825, 896, 1134.
hynde, see **hende.**
hyne, *n., pl.,* HOUSEHOLDERS, 505; SERVANTS, 632, 1211. OE hiwan. (See n. 505.)
hyr, see **he, her (1).**
hyre (1), *n.,* HIRE, WAGE, 523, 534, 539, 543, 583, 587. OE hyr.
hyre (2), *v., infin.,* HIRE, 507; *pret. 1 sg.,* 560. OE hyrian.
hys, *pron., poss.,* HIS, 307, 312, etc.; his, 285, 355, 526, etc.; hysse, 418. OE his.
hyt, see **he.**
hytteȝ, *v., pres. 3 sg.,* IS LIKELY, 132. ON hitta. (See n. 132.)
hyul, see **hylle.**

I

I, *pron., pers., 1 sg., nom.,* 3, 4, 7, etc.; *dat.* and *accus.,* me, 10, 13, 21, etc.; *pl.,* vus, 454, 520, 552, 553, etc. OE ic.
ichose, see **chose.**
if, *conj.,* IF, 147, 264, 265, etc.; *introduc. indir. question,* WHETHER, 914; ȝif, 45, 662, ȝyf, 482. OE gif.
ilke, *adj.,* SAME, VERY, 704; ilk, 995. OE ilca.
ille, *adv.,* WICKEDLY, 681; ILL, 1177. ON illa.
in, *prep.,* IN, ON, FOR, UPON, THROUGH, INTO, 2, 5, 8, 38, 63, etc.; IN THE CASE OF, 610; inne, 656; *adv.,* IN, 940. OE in; inne.

inlyche, *adv.*, FULLY, IN FULL, 546, 603. OE inlice. (See n. 603-6.)
inne, see **in.**
innocens, *n.*, INNOCENCE, 708. OF innocence.
innocent, *adj.* as *n.*, INNOCENT, 625, 720; innosent, 684, 696; innossent, 666; inoscente, 672. OF innocent.
innoghe, *adj.*, ENOUGH, 625, 649; innogh, 661; *adv.*, innoghe, 636; innogh, 660; innoȝe, 624; inoghe, 612; inoȝe, WELL ENOUGH, 637. OE genog.
innome, *pp.*, DENIED, NOT RECEIVED, 703. Cf. **nom.**
inoȝe, see **innoghe.**
into, *prep.*, INTO, 231, 245, 521, etc.; UNTO, 509. OE into.
inwyth, *adv.*, WITHIN, 970. OE in-, wiþ.
is, see **be.**
iuele, ieueler, see **juel, jueler.**
iwysse, *adv.*, SURELY, TRULY, CERTAINLY, 151, 394, 1128. OE gewis.

J

jacyngh, *n.*, JACINTH, 1014. OF jacincte.
jasper, *n.*, JASPER, 999, 1026; jasporye, 1018. OF jaspre.
Jerusalem, *n.*, JERUSALEM, 792, 793, 804, etc.
Jesus, *n.*, JESUS, 711, 717, 721, 820; Jesu, 453, 458.
John, *n.*, JOHN, 788, 818, 836, 867, 984, etc.
jolyf, *adj.*, BEAUTIFUL, FAIR, 842; joly, 929. OF jolif.
joparde, *n.*, JEOPARDY, UNCERTAINTY, 602. OF jeu parti.
Jordan, *n.*, JORDAN, 817.
joueler, see **jueler.**
joy., *n.*, JOY, 234, 395; joye, 577, 1196; ioy, 266, 796; ioye, 128, 1197. OF joye.
joyleȝ, *adj.*, JOYLESS, 252.
joyned, *v.*, *pret. 3 sg.*, ADDED, 1009. OF joindre.
Judee, *n.*, JUDA (JUDEA), 922; Judy (Judy londe), JUDA-LAND, 937.
juel, *n.*, JEWEL, 253, 277; iuel, 249; juelle, 795, 1124; iuele, 23; *pl.*, iueleȝ, 278; juele, 929. OF juel.
jueler, *n.*, JEWELER, 264, 265, 276, etc.; juelere, 252; iueler, 301; joueler, 734. OF jueler.
Jueȝ, *n.*, JEWS, 804. OF giu.
jugged, *v.*, *pret. 1 sg.*, JUDGED, APPRAISED, 7; *3 pl.*, iugged, 804. OF jugier.
justyfyet, *pp.*, JUSTIFIED, 700. OF justifier.

K

kasten, see **kesten.**
kene, *adj.*, KEEN, 40. OE cene.
kenned, *v.*, *pret. 3 sg.*, *subj.*, WOULD HAVE TAUGHT, 55. OE cennan.

keruen, *v., pres. 3 pl.,* CUT, 512; *pp.,* coruen, 40. OE ceorfan.

kesten, *v., pret. 3 pl.,* SCATTERED, 1122; *pp.,* kest, CAST AWAY, 861; keste, CAST, 66; kaste, HURLED, 1198. ON kasta.

keue, *v., infin.,* SINK, 320; *pp.,* keued, SUNKEN, LOW-PLACED, 981. Scand. kefja. (See n. 320.)

klyfeȝ, klyffeȝ, see **clyffe.**

klymbe, see **clym.**

knaw, *v., infin.,* KNOW, RECOGNIZE, PERCEIVE, 410, 541, 794, 1109; *pres. 1 sg.,* 673; *2 pl.,* knawe, 516; *3 pl.,* 505; *pret. 1 sg.,* knew, 66, 164, 168, 998, 1019; *3 pl.,* knewe, 890; *pp.,* knawen, 637. OE cnawan.

knelande, *pres. part.,* KNEELING, 434. OE cneowlian.

knot, *n.,* THRONG, 788. OE cnotta.

Kryst, *n.,* CHRIST, 55, 458, 776; Kryste, 569; Krysteȝ, 904, 1208; Crystes, 383. OE Crist.

Krysten, *adj.,* CHRISTIAN, 461; as *n.,* Krystyin, 1202. OE Cristen.

kyn, *n.,* KIND, SORT, MANNER OF, 619, 755, 771, 794; *pl.,* kynneȝ, 1028. OE cynn.

kynde (1), *n.,* NATURE, CHARACTER, 55, 74, 270, 271, 752. OE cynd.

kynde (2), *adj.,* NATURAL, RIGHTFUL, 276. OE cynde.

kyndely, *adv.,* KINDLY, 369; kyntly, FITTINGLY, 690. OE cyndelice. (See n. 689-94.)

kyndom, *n.,* KINGDOM, 445. OE cynedom.

kyng, *n.,* KING, 448, 468, 480, 596. OE cyning.

kynneȝ, see **kyn.**

kyntly, see **kyndely.**

kyrk, *n.,* CHURCH, 1061. ON kirkja.

kyste, *n.,* CHEST, 271. ON kista.

kyþe, *v., infin.,* REVEAL, 356. OE cyþan.

kyþeȝ, *n.,* REGIONS, REALMS, 1198. OE cyþþ.

L

labor, *v., infin.,* WORK, 504. OF laborer.

labour, *n.,* LABOR, 634. OF labour.

lad, see **lede (2).**

lade, *pp.,* LADEN; wern laste & l., WERE WEIGHTED AND LADEN, i.e., SUPERABOUNDED, 1146. OE hladan.

laden, see **ledden.**

lady, *n.,* LADY, 453, 491. OE hlæfdige.

ladyly, *adj.,* SUITABLE TO A LADY, NOBLE, 774.

ladyschyp, *n.,* LADYSHIP, 578.

laften, *v., pret. 3 pl.,* ABANDONED, 622. OE læfan.

laȝt, *v., pret. 1 sg.,* EXPERIENCED, FELT, 1128; laȝte, GRASP, UNDERSTAND, 1205. OE læccan.

lamb, lambeȝ, see **lombe.**

lande, *n.,* HEATH, 802. OF lande.

langour, *n.*, SUFFERING, 357. OF langour.
lantyrne, *n.*, LANTERN, 1047. OF lanterne.
lappeȝ, *n.*, LAPPETS, FOLDS, 201. OE læppa.
large, *adj.*, LARGE, AMPLE, ABUNDANT, 201, 609. OF large.
lasse, see **lyttel.**
laste (1), *v.*, *infin.*, LAST, 956; *pres. 3 pl.*, lasteȝ, 1198. OE læstan.
laste (2), *pp.*, LOADED, WEIGHTED, 1146; see **lade.** OE hlæstan.
laste (3), *adj.*, LAST, ENDURE, 547, 570, 571. OE læstest.
late, *adv.*, LATE, 392, 538, 574, 615. OE læt.
laueȝ, *v.*, *pres. 3 sg.*, POURS OUT, 607. OE lafian; OF laver.
launceȝ, *n.*, BOUGHS, BRANCHES, 978. OF lance.
laweȝ, *n.*, LAWS, 285. OE lagu.
layd, *pp.*, LAID, 958; layde, 1172. OE lecgan.
layned, *pp.*, CONCEALED, 244. ON leyna.
ledden, *n.*, OUTCRY, 878; laden, SOUND, 874. OE lædan.
lede (1), *n.*, MAN, 542. OE leod.
lede (2), *v.*, *infin.*, LEAD, 774; *pres. 1 sg.*, 409; *2 pl.*, 392; *pp.*, lad, 801. OE lædan.
lef (1), *n.*, LEAVES, 77; leueȝ, PAGES, 837. OE leaf.
lef (2), *adj.*, DEAR, 266; as *n.*, DEAR (ONE), BELOVED, 418. OE leof.
legg, *n.*, LEG, 459. ON leggr.
leghe, see **lyȝ.**
legyounes, *n.*, LEGIONS, 1121. OF legions.
leke, *n.*, RADIANCE, 210; see **lere (2).** ON leikr. (See n. 210.)
lelly, *adv.*, FAITHFULLY, 305. OF leial and suffix -ly.
leme, *v.*, *infin.*, GLEAM, 358; lemed, *pret. 3 sg.*, GLANCED, GLEAMED, 119, 1043. OE leomian.
lemman, *n.*, BELOVED, 763, 796, 805, 829. OE leof, mann.
lenge, *v.*, *infin.*, DWELL, 261; *pres. 2 pl.*, TARRY, LINGER, 933. OE lengan.
lenger, see **long.**
lenghe, *n.*, LENGTH, DURATION, 416; *in* on l., AT LENGTH, FOR A LONG INTERVAL, 167. OE lengu.
lenþe, *n.*, LENGTH, 1031. OE lengþu.
lere (1), *n.*, LURE, INDUCEMENT, RECOMPENSE, 616. OF loire, loerre, luerre. (See n. 616.)
lere (2), *n.*, FACE, 398; *in* l. leke, FACE-RADIANCE, 210. OE hleor. (See n. 210.)
lesande, *pres. part.*, UNBINDING, OPENING, 837. OE lesan.
lesse, les, see **lyttel;** also **neur þe les.**
lest, *conj.*, LEST, 187, 865. OE þy læs þe.
leste, *v.*, *pret. 1 sg.*, LOST, 9; *2 sg.*, lesteȝ, 269. OE -leosan; cf. **lose.**
lesyng, *n.*, LIE, 897. OE leasung.
let, *v.*, *infin.*, LET, 715; *2 sg.*, *imv.*, 901, 912, 964; *2 pl.*, SUFFER, 718; *pret. 3 sg.*, 20; lette, 813. OE lætan.
lette, *v.*, *pret. 3 sg.*, IMPEDED, STOPPED, 1050. OE lettan.

lettrure, *n.*, LITERATURE, WRITINGS, 751. OF littreure.
leþes, *v.*, *pres. 3 sg.*, IS ASSUAGED, 377. OE liþian.
leue (1), *n.*, LEAVE, PERMISSION, 316. OE leaf.
leue (2), *v.*, *infin.*, BELIEVE, 311; leuen, 69; *pres. 1 sg.*, leue, 469, 876; *3 sg.*, leueȝ, 302, 304; *1 pl.*, leuen, 425; *2 pl.*, leueȝ, 308; *2 sg.*, *subj.*, leue, 865. OE gelyfan.
leued, *adj.*, LEAVED, 978. See **lef (1)**.
leueȝ, see **lef (1)**; **leue (2)**.
liureȝ, *n.*, LIVERIES, APPAREL, 1108. OF livrée.
lo, *interj.*, LO!, 693, 740; BEHOLD, 822. OE la.
loȝe, *n.*, WATER, LOCH, 119. OE luh.
loke, *v.*, *infin.*, LOOK, 934; *pres. 3 sg.*, *subj.*, 710; *sg.*, *imv.*, 463; *pret. 1 sg.*, GAZED, 167; BEHELD, 1145. OE locian.
lokeȝ, *n.*, LOOKS, EXPRESSION, 1134.
lokyng, *n.*, VISION, SIGHT, 1049. OE -locung.
lombe (1), *n.*, LAMB, 413, 741, 795, etc.; lomp, 815; lompe, 945; lambe, 757, 771; loumbe, 867; *gen. sg.*, lombeȝ, 872; lambes, 785; lombe, 1047, 1141, etc. OE lamb. (See n. 811-15.)
lombe (2), *n.*, LAMP; *in* l. lyȝt, LAMPLIGHT, 1046. OF lampe. (See n. 811-15.)
londe, *n.*, LAND, 148. OE land, lond.
lone, *n.*, LANE, 1066. OE lone, lane.
long, *adj.*, LONG, 597; longe, 1024; *comp.*, lenger, 180, 186, 600, 977; *adv.*, long, FOR LONG, 586. OE long; lengra.
longe, *n.*, LENGTH, 477, 533. OE leng; cf. M.Du. lange.
longande, *pres. part.*, BELONGING TO, 462. OE langian.
longed, *v.*, *pret. 3 sg.*, *impers.*, LONGED, 144. OE langian.
longeyng, *n.*, LONGING, 244, 1180. OE langung.
lorde, *n.*, LORD, 285, 304, 362, etc.; LORD, MASTER, specif., MASTER OF THE VINEYARD, 502, 506, 513, etc.; *interj.*, 108, 1149. OE hlaford.
lore, *n.*, SPECIAL KNOWLEDGE, FOLK WISDOM; *in* womman l., WAY OF DOING A THING, FASHION, hence, WOMAN-FASHION, 236. OE lar.
lose, *v.*, *infin.*, LOSE, 265; BE LOST, DIE, 908; *pp.*, loste, 1092. OE losian; *infl. by* leosan.
lote (1), *n.*, LOT, DESTINY, 1205. OE hlot.
lote (2), *n.*, WORD, 238; SOUND, 876; APPEARANCE, 896. ON læti.
loþe, *n.*, WOE, 377. OE laþ.
loude, *adj.*, LOUD, 878. OE hlud.
loue, *v.*, *infin.*, PRAISE, 285, 342, 1124, 1127. OE lofian.
loueȝ, *v.*, *pres. 3 sg.*, LOVES, 403, 407. OE lufian.
loueloker, louely, see **lufly**.
loumbe, see **lombe**.
loute, *v.*, *pres. 2 pl.*, BEND, 933. OE lutan.
louyly, *adj.*, LAWFUL, 565. (See n. 565.)

lowe, *adv.*, LOW, 236; lowe, 547; *adj.*, *superl.*, lowest, 1001. ON lagr.

luf, *n.*, LOVE, 451, 467. OE lufu.

luf-daungere, *n.*, LOVE-DOMINION, 11. Cf. **daunger.** (See n. 11.)

luf-longyng, *n.*, LOVE-LONGING, 1152.

lufly, *adj.*, LOVELY, 962; louely, 693; *adv.*, lufly, PLEASINGLY, 880; BEAUTIFULLY, 880, 978. OE luflic.

lufsoum, *adj.* as *n.*, LOVELY (ONE), 398. OE lufsum.

lureȝ, *n.*, LOSSES, 339, 358. OE lyre.

lurked, *v.*, *pret. 1 sg.*, STEAL ON or ALONG, GO QUIETLY, 978. Cf. Norw. lurka.

lyf, *n.*, LIFE, 247, 305, 392, etc.; *gen. sg.*, lyueȝ, 477, 578, 908. OE lif.

lyfed, *v.*, *pret. 2 sg.*, LIVE, 483; *pres. part.*, lyuyande, 700; *pp.*, lyued, 477, 776. OE lifian.

lyfte, *pp.*, LIFTED, 567. ON lypta.

lygyngeȝ, *n.*, LODGINGS, 935. Cf. ON liggja.

lyȝ, *v.*, *infin.*, LODGE, 930; *3 sg.*, lys, LIES, 360, 602; *pret. 3 sg.*, leghe, 214. OE licgan.

lyȝe, *n.*, LIE, 304. OE lyge.

lyȝt, *n.*, LIGHT, BRILLIANCY, 69, 119, 1043, 1046, 1073. OE leoht; liht. See **lombe.**

lyȝte (1), *adj.*, CHEERFUL, 238; BRIGHT, 500; lyȝt, FREE OF BURDENS (GUILT), GUILTLESS, 682; *adv.*, LIGHTLY, 214; lyȝtly, GENTLY, 358. OE leoht.

lyȝte (2), *v.*, *pret. 2 sg.*, ARRIVE, 247; *3 sg.*, lyȝt, DESCEND, 943; *pp.*, 988. OE lihtan.

lyk, *adj.*, LIKE, 432, 501, 874, 896; lyke, 735. OE [ge]lic.

lykeȝ, *v.*, *pres. impers.*, IT PLEASES, 566. OE lician.

lykneȝ, *v.*, *pres. 3 sg.*, LIKENS, 500. Cf. **lyk**, *adj.*

lykyng, *n.*, JOY, 247. OE licung.

lym, *n.*, LIMB, 462; *pl.*, lymmeȝ, 464. OE lim.

lyne, *n.*, LINEAGE, ORDER OF BIRTH, 626. OF ligne.

lynne, *n.* as *adj.*, LINEN, 731. OE linen.

lys, see **lyȝ.**

lyste (1), *n.*, WISH, 173; JOY, 467, 908. ON lyst.

lyste (2), *v.*, *impers.*, *pret.*, WISH, DESIRE, LONG, 146, 181; *pres. 3 sg.*, *subj.*, HOPE, 1141. OE lystan. (See n. 1141.)

lysten, *v.*, *infin.*, HEAR, LISTEN, 880. OE hlystan.

lyth, *n.*, FORM, 398. OE liþ.

lyttel, *adj.*, LITTLE, 387, 575, 604, 1147; LOWLY, 574; *comp.*, lasse, LESS, 599, 600, 601, 853; LESSER, 491; lesse, 852; MINOR, 339; *adv.*, lyttel, LITTLE, 301; A SHORT WHILE, 172; *comp.*, les, LESS, 865. OE lytel.

lyþe, *v.*, *infin.*, RELIEVE, 357; *2 sg.*, *imv.*, lyþeȝ, YIELD, 369. OE liþian.

lyþer, *n.*, EVIL, 567. OE lyþre.

lyued, lyuyande, see **lyfed.**
lyueȝ, see **lyf.**

M

ma (1), *pron., poss.,* MY, 489. OF ma.
ma (2), see **man (1).**
mad, *adj.,* MAD, 267, 1199; madde, FOOLISH, 290; *adv.,* mad, MADLY, 1166. OE [ge]mæd. See **make (2).**
madde, *v., 2 sg., imv.,* RAGE, 359. Cf. OE mæden.
maddying, *n.,* MADNESS, 1154.
make (1), *n.,* SPOUSE, 759. ON maki; cf. OE [ge]maca.
make (2), *v., infin.,* CAUSE TO SEEM or APPEAR, 176; INVENT, 304; MAKE, 474; *pres. 1 sg.,* 281; *3 sg.,* matȝ, 610; *3 pl.,* man, MAKE *in* m. hit clos, MAKE IT CLOSE, or GATHER PARTS TOGETHER, hence, GATHER THE HARVEST, 512; *pret. 3 sg.,* made, MADE, 1149; *in* m. it toȝt, CAUSED IT TO BE BOUND, i.e., MADE AGREEMENT, 522; mad, 539; *2 pl.,* made, 371; *pp.,* mad, 274, 486, 953; made, 140. OE macian.
makeleȝ, *adj.,* MATCHLESS, PEERLESS, 435, 733, 757, 780, 784. Cf. **make (1).**
malte, *v., infin.,* DISSOLVE, 224; *pret. 3 sg.,* 1154. OE meltan.
man (1), *n., sg.,* MAN, 386, 675, 685, etc.; ma, 323; mon, 69, 95, 310, etc.; *pl.,* man, MANKIND, MAN, 165, 314; MEN, 1195; MORTALS, 290; MANKIND, MAN, 336; MEN, 674; *gen.,* maneȝ, MANKIND'S, 940; MAN'S, i.e., MORTAL, 154; manneȝ, MAN'S, 223; *pron., indef., sg.,* men, ONE, 194, 331; *pl.,* man, THEY, 334. OE man(n), mon(n).
man (2), see **make (2).**
maneȝ, manneȝ, see **man (1).**
maner, *n.,* MANOR, 918; manayre, CITY, 1029. OF manoir.
mankyn, *n.,* MANKIND, 637. OE mancynn.
mare, see **much.**
margyrye, *n.,* PEARL, MARGARITE, 1037; *pl.,* margarys, 199; mariorys, 206. OF margarie.
marked, *n.,* MARKET, 513. ONF market. (See n. 811-15.)
marreȝ, *v., pres. 2 sg.,* MARREST, 23; *2 sg., imv.,* marre, OBSTRUCT, 359. OE merran.
Mary, *n.,* MARY, 383; Marye, 425.
maryage, *n.,* MARRIAGE, 414; maryag, 778. OF mariage.
mas, *n.,* the MASS, 1115; messe, 497. OE mæsse.
maskelleȝ, *adj.,* SPOTLESS, 756, 768, 769, 780; maskelles, 744, 781; maskeleȝ, 745, 900, 923; mascelleȝ, 732. OF mascle and suffix -les.
masklle, *n.,* SPECK, SPOT, 843; mascle, 726. OF mascle.
mate, *v., infin.,* DEFEAT, 613; *pp.,* BALKED, 386. OF mater.
Mathew, *n.,* MATTHEW, 497.
matȝ, see **make (2).**

may (1), *n.*, MAIDEN, 435, 780. OE mæg.
may (2), *v.*, *pres. 1 sg.*, MAY, CAN, BE ABLE, 487, 783; *2 sg.*, 296, 347, 694, 703, 966, 970; *3 sg.*, 300, 310, 312, 355, 357, etc.; *2 pl.*, 918; moun, 536; *3 pl.*, 29, 336; *pret. 1 sg.*, moȝt, 188; *2 sg.*, myȝteȝ, 317; *3 sg.*, moȝt, 34, 194, 223, etc.; moȝte, 475; myȝt, 69, 135, 176, 722, 891, 1082, 1157; *2 pl.*, moȝt, 1051; *3 pl.*, moȝt, 92, 843, 1028; moȝten, 1196; myȝt, 579. OE mæg, mæhte, mihte.
mayden, *n.*, MAIDEN, 162; *pl.*, maydenneȝ, 869; maydeneȝ, 1115. OE mægden.
maynful, *adj.*, IN FULL MIGHT, 1093. OE mægn and suffix -ful.
mayster, *n.*, MASTER, 462, 900. OF maistre.
maysterful, *adj.*, MASTERFUL, 401.
me, see **I.**
mede, *n.*, REWARD, 620. OE med.
meke, *adj.*, MEEK, 404, 815, 832, 961. ON miukr.
mekenesse, *n.*, MEEKNESS, 406.
mele, *v.*, *infin.*, SPEAK, 925; melle, 797, 1118; *pres. 3 sg.*, meleȝ, RELATES, 497; *pret. 1 sg.*, meled, 589. OE mælan.
melle, *n.* in *prep. phrase* in m., AMID, AMIDST, 1127. ON i milli.
membreȝ, *n.*, MEMBERS, 458. OF membre.
men, see **man** (1).
mendeȝ, see **mynde.**
mendyng, *n.*, BETTERMENT, ENHANCEMENT, 452. OF amender.
mene, *v.*, *infin.*, MEAN, 293, 951; *pres. 2 sg.*, meneȝ, 937. OE mænan.
mensk, *n.*, DIGNITY, 783; menske, 162. ON menska.
menteene, *v.*, *infin.*, MAINTAIN, 783. OF maintenir.
mercy, *n.*, MERCY, 356, 623, 670; merci, 576; mersy, 383. OF merci.
mere (1), *n.*, MERE, 158. OE mere.
mereȝ (2), *n.*, BOUNDARIES, 140, 1166. OE mære.
merked, *pp.*, REACHED, 142. OE mearcian. (See n. 142.)
mersy, see **mercy.**
meruayle, *n.*, WONDER, 1130; MARVEL, 157; merwayle, 1081; *pl.*, meruayleȝ, WONDROUS THINGS, 64. OF merveille.
meruelous, *adj.*, MARVELOUS, MIRACULOUS, 1166. OF merveilleus.
mes, *n.*, COURSE OF A BANQUET or FEAST, 862. OF mes.
meschef, *n.*, TROUBLE, MISFORTUNE, 275. OF meschef.
mesure, *n.*, APPRAISAL, 224. OF mesure.
mete (1), *n.*, FOOD, 641. OE mete.
mete (2), *v.*, *infin.*, MEET, 918; COME UPON, FIND, 329; *pres. 1 pl.*, meten, 380; *pp.*, MEASURED, 1032. OE metan.
mete (3), *adj.*, EQUAL, 833; FITTING, MEET, 1063. OE mæte.
meten, see **mete** (2).
meuen, *v.*, *pres. 3 pl.*, MOVE, OCCUR, 64; *pret. 3 sg.*, meued, 156. OF movoir, mevoir.

meyny, *n.*, COMPANY, RETINUE, TRAIN, 542, 892, 899, 925, 960, 1127, 1145. OF maisnee.
mirþe, see **myrþe.**
mo, see **much.**
mod, *n.*, MOOD, 401; mode, TONE, 738; SPIRIT, 832. OE mod.
moder, *n.*, MOTHER, 435. OE modor.
modeȝ, *n.*, MODES (in music), 884. OF mode.
moȝt, moȝte, moȝten, see **may (2).**
mokke, *n.*, MUCK, 905. Cf. ON myki; OE -moc.
mol, see **mul.**
moldeȝ, *n.*, MOLDS, 30. OE molde.
mon (1), see **man (1).**
mon (2), *n.*, WOE, DOLE, 374. Cf. OE mænan; OF mene.
mone, *n.*, MOON, 923, 1044, 1045, 1056, 1057, 1068, 1069, 1072, 1080, 1081, 1092, 1093. OE mona.
mony, *adj.*, MANY, 160, 340, 572, 775. OE manig.
moote, see **mote (2).**
more, *see* **much.**
morne, *v.*, *2 sg.*, *imv.*, MOURN, 359. OE murnan.
mornyf, *adj.*, MOURNFUL, 386. OE murne.
mornyng, *n.*, MOURNING, 262. OE mornung.
moste (1), see **much.**
moste (2), *v.*, *pres. 2 sg.*, MUST, 319, 348; *3 pl.*, 623. OE moste.
mot, *v.*, *pres. 3 sg.*, MUST, 25, 31, 320, 397, 663. OE mot.
mote (1), *n.*, CITY, 142, 936, 937, 948, 973; *pl.*, motes, 949. OF mote.
mote (2), *n.*, SPECK, DEFECT, SPOT, 726, 764, 843, 924, 960; TRIFLE, 855; moote, 948. OE mot.
moteleȝ, *adj.*, FLAWLESS, SPOTLESS, 925, 961; moteles, 899.
moteȝ, *v.*, *pres. 2 sg.*, ARGUE, 613. OE motian.
moul, see **mul.**
moun, see **may (2).**
mount, *n.*, MOUNT, 868. OE munt.
mounteȝ, *v.*, *pres. 3 pl.*, AMOUNT TO, INCREASE, 351. OF mo(u)nter.
mouth, *n.*, MOUTH, 183, 803. OE muþ.
much, *adj.*, MUCH, GREAT, 244, 604, 776, 1118, 1130, 1149; *comp.*, mare, MORE, GREATER, *in* m. reȝ, ONRUSH, ELOQUENCE, 382; more, 128, 132, etc.; mo, 340, 850, 870, 1194; FURTHER, 151; *superl.*, moste, MOST, GREATEST, 1131; *adv.*, much, MUCH, 234, 303, etc.; *comp.*, more, MORE, 144, 145, 156, etc.; FURTHER, MOREOVER, IN ADDITION, BESIDES, ANYMORE, 565, 588, 589; mare, 145; ma, 283. OE micel; mare; ma, mæst. (See n. 382 *mare reȝ.*)
mul, *n.*, MOLD, EARTH, 905; mol, DUST, 382; moul, EARTH, 23. Cf. OE myl; ON mylja.
munt, *n.*, RESOLVE, 1161. Cf. OE myntan.

my, *pron.*, *poss.*, MY, MINE, 15, 16, 17, etc.; myn, 128, 174, 176, etc.; MINE (OWN), 566; myne, 335. OE min.

mydde3, *n.*, *gen.*, MIDDLE in *adv. phrase* in m., IN THE CENTER OF, 222, 740; *in* in myde3, IN THE MIDST OF, 835. Cf. OE to middes.

my3t (1), *n.*, MIGHT, POWER, STRENGTH, 630, 765; my3te, 1069; myste, 462. OE miht. (See n. 462.)

my3t (2), my3te, see **may (2)**.

myke3, *n.*, *pl.*, FRIENDS, COMPANIONS, i.e., CHOSEN ONES, 572. (See n. 572.)

mylde, *adj.*, MILD, GENTLE, 961, 1115; as *n.*, MEEK or TENDER ONES, 721. OE milde.

myn, *n.*, MEMORY, 1208. OE myne.

mynde, *n.*, MIND, 156, 224, 1130, 1154; *pl.*, mende3, OPINIONS, THOUGHTS, 351. OE [ge]mynd. (See n. 351 *mende3.*)

mynge, *v.*, *infin.*, BE MINDFUL OF, BE CONCERNED, 855. OE mynegian.

mynne, *v.*, *infin.*, RECALL, REMEMBER, 583. ON minna.

mynster, *n.*, MINSTER, CHAPEL, 1063. OE mynster.

myrþe, *n.*, MIRTH, JOY, 92; mirþe, MERRIMENT, 1149; *pl.*, myrþes, JOYANCES, 140. OE myrgþ.

myrþes, *v.*, *pres. 3 sg.*, REJOICES, 862.

myry, *adj.*, LOVELY, MERRY, JOYOUS, 23, 158, 781, 936; *comp.*, myryer, 850; *superl.*, myryeste, 199; myryest, 435. OE myrge.

mys, see **mysse (1)**.

myse, *adv.*, BADLY, ILL, 257. ON mis.

myself, *pron.*, MYSELF, ME, 52. OE min, self.

myserecorde, *n.*, MERCY, 366. OF misericorde.

mysse (1), *n.*, LOSS, 364; mys, 262. ON missa.

mysse (2), *v.*, *infin.*, LOSE, 329; *pres. 1 sg.*, LACK, 382. OE missan.

mysse3eme, *v.*, *infin.*, FAIL TO VALUE, MISESTEEM, 322. OE misgeman.

myste, see **my3t (1)**.

mysterys, *n.*, MYSTERIES, 1194. L. mysterium.

myte, *n.*, MITE, 351. OF mite.

myþe, *v.*, *2 sg.*, *imv.*, HIDE AWAY, 359. OE miþan.

N

na3t, na3te, see **ny3t**.

name, *n.*, NAME, 998, 1039; nome, 872. OE nama.

nature, *n.*, NATURE, 749. OF nature.

naule, *n.*, NAVEL, 459. OE nafela.

nauþeles, nawþeles, see **neuer þe les**.

nauþer, *see* **nawþer**.

nawhere, *adv.*, NOWHERE, 534, 932. OE nahwær.

nawþer, *conj.*, NEITHER (*correl.* with *ne*), 485, 1044, 1087; nauþer, 465, 484; ne . . . n., NOR . . . EITHER, 751. OE nahwæþer.

ne, *adv.*, NOT, 35, 65, 293, etc.; *intensifying one or two other negs.*, 4, 362, 403, etc.; *conj.*, NOR, 262, 334, 347, etc. OE ne.

nece, *n.*, NIECE, 233. OF niece.

nedde, *v.*, *pret. impers.*, NEED *in* hem n., THEY NEEDED, 1044. OE neodian.

nede, *n.*, NEED, 1045; *gen. sg.* as *adv.*, 25, 344. OE ned.

nem, see **nom.**

nemme, *v.*, *infin.*, NAME, 997. OE nemnan.

nente, *adj.*, NINTH, 1012. Cf. OE nigoþa; ON niundi.

ner, *adv.*, NEAR, 286; nere, 404; *comp.*, nerre, 233. OE near.

nesch, *adj.* as *adv.*, MILD, 606. OE hnesce.

neuer, *adv.*, NEVER, 4, 19, 71, etc.; in sense, NO, NEVER A, 841, 845. OE næfre.

neur þe les, *adv.*, NEVER THE LESS, NEVERTHELESS, NONE THE LESS, 876, 888, 900, 901; as *second neg.*, ANY *in* neuer . . . n. þ. l., NEVER . . . ANY THE LESS, 864; neuer þe lese, 912, 913; neuer þelesse, 852; nauþeles, 877; nawþeles, 950; nowþelese, 889. OE næfre þy læs; nohte þy læs.

newe, new, see **nwe.**

nieȝbor, *n.*, NEIGHBOR, 688. OE neahgebur.

nis, see **be (1).**

no, *adj.*, NO, 32, 69, 95, etc.; non, 206, 209, 215, etc.; *pron.*, none, 440, 586; non oþer . . . ne, NEITHER . . . NOR, 848; *adv.*, 347, 951, etc. OE na, nan.

noble, *adj.*, NOBLE, 922, 1097. OF noble.

noȝt, *n.*, NOTHING, 274, 337, 520, etc. OE nawiht.

nom, *v.*, *pret. 3 pl.*, RECEIVED, 587; *pres. 3 sg.*, nem, TAKE, SEIZE, 802. OE niman. (See n. 802 *nem.*)

nome, see **name.**

non, none, see **no.**

not, *adv.*, NOT, 29, 34, 92, etc. OE nawiht.

note (1), *n.*, A MATTER OF MOMENT, NEW CIRCUMSTANCE, hence, A WONDER, 155; PIECE OF WORK, CITY, 922. OE notu.

note (2), *n.*, NOTE (musical), 879; *pl.*, noteȝ, NOTES, TONES, 883. OF note.

noþynk, *n.*, NOTHING, NOUGHT, 308, 496, 587; noþyng, 1157. OE na, þing.

now, *adv.*, NOW, 271, 283, etc. OE nu.

nowþelese, see **neuer þe les.**

nwe, *adj.*, NEW, 155, 597, 792, 882, etc.; newe, FIRST, 894; *adv.*, nwe, AFRESH, 1080; ANEW, 1123; new, 662. OE niwe.

nyȝt, *n.*, NIGHT, 116, 1071; nyȝte, 243; naȝt, 523; naȝte, 1203. OE niht.

nys, see **be (1).**

O

O (1), *interj.*, O, 23, 241, 745, 1182.
o (2), *prep.*, see **of.**
obes, *v.*, *pres. 3 pl.*, OBEY, 886. OF obeir.
odour, *n.*, FRAGRANCE, 58. OF odor, odour.
of, *adv.*, OFF, 237; *prep.*, OF, 3, 12, 55, etc.; FROM, 31, 33, 36, etc.; BY, THROUGH, WITH, 11, 25, 76, etc.; *in* o. all, IN WHOLE, 584; o, 309, 429, 792, 1018; (MADE) OF, 1037. OE of.
offys, *n.*, OFFICE, RANK, 755. OF office.
ofte, *adv.*, OFTEN, 14, 340, 388; *comp.*, ofter, 621. OE oft.
oȝe, *v.*, *pres. impers.*, OUGHT, 552; *pres. 1 sg.*, owe, OWE, 543; *pret. 3 sg.*, aȝt, OUGHT, 1139; *impers.*, oȝte, 341. OE agan.
oȝt, *n.*, SOMETHING, 274; AUGHT, ANYTHING, 1200. OE awiht.
olde, *adj.*, OLD, ANCIENT, 941, 942; *comp.*, alder, 621; *superl.*, aldest, 1042. OE ald.
on (1), *num.*, ONE, 41, 293, 530, 551, etc.; *in* at o., AT ONE, IN ACCORD, 378; an, 869; *pron.* as *adj.*, 953; *gen. sg.*, oneȝ, ONE'S, 864; *indef. art.*, on, A, 9; *adj.*, ONE; SINGLE *in* by myn o., BY MY SINGLE or ONE (SELF), hence, ALONE, 243, 312. OE an.
on (2), *prep.*, ON, UPON, OVER, 45, 60, 78, etc.; IN, AT, 97, 155, 167; *adv.*, 255. OE on.
one, see **on (1).**
only, *adj.*, ALONE, 779. OE anlic.
onore, see **honour.**
onslydeȝ, *v.*, *pres. 3 pl.*, GLIDE ON, SLIP AWAY, 77. ME on, slide. Cf. OE aslidan.
onsware, *v.*, *infin.*, ANSWER, 680. OE andswarian.
onvunder, see **anvnder.**
open, *adj.*, OPEN, 183; vpen, 1066; vpon, 198. OE open.
or, see **oþer (1).**
oryent, *n.*, ORIENT, 3; Oryente, 82; *adj.*, 255. OF orient.
oþer (1), *conj.*, OR, 118, 130, 141, etc.; or, 233. OE ahwæþer.
oþer (2), *adj.*, OTHER, 206, 209, 219, etc.; ANOTHER, 319; *pron.*, 449; *gen. pl.*, oþereȝ, OTHERS', 450; *pl.*, 585, 773, 778. OE oþer.
ouer, *prep.*, OVER, ACROSS, ABOVE, BEYOND, 318, 324, 454, etc. OE ofer.
ouerte, *adj.*, EXPLICIT, 593. OF overt.
ouerture, *n.*, OPENING, 218. OF ouverture.
oure (1), *n.*, HOUR, 530, 551; *pl.*, houreȝ, 555. OF hore.
oure (2), *pron.*, OUR, 304, 322, 455, etc.; our, 851. OE ure.
out, *adv.*, OUT, 282, 365, 642, etc.; oute, 3. OE ut.
outdryf, *v.*, *infin.*, DRIVE OUT, 777. OE ut-drifan.
outfleme, *pp.*, EXPELLED, 1177. OE ut-fleman. (See n. 1177.)
outryȝte, *adv.*, OUT STRAIGHT, STRAIGHT FORTH, 1055. OE ut-riht.

outsprent, *v.*, *pret. 3 sg.*, GUSHED FORTH, 1137. OE ut, ON spretta.
owne, *adj.*, OWN, 559. OE agen.

P

pace, *n.*, PASSAGE, 677. OF pas.
pakke, *n.*, COLLECTION, 929. ON pakki.
pale, *v.*, *infin.*, PALE, 1004. OF palir.
pane, *n.*, SIDE, 1034. OF pan.
par, *prep.*, BY, 489. OF par.
Paradys, *n.*, PARADISE, 321; Paradys-erde, PARADISE-LAND, 248; Paradyse, 137. OF paradis.
parage, *n.*, MAJESTY, NOBILITY, 419. OF parage.
paraunter, *adv.*, PERCHANCE, 588. OF par aventure.
parfyt, *adj.*, PERFECT, 638, 1038; perfet, 208. OF parfit.
part, *n.*, SHARE, 573. OF part.
partleȝ, *adj.*, SHARELESS, DEPRIVED OF, 335. OF part.
passe, *v.*, *infin.*, PASS, 299, 707, 1110; *pres. 3 sg.*, passeȝ, SURPASSES, 753; *pret. 3 sg.*, passed, EXCELLED, 428; *pp.*, passed, PAST, 528. OF passer.
Pater, *n.*, PATER (for Pater Noster, the Lord's Prayer), 485. L. pater.
pay, *v.*, *infin.*, PAY, 635; PLEASE, 1201; *pres. 3 sg.*, payeȝ, 632; *2 sg.*, *imv.*, pay, 542; *pret. 3 sg.*, payed, 1165, 1177; *pp.*, payed, 584, 603. OF paier.
paye, *n.*, PLEASURE, FANCY, WILL, 1, 1164, 1176, etc.; pay, 1212. OF paye.
payment, *n.*, PAYMENT, 598. OF paiement.
payne, *n.*, PAIN, PENANCE, SUFFERING, 664, 954; *pl.*, payneȝ, 124. OF peine.
paynted, *v.*, *pret. 3 sg.*, PAINTED, 750. OF peindre.
payred, *pp.*, WORN, 246. OF empeirier.
pece, see **pyece**.
pechche, *n.*, PATCH, SHRED, 841. AN peche.
penaunce, *n.*, PENANCE, 477. OF penance.
pene, see **peny**.
pensyf, *adj.*, PENSIVE, 246. OF pensif.
peny, *n.*, PENNY, 546, 560, 614; pene, 510, 562. OE penig.
pere, *n.*, PEER, 4. OF per.
pereȝ, *n.*, PEARS, PEAR TREES, 104. OE peru.
perfet, see **parfyt**.
perle, *n.*, PEARL, 1, 12, 24, etc.; *pl.*, perleȝ, 82, 192, etc. OF perle.
perleȝ, *adj.* as *n.*, PEERLESS (ONE), 335. Cf. **pere**.
perre, *n.*, GEMS, JEWELS, PRECIOUS STONES, 730, 1028. OF pierre.
peryle, *n.*, PERIL, EXPOSURE TO RISKS, 695. OF peril.
pes, *n.*, PEACE, 742, 952, 953, etc. OF pais.
place, *n.*, PLACE, HOUSE, 175, 405, 440, etc. OF place.
planeteȝ, *n.*, PLANETS, 1075. OF planete.

plate3, *n.*, PLATES, METALS, 1036. OF plate.

play, *v.*, *infin.*, PLAY, 261. OE plegan.

playn, *adj.*, CLEAR, PLAIN, 178; *adv.*, 689; *n.*, PLAIN, 104; *pl.*, playne3, 122. OF plain.

playned, see **pleny.**

playnt, *n.*, PLAINT, 815. OF pleint.

pleny, *v.*, *infin.*, COMPLAIN, 549; *pret. 1 sg.*, playned, MOURNED, 53; *pp.*, 242. OF plaindre. (See n. 549.)

plesaunte, *adj.*, PLEASING, 1. OF plaisant.

plese, *v.*, *infin.*, PLEASE, 484. OF plaisir.

plete, *v.*, *infin.*, PLEAD, 563. OF plaidier.

plontte3, *n.*, PLANTS, 104. OE plante.

plye, *v.*, *infin.*, CREASE, MARK, 1039. OF plier.

ply3t, see **plyt.**

plyt, *n.*, STATE, CIRCUMSTANCE, CONDITION, PLIGHT, 647, 1015, 1114; ply3t, 1075. OF ploit; pleit.

pobbel, *n.*, PEBBLE, 117. OE papol- *in* papolstan.

pole, *n.*, STREAM, 117. OE pol.

porchace, *v.*, *infin.*, PURCHASE, 744; *pres. 3 pl.*, porchase3, SEEK, 439. OF porchacier.

pore, see **pouer.**

porfyl, *n.*, BORDER, 216. OF porfiler.

porpos, *n.*, INTENT, 508; porpose, 267; IMPORT, MEANING, 185. OF porpos.

portale3, *n.*, PORTALS, GATES, 1036. OF portal.

Poule, *n.*, PAUL, 457.

pourseut, *n.*, SUCCESSION, 1035. OF poursuite.

powdered, *pp.*, SCATTERED, POWDERED, 44. OF poudre.

poyned, *n.*, CUFF, 217. OF poignet. (See n. 811-15.)

poynt, *n.*, POINT, MARK, 309, 594; NOTE (musical), 891. OF point.

pray (1), *n.*, REWARD, 439. OF preie.

pray (2), *v.*, *infin.*, PRAY, 484; CALL FORTH, INVOKE, 524; *pret. 3 sg.*, PRAYED, 1192; *3 pl.*, 714. OF preier.

prayer, *n.*, PRAYER, 355; prayere, 618. OF preiere.

prayse, *v.*, *infin.*, PRAISE, 301; *pp.*, praysed, PRIZED, 1112. OF preisier.

precios, *adj.*, PRECIOUS, OF GREAT PRICE, 4, 36, 60, etc.; precious, 48, 82, 1212. OF precios.

pref, *n.*, TEST, 272. OF preve.

pres (1), *n.*, PRESS, MASS, 730; CROWDING, 1114. OF presse.

pres (2), *v.*, *pres. 1 pl.*, HASTEN, 957. OF presser.

prese, *n.*, VIRTUE, MERIT, 419. OF preis.

present, *n.*, PRESENCE, 1193; presente, 389. OF presence.

preste, *n.*, PRIEST, 1210. OE preost.

Pretermynable, *adj.*, INFINITE, ETERNAL, 596. L. prae-, terminabilis. (See n. 596.)

preued, see **proued.**

Prince, *n.*, PRINCE, 1201; *gen. sg.*, Prynceȝ, PRINCE'S, 1164, 1176, 1189; Prynces, 1188; prynces, OF A PRINCE, 1. OF prince. (See n. 1.)

proferen, *v.*, *pres. 3 pl.*, PROFFER, 1200; *pret. 3 sg.*, profered, 235. OF profrer.

professye, *n.*, PROPHECY, 821. OF profecie.

profete, *n.*, PROPHET, 797. OF prophete.

proper, *adj.*, OF BECOMING APPEARANCE, FAIR, 686. OF propre.

property, *n.*, PROPERTY, 446; *pl.*, propertyȝ, 752. OF propriete.

prosessyoun, *n.*, PROCESSION, 1096. OF procession.

proudly, *adv.*, MAJESTICALLY, PROUDLY, 1110. OE prutlice.

proued, *v.*, *pret. 1 sg.*, TESTED, 4; *pp.*, preued, PROVED, SHOWN, 983. OF prover.

pryde, *n.*, PRIDE, 401. OE pryte.

prys, *n.*, VALUE, PRICE, 193; WORTH, 419; of p., OF GREAT PRICE, 272, 746. OF pris.

pryse, *v.*, *infin.*, PRIZE, 1131. OF prisier.

pryuy, *adj.*, PRIVATE, ONE'S OWN, 12; priuy, 24. OF privé.

pure, *adj.*, PURE, 227, 745, 1088. OF pur.

purly, *adv.*, TRANSLUCENTLY, 1004.

purpre, *adj.*, PURPLE, 1016. OF purpre.

put, *pp.*, PUT, SET, 267, 272. OE putian.

pyece, *n.*, PERSON, BEING, 192; pece, 229. OF pece.

pyȝt, *v.*, *pret. 3 sg.*, FIXED FIRMLY, SET IN PLACE, 742; SET (as with jewels), ADORNED, ORNAMENTED, 768; *pp.*, 192, 205, 217, 229, 241; SET, SET IN PLACE, FIXED FIRMLY, 117, 228, 991; pyȝte, 193, 216; ADORNED, 240. Etymology uncertain; cf. **pykeȝ.**

pykeȝ, *v.*, *pres. 3 pl.*, PICK, GATHER, 573; *pp.*, pyked, ADORNED, 1036. Cf. OE picung.

pyle, *n.*, MASS OF BUILDINGS, CITY, 686. Cf. OF piler.

Pymalyon, *n.*, PYGMALION, 750.

pynakled, *pp.*, POINTED, 207. OF pinacle.

pyne, *n.*, ANGUISH, 330; PAIN, 511. OE pin.

pyonys, *n.*, PEONIES, 44. OF pione.

pytosly, *adv.*, PITYINGLY, IN PITY, 370; pitously, COMPASSIONATELY, 798. OF pitous, -ly.

pyty, *n.*, SORROW, 1206; pyte, PITY, 355. OF pité.

Q

quat, see **quo.**

quayle, *n.*, QUAIL, 1085. OF quaille.

quelle, *v.*, *infin.*, KILL, 799. OE cwellan.

queme, *adj.*, DEAR, 1179. OE cweme.

quen, *conj.*, WHEN, 40, 79, 93, etc.; when, 332, 335, 347, etc.; AFTER, 170. OE hwænne.

quene, *n.*, QUEEN, 415, 423, 456, etc.; quen, 432, 433, 444, etc. OE cwen.
quere, *conj.*, WHERE, 65, 376; where, 68, 617. OE hwær.
query, *n.*, QUESTIONING, INTERROGATION, 803. (See n. 803.)
queresoeuer, *conj.*, WHERESOEVER, 7.
queþersoeuer, *conj.*, WHETHER, 606.
quo (1), *pron.*, *inter.*, WHO, 427, 678, 747, 827; who, 1138; *neut.*, quat, 755, 771; what, 249, 331, 336, etc.; *adv.*, WHY, 1072; *conj.*, what, WHETHER, 463. OE hwa.
quo (2), *pron.*, *rel.*, ONE WHO, 693; HIM WHO, 709; who, WHO, 344; quom, WHOM, 453; wham, 131; *neut.*, quat, 186, 293; what, 392, 523, 794. OE hwa.
quam, see **quo (2)**.
quoþ, *v.*, *pret. 1 sg.*, SAID, 241, 279, 325, etc.; *3 sg.*, 569, 758, 781. OE cweþan.
quoynt, *adj.*, SKILLED, 889. OF cointe.
quy, see **why**.
quyke, *adj.*, VIVID, 1179. OE cwic.
quyt, *adj.*, WHITE, 207, 842, 1011, 1150; quyte, 220, 844, 1137; qwyte, 1102; whyt, 163, 178, 197, 1133; whyte, 219. OE hwit.
quyteȝ, *v.*, *pres. 2 sg.*, REQUITEST, 595. OF quiter.
qwyte, see **quyt**.

R

raas, *n.*, A RUSHING ONWARD, ONRUSH, 1167. ON ras.
ran, *v.*, *pret. 3 sg.*, RAN, FLOWED, 646, 1055; *pp.*, runne, 26; ACCRUED, 523; *pp.*, runnen, RUN TOGETHER, BLENDED, 874. OE rinnan.
randeȝ, *n.*, BORDERS, 105. OE rand.
rapely, *adv.*, RECKLESSLY, 363; SWIFTLY, 1168. ON hrapalliga.
rasch, *adj.*, RASH, 1167. Cf. ON röskr.
raue (1), *v.*, *infin.*, ERR, 665. Cf. ON rafa.
raue (2), *v.*, *pres. 1 sg.*, RAVE, 363. OF raver.
rauþe, *n.*, GRIEF, 858. Cf. ON hrygþ; OE hreow.
rauyste, *pp.*, RAPTURED, 1088. OF ravir.
rawe, *n.*, ROW, 545; *pl.*, raweȝ, HEDGEROWS, 105. OE raw.
raxled, *v.*, *pret. 1 sg.*, START UP (as from a swoon), 1174. (See n. 1174.)
ray, *n.*, RAY, 160. OF rai.
raykande, *pres. part.*, COURSING, 112. ON reika.
rayse, *v.*, *infin.*, RAISE, 305. ON reisa.
raysoun, see **resoun**.
rebuke, *v.*, *2 sg.*, *imv.*, REBUKE, 367. OF rebuchier.
recen, *v.*, *infin.*, RECOUNT, 827. OE [ge]recenian.
rech, *v.*, *pres. 1 sg.*, CARE, 333. OE reccan.
recorde, *n.*, RECORD, 831. OF record.
red, *adj.*, RED, 1111; rede, 27. OE read.
rede, *v.*, *infin.*, READ, 709; *pres. 1 sg.*, COUNSEL, 743. OE rædan.

redy, *adj.*, PROMPT, 591. OE ræde.
refete, *v.*, *infin.*, REVIVE, 88. OF refaire.
reflayr, *n.*, FRAGRANCE, 46. OF reflair.
reget, *v.*, *infin.*, GET AGAIN, REDEEM, 1064. ME re-, ON geta. (See n. 1064.)
regne, *n.*, KINGDOM, 501; rengne, 692. OF regne.
regretted, *pp.*, GRIEVED OVER, 243. OF regreter.
reȝ, see **resse**.
reiateȝ, *n.*, MARKS OF ROYALTY, 770. OF reiaute.
reken, *adj.*, PERFECT, 5, 92, 906. OE recen. (See n. 5.)
reles, *n.*, SURCEASE, 956. OF reles.
relusaunt, *adj.*, RELUCENT, 159. OF reluisant.
reme (1), *n.*, REALM, 448; KINGDOM, 735. OF reaume.
reme (2), *v.*, *infin.*, CRY ALOUD, 1181; *pres. 2 pl.*, remen, LAMENT, 858. OE hreman.
remnaunt, *n.*, REST, 1160. OF remenant.
remorde, *pp.*, AFFLICTED, DISTURBED, 364. OF remordre.
remwe, *v.*, *infin.*, REMOVE, 427; DEPART, 899. OF removoir.
rengne, see **regne**.
renoun, *n.*, RENOWN, 986, 1182. OF renon.
renowleȝ, *v.*, *pres. 3 pl.*, RENEW, 1080. OF renoveler.
rent, *pp.*, RENT, RENDED, 806. OE rendan.
reparde, *pp.*, KEPT BACK, WITHHELD, 611. Cf. ME parre; L. partire.
repayre, *v.*, *infin.*, GATHER, COLLECT, 1028. OF repairer.
repente, *v.*, *pres. impers.*, *subj.*, REPENT, 662. OF repentir.
repreny, *v.*, *infin.*, REPROACH, 544. OF reprendre.
requeste, *n.*, REQUEST, 281. OF requeste.
rere, *v.*, *infin.*, ARISE, RISE, 160; *pp.*, rert, ESTABLISHED, 591. OE ræran.
rescoghe, *n.*, RESCUE, 610. OF rescourre.
reset, *n.*, REFUGE, 1067. OF recet.
resonabele, *adj.*, REASONABLE, JUST, 523. OF resonable.
resoun, *n.*, REASON, UNDERSTANDING, 52; SENTENCE, 665; raysoun, CAUSE, 268; *pl.*, resouneȝ, OBJECTIONS, 716. OF raison.
respecte, *n.*, RESPECT, 84. OF respect.
respyt, *n.*, SURCEASE, 644. OF respit.
resse, *n.*, RUSH; on r., IN A RUSH, RUSHINGLY, 874; reȝ *in* mare r., ON-RUSH, ELOQUENCE, 382. OE ræs. (See n. 382 *mare reȝ*.)
rest, *v.*, *infin.*, REST, 679. OE restan.
restay, *v.*, *infin.*, RESTRAIN, 437; *pret. 3 pl.*, restayed, 716; *pp.*, 1168. OF restaier.
reste, *n.*, REST, REPOSE, 858, 1087. OE rest.
restored, *pp.*, RESTORED, 659. OF restorer.
retrete, *v.*, *infin.*, RETRACE, REPRODUCE, 92. OF retraitier, retreter.
reue, *n.*, REEVE, OVERSEER, 542. OE [ge]refa.
reuer, *n.*, RIVER, 1055; *pl.*, reuereȝ, 105. OF rivere.

rewarde, *n.*, REWARD, 604. ONF rewarde.
rewfully, *adv.*, RUEFULLY, REPENTANTLY, 1181. Cf. OE *v.* hreowan.
rode, *n.*, ROOD, CROSS, 646, 705, 806. OE rod.
roghe, *adj.*, ROUGH, 646. OE ruh.
rokkeȝ, *n.*, ROCKS, 68. ONF roque; OF roche.
ronk, *adj.*, RICH, IN ABUNDANCE, 844; PROUD, 1167. OE ranc.
ros, see **ryse.**
rose, *n.*, ROSE, 269, 906. OE rose.
rot, see **rote (2).**
rote (1), *n.*, ROOT, 420. OE rot; prob. fr. ON rot.
rote (2), *v.*, *infin.*, ROT, 958; *n.*, DECAY, 26. OE rotian.
rounde, *adj.*, ROUND, 5, 738; WHOLE, 657. OF roont (roonde, *fem.*).
rourde, *n.*, SOUND, 112. OE reord.
route, *n.*, THRONG, 926. OF route.
rownande, *pres. part.*, MURMURING, 112. OE runian.
ruful, *adj.*, RUEFUL, MOURNFUL, 916. Cf. OE hreowan.
runne, runnen, see **ran.**
ryal, *adj.*, ROYAL, 160, 193; ryalle, 191, 919. OF real.
ryally, *adv.*, ROYALLY, 987.
rybe, *n.*, RUBY, 1007. OF rubi.
ryche (1), *adj.*, PRECIOUS, RICH, GREAT, 646, 770, 906, 1097; rych, 68, 105, 1036, 1182; riche, 993. OE rice.
ryche (2), *n.*, KINGDOM, 601, 722, 919. OE rice.
rycheȝ, *n.*, WEALTH, 26. OF richece.
ryf, *adj.*, RIFE, ABUNDANT, 770, 844. OE rife.
ryȝt, *n.*, RIGHT, VIRTUE, JUSTICE, 496, 580, 591, etc.; ryȝte, 708; by r., BY RIGHT, i.e., JUSTLY, 684, 696, etc.; *adj.*, JUST, 673; *adv.*, JUSTLY, RIGHTLY, 298, 461, 672, etc.; EVEN, 723. OE riht.
ryȝtwys, *adj.*, JUST, RIGHTEOUS, 675, 685, 697, 739; as *n.*, RIGHTEOUS or JUST (MAN), 689. OE rihtwis.
ryȝtwysly, *adv.*, CORRECTLY, RIGHTLY, 709.
ryse, *v.*, *infin.*, RISE, 103; rys, 1093; *pres. 3 sg.*, ryseȝ *in* r. vp, ARISES, 191; *pret. 3 sg.*, ros, 437, 506, 519. OE risan.

S

sadde, *adj.*, SERIOUS, GRAVE, 887; sade, 211. OE sæd.
sade, *v.*, see **say.**
saf, *adj.*, SAFE, SAVED, 672, 684, 720; saue, 696. OF sauf.
saffer, *n.*, SAPPHIRE, 118, 1002. OF safir.
saghe, *n.*, WORD, STATEMENT, 226; *pl.*, saweȝ, 278. OE sagu.
saȝ, see **se.**
saȝt, *n.*, PEACE, 52; saȝte *in* sette s., MAKE PEACE, BE RECONCILED, 1201. OE seht.
sake, *n.*, CAUSE, SAKE, 800, 940. OE sacu.
Sakerfyse, *n.*, SACRIFICE, 1064. OF sacrifice.

Salamon, *n.*, SOLOMON, 689.
same, *adj.*, SAME, 1099, 1101. ON same.
samen, *adv.*, TOGETHER, 518. OE samen.
sample, *n.*, PARABLE, 499. OF ensample.
sange, see **songe (1)**.
sant, see **saynt**.
sardonyse, *n.*, SARDONYX, 1006. L., from Gr. sardonyx.
satȝ, see **say**.
saue (1), see **saf**.
saue (2), *v.*, *infin.*, SAVE, 674; *pres. 3 sg.*, saueȝ, 666. OF sauver.
sauerly, *adj.*, SAVORY, APPRECIATIVE, 226. Cf. OF savor.
Sauter, *n.*, PSALTER, 593, 677, 698. OF sautier.
saweȝ, see **saghe**.
sawle, *n.*, SOUL, 461; saule, 845. OE sawel.
say, *v.*, *infin.*, SAY, REPORT, DECLARE, STATE, UTTER, 226, 256, 258, etc.; saye, 482; *pres. 1 sg.*, 3; *2 sg.*, says, 295, 297, 409; sayȝ, 615; saytȝ, 315; *3 sg.*, says, 693, 867; saytȝ, 457, 697, 836; satȝ, 677; *pret. 1 sg.*, sayde, 589, 962; sade, 784; sayd, 1175; *3 sg.*, sayde, 289, 338, 398, etc.; sade, 532; *3 pl.*, sayden, 534, 550; *pp.*, sayd, 593. OE secgan.
saynt, *n.*, SAINT, 457, 818; sant, 788; *pl.*, sayntеȝ, 835. OF saint.
sayȝ, saytȝ, see **say**.
scale, *n.*, SCALE, 1005. OF escale.
schadowed, *v.*, *pret. 3 sg.*, SHADOWED, 42. OE sceadwian.
schafteȝ, *n.*, RAYS, 982. OE sceaft.
schal, *v.*, *fut. aux.*, SHALL, *1 sg.*, 283; *2 sg.*, 405; *3 sg.*, 348 (and in this use *passim*); MUST, 328, 329, 332, etc.; *1 sg.*, schulde, OUGHT, SHOULD, 903; *3 pl.*, 668, 924; *1 sg.*, WAS ABOUT, INTENDED, 1162; *pres. 3 sg.*, *conting. subj.*, 186, 314, 930, 1159. OE sculan.
scharpe, *adv.*, SHARPLY, PIERCINGLY, 877. OE scearpe.
schede, *v.*, *infin.*, SEPARATE, FALL, 411; *pret. 3 sg.*, SHED, 741. OE sceadan.
schene, *adj.*, BEAUTIFUL, BRIGHT, FAIR, GLITTERING, 42, 80, 203, 1145; as *n.*, SHINING or BRIGHT (ONE), 166, 965. OE scene.
schente, *pp.*, CONFOUNDED, 668. OE scendan.
schep, *n.*, SHEEP, 801. OE sceap.
schere (1), *v.*, *infin.*, CUT, CARVE, 165; *pp.*, schorne, CARVED, 213. OE sceran, scieran.
schere (2), *v.*, *pres. 3 sg.*, SWERVES, WINDS, 107. Etymology uncertain; cf. **schere (1)**.
scheweȝ, *v.*, *pres. 3 sg.*, SHOWS, 1210; *pret. 3 sg.*, sheued, 692. OE sceawian.
scho, see **he**.
schon, see **schyneȝ**.

schore, *n.*, SHORE, STRAND, 107; BANK, 230; HILL, 166. OE scora; prob. fr. OE scieran; cf. **schere.**

schorne, see **schere.**

schot, *v.*, *pret. 3 sg.*, SHOT, 58. OE sceotan.

schowted, *v.*, *pret. 3 sg.*, SHOUTED, 877. Etymology uncertain.

schrylle, *adv.*, BRIGHTLY, BRILLIANTLY, 80. Cf. LG schrell (*STR-BR*).

schylde, *v.*, *infin.*, THWART, 965. OE scildan.

schylderez, *n.*, SHOULDERS, 214. OE sculdor.

schym, *adj.*, BRIGHT, 1077. Cf. OE *n.* scima.

schymeryng, *n.*, GLIMMER, 80. OE scimrian.

schynez, *v.*, *pres. 3 sg.*, SHINES, 1074; *pres.* for *fut. 3 pl.*, 28; *pret. 3 sg.*, schon, 166, 213, 982, 1018, 1057; *3 pl.*, schynde, 80. OE scinan. (See n. 28.)

schyr, *adj.*, BRIGHT, CLEAR, 28, 213, 284; schyre, 42; *comp.*, 982. OE scir.

sclade, see **slade.**

scrypture, *n.*, WRITING, 1039. OF escripture.

se, *v.*, *infin.*, SEE, LOOK, GAZE, ENVISION, 96, 146, 296, etc.; sene, 45; *pres. 1 sg.*, 377, 385, 932; *3 sg.*, sez, 302; *2 pl.*, *subj.*, syze, 308; *pret. 1 sg.*, sez, 158, 175, 200, 1155; seghe, 867; saz, 1021, 1147; syze, 986, 1033; *3 sg.*, syz, 985, 1032; saz, 689, 836; sez, 531; segh, 790; *2 pl.*, sez, NOTED, 698; *pp.*, sen, 164; sene, 194, 787, 1143. OE seon.

sech, *v.*, *imv.*, SEEK, 354; *pret. 3 sg.*, sozte, 730. OE secan.

secounde, *adj.*, SECOND, 652, 1002. OF second.

sede, *n.*, SEED, 34. OE sæd.

selden, *adv.*, SELDOM, 380. OE seldan.

self, *adj.*, SAME, 203; OWN, 446; VERY, TRUE, 1076; *in* þe S. God, THE VERY GOD, hence, GOD HIMSELF, 1046; *n.*, BEING, SELF, 414; SELF *in* Godez S., GOD'S SELF, hence, GOD HIMSELF, 1054. OE self.

sely, *adj.*, BLESSED, 659. OE sælig.

semblaunt, *n.*, EXPRESSION, 211; sembelaunt, 1143. OF semblant.

seme (1), *n.*, SEAM, LINE, 838. OE seam.

seme (2), *adj.*, SEEMLY, 1115; *adv.*, PLEASINGLY, 190. Cf. ON sœmr.

semed, *v.*, *pret. 3 sg.*, SEEMED, APPEARED, 760. Cf. ON soma.

semly, *adj.*, BEAUTIFUL, LOVELY, 34, 45, 789. Cf. ON sœmiligr.

sende, *v.*, *pres. 3 sg.*, *subj.*, SEND, 130. OE sendan.

sengeley, *adv.*, ALONE, APART, 8. OF sengle.

serlypez, *adj.* (*adv.* form), SEPARATE, 994. ON ser, OE -lepes.

sermoun, *n.*, TEACHING, 1185. OF sermon.

sertayn, *adv.*, UNDOUBTEDLY, 685. OF certain.

seruaunt, *n.*, SERVANT, 699. OF servant.

seruez, *v.*, *pres. 3 sg.*, SERVES, 331; *pp.*, serued, 553. OF servir.

sesed, *pp.*, SEIZED; *in* s. in, POSSESSED OF, 417. OF seisr.

set (1), *v.*, *pret. 3 sg.*, SAT, 1054; sete, 161; *3 pl.*, 835. OE sittan.

set (2), see **sete (1).**

sete (1), *v.*, *infin.*, MAKE, 1201; *pres. 2 pl.*, setten, 307; *imv.*, set, DRAW, 545; *pret. 1 sg.*, sette, SET, 8; *3 sg.*, set, PUT, 255; SET, 811; *3 sg.*, *subj.*, sette, WOULD HAVE BROUGHT, 52; *pp.*, SET, 222, 838; set, BUILT, 1062. OE settan.

sete (2), see **set** (1).

seuen, *num.*, SEVEN, 838, 1111. OE seofon.

seuenþe, *adj.*, SEVENTH, 1010. OE seofoþa.

sexte, *adj.*, SIXTH, 1007. OE siexta.

seysoun, *n.*, SEASON, 39. OF seison.

Sir, *n.*, SIR, 257, 439. OF sire.

skyfte, *v.*, *infin.*, SHIFT, ARRANGE, 569. OE sciftan.

skyl, *n.*, REASON, 312; JUDGMENT, 674; *pl.*, skylleȝ, REASONINGS, 54. ON skil.

slade, *n.*, DALE, 141; sclade, 1148. OE slæd.

slaȝt, *n.*, SLAUGHTER, 801. OE sleaht.

slake, *v.*, *infin.*, SLAKE, SUBSIDE, 942. OE [a-]sleacian.

slayn, *pp.*, SLAIN, 805. OE slean.

slente, *n.*, SLOPE, 141. Etymology uncertain.

slepe, *v.*, *pres. 3 pl.*, SLEEP, 115. OE slæpan.

slepyng-slaȝte, *n.*, SLEEPING-STROKE, DEATHLIKE SLEEP, 59. Cf. **slaȝt**.

slode, *v.*, *pret. 1 sg.*, SLIPPED, FELL, 59. ME slyde; OE slidan.

slyȝt, *adj.*, SLIGHT, 190. ON slëttr.

smal, *adj.*, FINE, 6; GRACEFUL, 190; smale, SMALL, 90. OE smæl.

smelle, *n.*, FRAGRANCE, 1122. Etymology uncertain.

smoþe, *adj.*, SMOOTH, 6; FLAWLESS, 190. OE smoþ.

so, *adv.*, SO, THUS, THEREFORE, FOR THAT REASON, VERY, EXCEEDINGLY, etc., 2, 5, 6, etc. OE swa.

sobre, *adj.*, SERIOUS, 391, 532; *adv.*, soberly, SERIOUSLY, 256. OF sobre.

sodanly, *adv.*, SUDDENLY, 1095, 1098; sodenly, 1178. OF sodain.

soffer, see **suffer**.

soȝt, *pp.*, SIGHED, MURMURED, 518. OE swogan. (See n. 518.)

solace, *n.*, SOLACE, 130. OF solaz.

solde, *v.*, *pret. 3 sg.*, SOLD, 731. OE sellan.

sommoun, *n.*, SUMMONS, SUMMONING, 1098; sumoun, 539. Cf. OF *v.* somondre.

sonde, *n.*, COMMAND, 943. OE sond.

sone, *adv.*, SOON, 537, 626, 1127; ful s., QUITE SOON, QUICKLY, 1078. OE sona.

songe, *n.*, SONG, 882, 888, 891; sange, 19. OE sang, song.

sore (1), *adv.*, SORELY, 550; sor, 940. OE sare.

sore (2), *n.*, SORROW, WOE, 130. OE sar.

sorȝ, *n.*, SORROW, 663; sorȝe, 352. OE sorg.

sorquydryȝe, *n.*, PRESUMPTION, 309. OF surcuiderie.

soth, *n.*, TRUTH, 482; soþe, 653; *adj.*, soth, TRUE, 1185; *adj.*, sothfol, TRUTHFUL, 498. OE soþ.

sotyle, *adj.* as *adv.*, SUBTLY, 1050. OF soutil.
soun, *n.*, TONE, 532. OF soun.
sounande, *pres. part.*, RESOUNDING, 883. OF soner.
space, *n.*, MOMENT; in s., IN A MOMENT, AT ONCE, 61; INTERVAL (of time), 438; SPACE, 1030. OF [e]space. (See n. 61.)
spakk, see **speke.**
sparred, *v.*, *pret.* *1 sg.*, MADE ONSET, CHARGED, 1169. Etymology uncertain; cf. OF [e]sparer.
spece, see **spyce.**
speche, *n.*, SPEECH, 37, 235, 400, etc.; spech, 704. OE spæc.
special, *adj.*, PEERLESS, RARE, 235; specyal, 938. OF special.
spede, *v.*, *pres.* *3 sg.*, *subj.*, SPEED, PROSPER, 487. OE spedan.
speke, *v.*, *pres.* *1 sg.*, UTTER, SPEAK, 422; *3 sg.*, speke3, EXPRESSES, 594; *pret.* *3 sg.*, speke, SPEAK *in* s. . . . towarde, CONTRADICT, 438; spakk, 938; *pp.*, spoken, 291. OE specan.
spelle (1), *v.*, *pres.* *1 sg.*, DISCOURSE, 793. OE spellian.
spelle (2), *n.*, SPEECH, 363. OE spel.
spenned, *v.*, *pret.* *1 sg.*, WRUNG, 49; *pp.*, LOCKED, 53. ON spenna.
spent, *pp.*, SPENT, 1132. OE spendan.
sponne, *v.*, *pret.* *3 pl.*, *subj.*, WOULD GROW, 35. OE spinnan.
spornande, *pres. part.*, RESISTING, 363. OE spornan.
spot, *n.*, SPOT (place), 25, 37, 49, 61; spote, 13; SPOT, BLOTCH, FLAW, SPECK, 12, 48, 60, etc.; spotte, 24, 36; *pl.*, spotte3, FLECKS, 945. Cf. M.Du. spotte.
spotle3, *adj.*, SPOTLESS, 856.
spotty, *adj.*, SPOTTY, 1070.
sprede, *v.*, *infin.*, EXPAND, BE OVERSPREAD, 25. OE sprædan.
spryg, *n.*, SPRIG, 35. Cf. OE spræc.
spryng, *v.*, *infin.*, SPRING, 453; *pret.* *3 sg.*, sprang, 61; sprange, 13. OE springan.
spyce, *n.*, PERSON, ONE, 938; spece, BEING, 235; spyse, SPICE, 104; *pl.*, spyce3, SPICE-BLOOMS, 35; spyse3, 25. OF espice.
spyryt, *n.*, SPIRIT, 61. OF espirit.
spyse, spyse3, see **spyce.**
spyt, *n.*, WRONG, 1138. OF despit.
stable, *adj.*, FIRM, 597; as *adv.*, 683. OF estable.
stage, *n.*, STATE, 410. OF estage.
stale, *n.*, PLACE, POSITION, 1002. OF estal.
stalked, *v.*, *pret.* *1 sg.*, STOLE, 152. OE -stealcian.
stalle, *v.*, *infin.*, FORESTALL, ANTICIPATE, 188. OE steallian.
stande, *v.*, *infin.*, STAND, 514, 867; *pres.* *3 sg.*, stande3, 547; *2 pl.*, stande, 515; stonde, 533; *3 pl.*, stonden, 113; *pret.* *1 sg.*, stod, 182, 184, 1085; *3 sg.*, 597, 1023; *pp.*, standen, 519, 1148. OE standian.
stare, *v.*, *infin.*, GAZE, 149; *pres.* *3 pl.*, staren, SHINE, 116. OE starian.
start, *v.*, *infin.*, SPRING, DIVE, 1159; LEAP, 1162. ON sterta.

stayre, *adj.*, STEEP, 1022. OE stæger.
stele, *v.*, *infin.*, STEAL, 20. OE stelan.
step, *n.*, STEP, FOOTSTEP, 683. OE stæpe.
stepe, *adj.*, GLISTENING, 113. OE steap.
stere, *v.*, *infin.*, GUIDE, 623; CHECK, 1159. OE steoran.
sterneȝ, *n.*, *pl.*, STARS, 115. ON stiarna.
steuen, *n.*, SOUND, CALL, 188, 1125. OE stefn.
stode, *n.*, PLACE, 740. OE stede; ME var., stude.
stok, *n.*, STOCK, 380. OE stocc.
stoken, *pp.*, FASTENED, 1065. Cf. OLG stecan.
ston, *n.*, STONE, 206, 380, 822, etc.; *pl.*, stoneȝ, 113, 997. OE stan.
stonge, *v.*, *pret. 3 sg.*, PIERCED, 179. OE stingan.
store, *n.*, GREAT NUMBER, 847. OF estore.
stote, *v.*, *infin.*, PAUSE, 149. Etymology uncertain; cf. OF estoutoier.
stounde, *n.*, TIME, HOUR, 20, 659. OE stund.
stout, *adj.*, PROUD, 779; stoute, STRONG, 935. OF estout.
strange, *adj.*, STRANGE, 175. OF estrange.
strateȝ, see **strete.**
stray, *adv.*, DISTRACTEDLY, TO DISTRACTION, 179. Cf. OF estraier.
strayd, *v.*, *pret. 3 sg.*, STRAYED, 1173. OF estraier.
strayn, *v.*, *infin.*, CONSTRAIN, 691; streny, EXERT, 551; *pres. 3 sg.*, strayneȝ, 128. OF estraindre.
streche, *v.*, *infin.*, REACH, 843; strech, EXTEND, 971. OE streccan.
streȝt, *adj.*, STRAIGHT, 691. Fr. OE streht, *pp.* of streccan; cf. **streche**, *v.*
strem, *n.*, STREAM, 125, 1159, 1162. OE stream; ON streyma.
stremande, *pres. part.*, STREAMING, RADIANT (as of stars), 115. Cf. **strem**, *n.*
strenghþe, *n.*, STRENGTH, 128. OE strengþu.
streny, see **strayn.**
stresse, *n.*, DISTRESS, 124. OF destresse.
strete, *n.*, STREET, 971, 1059; *pl.*, streteȝ, 1025; strateȝ, 1043. OE stræt.
strok, see **stryke.**
stronde, *n.*, SHORE, 152. OE strand.
stronge, *adj.*, STRONG, 531; *adv.*, 476. OE strong.
strot, *n.*, CONTENTION, STRIFE, 353, 848. Etymology uncertain.
stroþe-men, *n.*, MORTALS, 115. (See n. 115.)
stryf, *n.*, STRIFE, 248, 848; CONFLICT, 776. OF estrif.
stryke, *v.*, *infin.*, STRIKE, 1125; *pres. 3 sg.*, strykeȝ, GOES, 570; *pret. 3 sg.*, strok, 1180. OE strican.
stryuen, *v.*, *pres. 3 pl.*, STRIVE, 1199. OF estriver.
styf, *adj.*, STRONG, 779. OE stif.
stykeȝ, *v.*, *pres. 2 sg.*, STICKEST, ART SET, 1186. OE stician. (See n. 1186.)
stylle (1), *adj.*, STILL, QUIET, 20, 182, 1085. OE stille.
stylle (2), *v.*, *infin.*, REST, 683. OE stillan.
stynt, *v.*, *2 sg.*, *imv.*, DESIST, 353. OE styntan.

such, *adj.*, SUCH, 26, 176, 407, etc.; suche, 58, 171, 719. OE swylc.
sve, *v.*, *infin.*, FOLLOW, 976; *pres. 3 pl.*, swe, 892. OF suir.
suffer, *v.*, *infin.*, SUFFER, 954; soffer, 940; *pp.*, suffred, ENDURED, 554. OF sufrir.
suffyse, *v.*, *infin.*, SUFFICE, 135. OF soufire.
sulpande, *pres. part.*, POLLUTING, 726. Etymology uncertain.
sum (1), *adj.*, SOME, 428, 619; *pl.*, summe, 508. OE sum.
sum (2), *n.*, MAXIMUM AMOUNT, SUM; *in* al & s., IN WHOLE AND IN FULL, WHOLLY AND FULLY, 584. OF summe.
sumoun, see **sommoun.**
sumtyme, *adv.*, SOMETIME, 620; FORMERLY, 760. OE sum, tima.
sunne, *n.*, SUN, 28, 519, 538, etc.; sonne, 530. OE sunne.
sunnebemeȝ, *n.*, *pl.*, SUNBEAMS, 83. OE sunnebeam.
supplantoreȝ, *n.*, SUPPLANTERS, USURPERS, 440. OF supplanter.
sure, *adj.*, SURE, 1089; *adv.*, SO S., EXCEEDINGLY SURE, SECURELY, 222. OF sur.
sute, *n.*, MODE, FASHION, 203; TONE, 738; in s., IN ONE FASHION, i.e., ALIKE, 1108. OF seute.
swalt, *v.*, *pret. 3 sg.*, DIED, 816; *1 sg.*, *subj.*, swalte, 1160. OE sweltan.
swange, *v.*, *pret. 3 sg.*, FLOWED, COURSED, 1059; *3 pl.*, SWUNG (as a scythe), hence, TOILED, LABORED, 586; *pres. part.*, swangeande, SWINGING, MOVING RHYTHMICALLY, 111. OE swingan.
swangeande, see **swange.**
sware (1), *adj.*, SQUARE, 837; FOURSQUARE, 1023; *n.*, 1029. OF esquarre.
sware (2), *v.*, *infin.*, ANSWER, 240. ON svara.
swat, *v.*, *pret. 3 pl.*, SWEATED, 586; *3 sg.*, swatte, BLED, 829. OE swætan.
swe, see **sve.**
swefte, see **swyft.**
sweng, *n.*, SWING, STROKE, 575. OE sweng.
swepe, *v.*, *infin.*, SWEEP, 111. Cf. OE swapan.
swete, *adj.*, SWEET, 19, 94, 763, 1122; as *n.*, SWEET (ONE), 240; SWEET, 325; *adv.*, SWEETLY, 111; BRIGHT, 1057. OE swete.
swetely, *adv.*, SWEETLY, 717. OE swetlice.
sweuen, *n.*, SLEEP, 62. OE swefen.
swone, *n.*, SWOON, 1180. Cf. OE [ge]swogen.
swyft, *adj.*, SWIFT, 571; *adv.*, swefte, 354. OE swift.
swymme, *v.*, *infin.*, SWIM, 1160. OE swimman.
swyþe, *adv.*, EARNESTLY, 354; STRONGLY, 1059. OE swiþe.
syde, *n.*, SIDE, 975, 1137; *pl.*, sydeȝ, 6, 198, 218; MARGINS, 73. OE side.
syȝ, **syȝe**, see **se.**
syȝt, *n.*, SIGHT, 226, 839, 968, 1151; VISION, 952; *pl.*, syȝteȝ, VISIONS, 1179; SPIRITUAL PERCEPTION *in* wyth s., hence, IN A VISION, 985. OE [ge]siht.
sykyng, *pres. part.*, SIGHING, GRIEVING, 1175. OE sican. (See n. 1175.)
syluer, *n.*, SILVER, 77. OE sylfor.

sympelnesse, *n.*, SIMPLICITY, DIRECTNESS, 909. Cf. OF simple.
symple, *adj.*, SINCERE, ARTLESS, 1134. OF simple.
syn, see **syþen.**
synge, *v.*, SING, 891; *pret. 3 pl.*, songen, 94, 882, 888; songe, 1124. OE singan.
synglerty, *n.*, SINGULARITY, UNIQUE QUALITY, 429. OF singulierté.
syngnetteȝ, *n.*, SEALS, 838. OF signet.
synglure, *adj.*, SINGULAR; in s., IN PARTICULAR, 8. OF singuler. (See n. 8.)
synne, *n.*, SIN, INIQUITY, 610, 726, 811; *pl.*, synneȝ, 823. OE syn(n).
synneȝ, *v.*, *pres. 3 sg.*, SINS, 662. OE syngian.
Syon, *n.*, SION (ZION), 789, 868.
syt, *n.*, GRIEF, 663. ON syti.
sytole-streng, *n.*, CITOLE STRING, 91. OF citole; OE streng.
syþen, *adv.*, THEN, AFTERWARD, 643, 1207; *conj.*, SINCE, 13, 245; syn, 519. OE siþþan.
syþeȝ, *n.*, *pl.*, TIMES, 1079. OE siþ.

T

tabelment, *n.*, PLINTH, 994. OF tablement.
table, *n.*, TABLE, 1004. OF table.
tached, *pp.*, FIXED, 464. OF atachier.
take, *v.*, *infin.*, TAKE, GET, RECEIVE, OBTAIN, 539, 552, 599, etc.; TAKE *in* t. me halte, TO TAKE MYSELF HIGH, i.e., TO SPRING HIGH, 1158; *imv.*, 559; *pres. 2 sg.*, 387; *3 sg.*, totȝ, TAKES (HIMSELF), i.e., GOES, 513; *3 pl.*, takeȝ, USE, CONSUME, 687; *pret. 3 sg.*, toke, 414, 808; *3 pl.*, 585; *pp.*, taken, 830; tan, 614. OE tacan. (See n. 1157-60.)
tale, *n.*, REPORT, ACCOUNT, SPEECH, TALE, 257, 311, 590, etc. OE talu.
tan, see **take.**
tech, *v.*, *2 sg.*, *imv.*, DIRECT, 936. OE tæcan.
teche, *n.*, STAIN, 845. OF teche.
telle, *v.*, *infin.*, TELL, 134, 653; *pres. 2 sg.*, telleȝ, 919; *pret. 3 sg.*, tolde, UTTERED, 815. OE tellan.
temen, *v.*, *pres. 3 pl.*, 'TEAM UP,' YOKE, CONNECT, 460. OE teman.
temple, *n.*, TEMPLE, 1062. OE tempel; OF temple.
tempte, *v.*, *infin.*, TEST, 903. OF tempter.
tender, *adj.*, TENDER, 412. OF tendre.
teneȝ, *n.*, *pl.*, SUFFERINGS, 332. OE teona.
tenoun, *n.*, TENON, JOINING, 993. OF tenon.
tente, *n.*, HEED, 387; *pp.*, CONSIDERED, 257. OF entente.
tenþe, *adj.*, TENTH, 136, 1013. Cf. OE teoþa.
terme, *n.*, END, 503; *pl.*, termeȝ, TERMS, PRECISE WORDS *in* in t., hence, PRECISELY, CLEARLY, 1053. OF terme.
that, see **þat (2).**
the, see **þe (1).**

theme, *n.*, THEME, 944. OF teme. (See n. 944.)
then, thenne, see **þenne (1).**
this, see **þys.**
thow, see **þou.**
thynge, see **þyng.**
thys, see **þys.**
throne, see **trone.**
to, *prep.*, TO, 1, 2, 10, etc.; INTO, 507; FOR, AS, 272, 638, etc.; ON, 434; to . . . warde, TOWARD, 820; *adv.*, TOO, ALSO, 481, 492, 615, etc. OE to.
todrawe3, *v.*, *pres. 2 sg.*, REMOVEST, 280. Cf. **dra3.**
togeder, *adv.*, TOGETHER, 1121. OE togædere.
to3ere, *adv.*, THIS YEAR *in* t. more, ANYMORE THIS YEAR, 588. OE to geare.
to3t, *adj.*, SECURE, BOUND, 522. Cf. OE togian.
toke, see **take.**
token, *n.*, SYMBOL, TOKEN, 742. OE tacen.
tolde, see **telle.**
tom, *n.*, LEISURE, TIME, 134, 585. ON tom.
tonge, *n.*, TONGUE, 100, 898; tong, 225. OE tunge.
topasye, *n.*, TOPAZ, 1012. OF topase.
tor (1), *adj.*, DIFFICULT, 1109. ON tor.
tor (2), *n.*, TOWER, 966; *pl.*, torre3, TORS, CRAGS, 875. OE tor.
torente, *pp.*, RENT, 1136. OE torendan.
toriuen, *pp.*, SHATTERED, 1197. OE to-, ON rifa.
torre3, see **tor.**
tot3, see **take.**
touch, *v.*, *infin.*, TOUCH, 714; *pret. 3 sg.*, towched, 898. OF toucher.
toun, *n.*, CITY, 995. OE tun.
towarde, *prep.*, AGAINST, 438; TOWARD, 974, 1113. OE toweard.
towen, *pp.*, DRAWN BY FORCE, hence, FORCED, 251. OE togian.
tras, *n.*, TRAIN, RETINUE, 1113. OF trace.
trauayle, *n.*, TOIL, 1087. OF travail.
trauayled, *pp.*, TOILED, 550. OF travailler.
traw, *v.*, *infin.*, BELIEVE, 487; *pres. 1 sg.*, trowe, SUPPOSE, 933; *2 sg.*, trawe3, 295; *pret. 1 sg.*, trawed, 282. OE treowian.
trawþe, *n.*, TRUTH, 495. OE treowþ.
trendeled, *v.*, *pret. 3 sg.*, ROLLED, WENT ROLLING, 41. OE a-trendlian.
tres, *n.*, TREES, 1077. OE treo.
tresor, *n.*, TREASURE, 331; tresore, WORTH, VALUE, 237. OF tresor.
trone (1), *n.*, THRONE, 835, 920, 1051, 1055; throne, 1113. OF trone. (See n. 944 *theme.*)
trone (2), *v.*, *pret. 3 pl.*, WENT, 1113. Cf. Swedish trina.
trowe, see **traw.**
trwe, *adj.*, TRUE, 421, 460, 725, etc.; true, 311; trw, 831. OE treowe.

tryed, *pp.*, TRIED, 707. OF trier.
try3e, *v., infin.*, TRUST, 311. OE triewan.
trylle, *v., infin.*, QUIVER, 78. Cf. Danish trille.
tryste, *adj.*, TRUSTED, TRIED, 460. Cf. ON treysta.
twayned, *pp.*, SEVERED, SEPARATED, 251. Cf. OE twegen, *adj.*
twelfþe, *adj.*, TWELFTH, 1015. OE twelfta.
twelue, *num.*, TWELVE, 992, 993, 1022, etc. OE twelf.
two, *num.*, TWO, 483, 555, 674, etc. OE twa.
twye3, *adv.*, TWICE, 830. OE twiga.
twynne, *adj.*, TWO; *in adv. phrase* in t., IN TWO, APART, 251; twynne-how, TWI-HUED, 1012. OE [ge]twinn.
ty3ed, see **ty3t** (2).
ty3t (1), *v., infin.*, APPROACH, COME, 718; *pret. 3 sg.*, ty3te, MADE CLEAR, EXPOUNDED, 1053; *pp.*, ty3t, ARRIVED, AT HAND, 503. OE tyhtan; cf. OE dihtan.
ty3t (2), *pp.*, FIXED, FASTENED, SET, 1013; ty3ed, 464. OE tigan.
ty3te, see **ty3t** (1).
tyl, *conj.*, UNTIL, TILL, 548, 976, 979; *prep.*, tylle, TO, 676. ON til.
tyme, *n.*, TIME, 833; t. of 3ere, SEASON OF YEAR, i.e., HARVEST SEASON, 503. OE tima.
tynde, *n.*, BRANCH, 78. OE tind.
tyne, *v., infin.*, LOSE, 332. ON tyna.
tyt, *adv.*, QUICKLY, 728; as t., AS QUICKLY (AS POSSIBLE), i.e., IMMEDIATELY, 645. ON titt.

Þ

þa, see **þat**(3).
þa3, *conj.*, THOUGH, ALTHOUGH, 52, 55, 134, etc.; þo3, 345. OE þeah.
þar, þara, þare, see **þer.**
þat (1), *conj.*, THAT, 65, 137, 185, etc.; SO THAT, 35, 119, 356, etc.; IN ORDER THAT, 471, 544. OE þæt.
þat (2), *pron., dem.*, THAT, 12, 13, 14, etc.; that, 253, 481, 937; þo, 136; *pl.*, 73, 85, 109, etc.; þose, 93, 127; þos, 516, 953, 955. OE þæt.
þat (3), *pron., rel.*, THAT, 15, 17, 37, etc.; WHO, 609; HE WHO, 705; THAT WHICH, i.e., THAT SORT, SUCH AS, 687; THAT WHICH, 312, 327, 521, 657; þa, WHO, 856; *pron., pers.*, 195, 843, 1209. OE þæt. (See n. 685-88 *þat.*)
þay, see **he.**
þe (1), *def. art.*, THE, 28, 67, 69, etc.; the, 85, 109, 121, etc. OE þe.
þe (2), see **þou.**
þede, *n.*, LAND, 483. OE þeod.
þef, *n.*, THIEF, 273. OE þeof.
þen, *conj.*, THAN, 134, 181, 212, etc.; þenn, 555. OE þænne.
þenke, *v., infin.*, MUSING ON (*gerund.*), 22; þenk, THINK, 1151; *pres.*

part., þenkende, REFLECTING, 370; *pret. 1 sg.*, þoȝt, THOUGHT, 137, 1138; PROPOSED, 1157. OE þencan.

þenne (1), *adv.*, THEN, 155, 177, 213, etc.; THEREUPON, 632; AFTERWARD, 1181; thenne, 361; þen, 277, 398, 494, etc.; þenn, 555; then, 589. OE þænne, þanne.

þenne (2), *adv.*, THENCE, 631. OE þanon.

þer, *adv.*, THERE, 28, 47, 53, etc.; WHEN, SINCE, 262; THITHER, 61; þere, 167, 194, 742, etc.; *adv., rel.*, WHERE, 385; þare, 830, 1021; þore, THEN, 562; þer, 21, 61, 113, etc.; *conj.*, WHERE, 26, 30, 41, etc.; þere, 835, 838. OE þær.

þer-as, *conj.*, WHEN-AS, WHENEVER, 129; WHERE, 1173. OE þær, eal swa.

þerate, *adv.*, THERE, 514. OE þær, æt.

þerefore, *conj.*, THEREFORE, 1197. OE þær, for.

þerinne, *adv.*, THEREIN, THITHER, 447, 644, 724, etc.; þereine, 633. OE þærinne.

þerof, *adv.*, THEREOF, 99, 161, 410, etc.; THEREFROM, 1089. OE þær, of.

þeron, *adv.*, THEREON, 645, 1042; THEREOF, 387. OE þæron.

þeroute, *adv.*, OUTSIDE, WITHOUT, 930. OE þær, ut.

þerto, *adv.*, THERETO, 172, 664, 833; THEREIN, 1140. OE þærto.

þese, see **þys.**

þike, *adv.*, THICK(LY), IN DENSE GROWTH, 78. OE þicce.

þis, **þise**, see **þys.**

þo, *adv.*, THEREUPON, 451; þoo, THEN, 873. OE þa.

þo, **þos**, **þose**, *pron.*, see **þat** (2).

þoȝt, see **þenke, þynk.**

þoȝte, *n.*, THOUGHT, INTENT, 524. OE þoht.

þole, *v., infin.*, SUFFER, 344. OE þolian.

þonc, *n.*, PARDON, 901. OE þanc.

þore, see **þer.**

þou, *pron., pers.*, THOU, 23, 242, 245, etc.; þow, 411; thow, 337; *dat.* and *accus. sg.*, þe, 244, 263, 266, etc.: *nom. pl.*, ȝe, 290, 515, 516, etc.; as *sg.*, 307, 308, 371, etc.; *dat.* and *accus.*, yow, 470, 471, 524, etc.; as *dat.*, and *accus.*, *sg.*, 287, 913, 951. OE þu, ge, eow.

þow, see **þou.**

þowsande, *n.*, THOUSAND, 786, 869, 870; þowsandeȝ, 1107; þousandeȝ, 926. OE þusend.

þrange, *adv.*, CRUSHINGLY, 17. ON þröngr.

þre, *num.*, THREE, 291, 292, 1034. OE þreo.

þrete, *v., infin.*, REBUKE, 561. OE þreatian.

þro, *adj.*, BOLD, FIERCE, 344; STRONG, 868. Cf. ON þrar.

þroweȝ, *v.*, ROLLS, 875. OE þrawan.

þrych, *v., infin.*, AFFLICT, 17; *pp.*, þryȝt, 706; IMPELLED, 670; MASSED, 926. OE þryccan.

þrydde, *adj.*, THIRD, 299; þryd, 1004; þryde, 833. OE þridda.

þryf, *v.*, *infin.*, THRIVE, 851; *pp.*, þryuen, VIGOROUS, 868; BLESSED, 1192. ON þrifa.

þry3t, see **þrych.**

þryuen, see **þryt.**

þunder, *n.*, THUNDER, 875. OE þunor.

þur3, *prep.*, THROUGH, 10, 114, etc.; BY REASON OF, BECAUSE OF, 271. OE þurh.

þur3outly, *adv.*, THROUGHOUT, 859. OE þurhut, -lice.

þus, *adv.*, THUS, SO, 526, 569, 573, etc.; THEREFORE, 673; AS, 673. OE þus.

þy, *pron.*, *poss.*, THY, 266, 273, 275, etc.; þyn, 559, 567, 754. OE þin.

þyder, *adv.*, THITHER, 723, 946. OE þider.

þyn, see **þy.**

þyng, *n.*, BEING, 771; thynge, THING, 910. OE þing.

þynk, *v.*, *pres.*, *impers.*, IT SEEMS, APPEARS; *in* vs þ., IT SEEMS TO US, 552, 553; METHINKS *in* me þ., 267, 316, 590; þo3t, *pret. 1 sg.*, I IMAGINED *in* þ. me, 19; I FELT *in* me þ., 153. OE þyncan (*pret.*).

þys, *pron.*, *dem.*, THIS, 250, 277, 297, etc.; þis, 65, 260, 295, etc.; thys, 841; this, 733; þysse, 370; þise, 533; *pl.*, 287, 384, 997, etc.; þys(e), 505, 555, 921, 931; þis, 42; þese, 531, 752. OE þis.

þyse, þysse, see **þys.**

þyself, *pron.*, *reflex.*, THYSELF, 473; *intens.*, þyseluen, 341; þyself, 298, 313, 779. OE þin, self.

(U)V

vale3, *n.*, VALES, 127. OF val.

vayl, *v.*, *infin.*, AVAIL, 912. OF valoir.

vayn, *adj.*, VAIN; in v., AT NOUGHT, 811; *n.*, vayne, VANITY, 687. OF vain.

vayned, see **wayne3.**

vch, *adj.*, EACH, EVERY, 31, 323, 603, etc., vch a, 78, 375, 436, etc.; vche, 5, 33, 310, etc.; vche a, 117, 217, 1066, etc. OE ælc.

vchon, *pron.*, EACH ONE, 450, 546, 595, etc.; *gen.*, vchone3, 836, 1103.

veray, *adj.*, TRUE, REAL, 1184; ueray, 1185. OF verai.

verce, *n.*, VERSE, 593. OF vers.

vere3, *v.*, *pres. 3 sg.*, LIFTS, 177; *pret. 3 sg.*, vered, 254. OF virer.

vergyne3, *n.*, *pl.*, VIRGINS, 1099. OF virgine.

vergynte, *n.*, VIRGINITY, 767. OF virginité.

Vertues, *n.*, VIRTUES, 1126. OF vértu. (See n. 1126.)

uesture, *n.*, VESTURE, 220. OF vesture.

veued, *pp.*, SIGHTED, VIEWED; *in* to . . . be v., BE SIGHTED TOWARD, i.e., BE IN SIGHT OF, 976. OF veoir (*pp.*, veü).

vmbe, *prep.*, ABOUT, AROUND, 210. OE ymbe.

vmbepy3te, *pp.*, SET AROUND, 204; RANGED ABOUT, 1052. OE ymbe; cf. py3t.

vnavysed, *adj.*, ILL-ADVISED, 292. OE un-, OF aviser.
vnblemyst, *adj.*, UNBLEMISHED, 782. OF blesmir.
vncortoyse, *adj.*, DISCOURTEOUS, 303. Cf. OF corteis.
vndefylde, *adj.*, UNDEFILED, 725. OE un-, OF defouler.
vnder (1), *n.*, THIRD HOUR, 513. OE undern.
vnder (2), *prep.*, UNDER, 923. OE under.
vnderstonde, *v.*, *infin.*, UNDERSTAND, 941. OE understandan.
vnhyde, *v.*, *infin.*, REVEAL, 973. OE un-, hydan.
vnlapped, *pp.*, UNBOUND, 214. OE un-, læpped.
vnmete, *adj.*, NOT FIT, in sense, UNDESERVED, 759. OE un-, mæte.
vnpynne, *v.*, *infin.*, UNBOLT, 728. Cf. OE pinn.
vnresounable, *adj.*, UNREASONABLE, 590.
vnstrayned, *pp.*, SET FREE, 248. Cf. **strayn.**
vnto, *prep.*, UNTO, 712, 718, 1212; AS, 772; UP TO, 1169; TOWARD, 362.
vntrwe, *adj.*, UNTRUE, 897. Cf. **trwe.**
uoched, *pp.*, CALLED, 1121. OF vochier.
vp, *adv.*, UP, 35, 177, 191, etc. OE up.
vpen, vpon, see **open.**
vpon, *adv.*, ON, 208; *prep.*, UPON, 57, 59, 370, etc.; vpone, 1054. OE up, on.
vrþe, vrþely, see **erþe.**
vtwyth, *adv.*, OUTSIDE, 969. OE ut-, wiþ.
vus, see **I.**
vyf, see **wyf.**
vygour, *n.*, POWER, 971. OF vigor.
vyne, *n.*, VINEYARD, 504, 507, 521, etc.; uyne, 502. OF vigne.
vyrgynflor, *n.*, VIRGINITY, 426. OF virgine, flor.
vys, *n.*, FACE, 750; vye, 254. OF vis.
vysayge, *n.*, FACE, 178. OF visage.
vyueȝ, see **wyf.**

W

wace, see **be.**
wade, *v.*, *infin.*, CROSS, 143, 1151. OE wadan.
wage, *v.*, *infin.*, KEEP TROTH or FAITH, 416. OF wager.
wakned, *v.*, *pret. 1 sg.*, AWAKENED, 1171. OE wæcnan.
wal, *n.*, WALL, 1017, 1026. OE weall.
wale, *v.*, *infin.*, DISCERN, 1000; SINGLE OUT, 1007. ON velja.
walk, *v.*, *infin.*, 399; *pret. 3 sg.*, welke, 101, 711. OE wealcan.
wallande, *pres. part.*, WELLING, 365. OE weallan.
walte, *pp.*, VEXED, 1156. OE -wælan. (See n. 1156.)
wan, see **wynne (2).**
wanig, *adj.*, LACKING, 558. OE wan, -ig. (See n. 558.)
war, *adj.*, AWARE, 1096. OE a-, wær.
warde, *adv.*, -WARD, 820, 981. OE weard.

ware, see **be.**

warpe, *v., infin.,* UTTER, SOUND FORTH, 879. ON varpa.

wasche3, *v., pres. 3 sg.,* WASHES, 655; *pret. 3 pl.,* wesch, 766. OE wascan.

wasse, see **be.**

wate, see **wot.**

water, *n.,* WATER, CURRENT, RIVER, STREAM, 107, 111, 122, etc. OE wæter.

wat3, see **be.**

wawe3, *n.,* WAVES, 287. Cf. OE wafian; wagian.

wax, *v., pret. 3 sg.,* FLOWED, 649; wex, GREW, 538, 648. OE weaxan.

way (1), *n.,* WAY, 350, 580; *pl.,* waye3, 691. OE weg.

way (2), *adv.,* AWAY, 718. OE [on]weg.

wayne3, *v., pres. 3 sg.,* GAINS, WINS, 131; *pp.,* vayned, FETCHED, BROUGHT, 249. OE wægn.

wayted, *pp.,* WATCHED, 14. ONF waitier.

we, see **I.**

webbe3, *n.,* WEBS, FABRICS, 71. OE webb.

wedde, *v., infin.,* WED, 772. OE weddian.

weddyng, *n.,* WEDDING, 791. OE weddung.

wede, *n.,* DRESS, ROBE, GARMENT, RAIMENT, 748, 766; *pl.,* wede3, 1102, 1112, 1133. OE wæde.

weete, *adj.,* WET, 1135. OE wæta.

wel, *adj.,* WELL, FORTUNATE *in* w. wat3 me, FORTUNATE FOR ME, 239; HAPPY *in* w. is me, HAPPY AM I, 1187; *adv.,* 164, 302, 411, etc.; VERY, 537; STILL, MUCH, 145, 148; *comp.,* better, RATHER, 341. OE wel; *better* fr. OE *adv.* bet.

welcum, *adj.,* WELCOME, 399. Cf. OE wilcuma.

wele, *n.,* WEALTH, 14; HAPPINESS, 133; WEAL, 342; BLISS, 394; *pl.,* wele3, JOYS, 154. OE wela.

welke, see **walk.**

welkyn, *n.,* SKY, 116. OE wolcen.

welle, *n.,* WELL, SPRING, 365, 649. OE wella.

welnygh, *adv.,* ALMOST, WELL-NIGH, 581; wel-ne3, 528. OE welneah.

wely, *adj.,* HAPPY, 101. OE welig.

wemle3, *adj.,* SPOTLESS, 737. Cf. **wemme.**

wemme, *n.,* FLAW, 221, 1003. OE wamm (*infl. by v.* wemman).

wende (1), *v., infin.,* GO, 643; *pret. 1 sg.,* wente, 761; *3 sg.,* went, 1130; *3 pl.,* wente, 525, 631. OE wendan.

wende (2), see **wene.**

wene, *v., infin.,* THINK, IMAGINE, 1141; *pres. 1 sg.,* 47, 201; *pret. 1 sg.,* wende, 1148. OE wenan.

went, wente, see **wene.**

wer (1), *v., pret. 3 sg.,* WORE, 205. OE werian.

wer (2), were, see **be.**

werke, *n.,* WORK, 599. OE weorc.

werkmen, *n.*, WORKMEN, 507.
werle, *n.*, CIRCLET, 209. (See n. 209.)
wern, see **be.**
west, *adj.*, EMPTY, 307. OE weste. (See n. 307.)
wete, *n.*, WOE, 761. OE wite. (See n. 761.)
weþer, see **wheþer.**
weue, *v., infin.*, GO, MOVE, 318. Cf. OE wæfan.
weuen, *v., pres. 3 pl.*, WEAVE, 71. OE wefan.
wex, see **wax.**
whalleȝ, *n., gen. sg.*, OF A WHALE, 212. OE hwæl.
wham, see **quo (2).**
what, see **quo (1), (2).**
whateȝ, see **byrþ whateȝ.**
when, see **quen.**
where, see **quere.**
whete, *n.*, WHEAT, 32. OE hwæte.
wheþer, *adv.*, YET, NEVERTHELESS, 581; *pron., rel.*, WHICH, 826; *inter. adv. in* w. . . . oþer, WHETHER . . . OR, 130, 604; weþer, *introduc. direct question*, 565. OE hwæþer.
who, see **quo (1), (2).**
why, *inter. adv.*, WHY, 329, 338, 515, 634; wy, 290, 533, 564; quy, 561; *interjec.*, 769. OE hwy.
whyle, *adv.*, FOR A WHILE, 15. OE *n.* hwil.
whyt, whyte, see **quyt.**
win, see **wynne (2).**
wlonc, *adj.*, SPLENDID, FAIR, FINE, 903; wlonk, 122, 1171. OE wlanc.
wo, *n.*, WOE, SUFFERING, 56, 342; FAILURE, 154. OE wa.
wod, *n.*, WOOD, 122. OE wudu.
wode, *adj.*, SENSELESS, FOOLISH, 743. OE wod.
wod-shaweȝ, *n., pl.*, WOOD-SHAWS, WOODLANDS, 284. OE wudu, sceaga.
woghe, *n.*, EVIL, 622. OE woh.
woȝe, *n.*, WALL, 1049. OE wah.
wolde (1), *v., infin.*, CONTROL, SUBDUE, RULE, 812. OE wealdan.
wolde (2), woldeȝ, see **wyl (2).**
wolen, *adj.*, WOOLEN, 731. Cf. OE wyllen.
wolle, *n.*, WOOL, 844. OE wull; wyll.
wommon, *n.*, WOMAN, 236. OE wimman.
won (1), *n.*, DWELLING, HOME, 1049; *pl.*, woneȝ, 32, 917, 924, 1027. OE [ge]wuna.
won (2), *v., infin.*, DWELL, ABIDE, 298, 315, 644, 918; wony, 284; *pres. 3 sg.*, wonys, 47; *3 pl.*, woneȝ, 404. OE wunian.
wonde, *v., infin.*, RETREAT, TURN BACK, 153. OE wandian.
wonder, *n.* as *adj.*, WONDROUS, 221, 1095. OE wundor.
wonne, see **wynne (2).**
wont, *adj.*, WONT, CUSTOMARY, 15; wonte, 172. OE wunian.

wonted, *v.*, *pret. 3 sg.*, WANTED, LACKED, 215. ON vanta.

worchen, *v.*, *pres. 3 pl.*, TOIL, 511; *2 pl.*, *imv.*, wyrkeȝ, WORK, 536; *pret. 3 sg.*, wroȝt, WROUGHT, 748; wraȝte, TOSSED, 56; *3 pl.*, wroȝt, LABORED, 555; WROUGHT, 631, 825; wroȝten, 622; wroȝte, WORKED, 525; *pp.*, wroȝt, FASHIONED, 638; w. vpon, WROUGHT UPON, i.e., COMMITTED, 824. OE wyrcan.

worde, *n.*, WORD, SAYING, REMARK, STATEMENT, 294; *pl.*, wordeȝ, 291, 307, 314, 367, 819. OE word.

wore, see **be.**

worlde, *n.*, WORLD, EARTH, 293, 424, 476, etc.; *gen. sg.*, 761. OE worold.

worschyp, *n.*, HONOR, 394, 479. OE weorþscipe.

worteȝ, *n.*, *pl.*, PLANTS, 42. OE wyrt.

worþe (1), *adj.*, WORTHY, 100; WORTH, 451; worþy, NOBLE, 494; WORTHY, 616. OE weorþ.

worþe (2), *v.*, *pres. 3 sg., subj.*, CONSIDERED, COUNTED, 362; pp. worþen, CHANGED, 394. OE weorþan.

worþly, *adj.*, VALUED, PRECIOUS, 1073; worthyly, WORTHY, 846; *adv.*, worþyly, FITTINGLY, 47; worþly, 1133. OE weorþlic.

wost, woste, see **wot.**

wot, *v.*, *pres. 1 sg.*, KNOW, 47, 201, 1107; wate, 502; *2 sg.*, wost, 411; woste, 293; *pret. 1 sg.*, wyste, 65, 376; *2 sg.*, wysteȝ, 617. OE witan.

woþe, *n.*, HUNT, SEARCH, 375; *pl.*, woþeȝ, SEARCHINGS, 151. Cf. OE waþ.

wounde, *n.*, WOUND, 650, 1135, 1142. OE wund.

wraȝte, see **worchen.**

wrang, *n.*, EVIL, SIN, FAULT, 631; wrange, 15; *adv.*, WRONGLY, UNJUSTLY, 488; wrang, 614. OE wrang. (See n. 14-18.)

wrathþe, *n.*, ANGER, 362. OE wræþþo.

wrekan, see **wroken**, *pp.*

wreched, *adj.*, WRETCHED, 56. Cf. OE wræcca.

wro, *n.*, ANGLE, SECTION (of a book), PASSAGE, 866. ON (v)ra.

wroȝt, wroȝte, wroȝten, see **worchen.**

wroken (*pp.* of *wrekan*), EXPELLED, CUT OFF, 375. OE wrecan ('outcast').

wroþe, *adj.*, WROTH, 379. OE wraþ.

wryt, *n.*, (HOLY) WRIT, SCRIPTURE, 592; writ, 997. OE writ.

wryteȝ, *v.*, *pres. 3 sg.*, WRITES, 1033; *pp.*, wryten, 834, 866, 871. OE writan.

wryþe, *v.*, *infin.*, TURN, DEVIATE, 350, 488; *pres. 3 pl.*, wryþen, TWIST, 511. OE wriþan.

wy, see **why.**

wyde, *adj.*, WIDE, 1135. OE wid.

wyf, *n.*, WIFE, SPOUSE, 846; vyf, 772; *pl.*, vyueȝ, 785. OE wif.

wyȝ, *n.*, PERSON, MORTAL, MAN, 100, 131, 722; *pl.*, wyȝeȝ, MORTALS, 71, 579. OE wiga.

wyȝt, *n.,* PERSON, BEING, 338; wyȝte, ONE, 494; *adj.,* BRAVE, VALIANT, 694. OE wiht; cf. ON vigt.

wyl (1), *adv.,* ALMOST, 528. OE hwil.

wyl (2), *v.,* WILL, WISH, and as *aux.: pres. 1 sg.,* 558; *3 sg.,* 350, 443, 965; *2 sg., subj.,* 794; *pret. 1 sg.,* wolde, 390, 910; *2 sg.,* woldeȝ, 410; *3 sg., wolde,* 304, 451, 488, 772, 1195; *pl.,* 391, 849; *1 sg.,* 977, 1155. OE willan.

wylle, *n.,* WILL, DECISION, 56; INTENT, 131. OE willa.

wylneȝ, *v., pres. 2 sg.,* WISH, 318. OE wilnian.

wyn, *n.,* WINE, 1209. OE win.

wyngeȝ, *n.,* WINGS, 93. Cf. ON vængr.

wynne (1), *adj.,* BLESSED, 154, 647. Cf. OE *n.* wynn.

wynne (2), *v., infin.,* WIN, 579, 694, 722; *pret. 1 sg.,* wan, REACHED AT LAST, FINALLY CAME TO (GOT), 107; *pp.,* wonne, 32, 517. OE winnan.

wynter, *n.,* WINTER, 116. OE winter.

wyrde, *n.,* FATE, 249, 273. OE wyrd.

wyrkeȝ, see **worchen.**

wys, *adj.,* WISE, 748. OE wis.

wyschande, *pres. part.,* WISHING, 14. OE wyscan.

wyse (1), *n.,* WISE, WAY, 101, 133, 1095. OE wise.

wyse (2), *v., infin.,* EXTEND, RUN, 1135. OE wisian.

wyste, wysteȝ, see **wot.**

wyt, *n.,* WIT, MIND, 903; wytte, 294. OE witt.

wyth, *prep.,* WITH, BY, 40, 54, 74, etc.; with, 200, 203, 837. OE wiþ.

wythdroȝ, *v., pret. 3 sg.,* TOOK AWAY, 658. OE wiþ, dragan.

wyth-inne, *adv.,* WITHIN, 1027; *prep.,* 440, 679, 966. OE wiþinnan.

wythnay, *v., imv.,* DENY, 916. OE wiþ, ON nei.

wythouten, *prep.,* WITHOUT, BEYOND, 12, 24, 36, etc.; wythoute, 644, 695. OE wiþutan.

wyþer, *adj.,* OPPOSITE, OTHER; *in* on w. half, ON THE OTHER SIDE, ACROSS, 230. OE wiþer.

XYZ

ydel, *adj.,* IDLE, 514, 515, 531, 533. OE idel.

yȝe, *n.,* EYE, 302, 567, 1153; *pl.,* yȝen, 183, 200, 254, 296. OE eage.

yle, *n.,* ISLE, 693. OF ile.

ynde, *n.,* IND, 76; INDIGO, DEEP BLUE, 1016. OF inde.

yot, see **gon.**

your, *pron., poss.,* YOUR, 257, 258, 305, etc.; yor, 761. OE eower.

you, see **þou.**

Ysaye, *n.,* ISAIAS (ISAIAH), 797, 819.

yuore, *n.,* IVORY, 178. OF ivoire.

Date Due

OC 22 '62			

AUTHOR
Pearl (Middle English poem)

TITLE
The pearl, medieval text with a literal trans.

DATE DUE	BORROWER'S NAME	ROOM NUMBER
	~~D. Preston~~	
OC 22 '62	~~Martha Moore~~	~~386~~ M
NO 2 '62	~~Sr. Richard~~ Clare	301 M
NO 16 '62		

Pearl (Middle English poem)

The pearl, medieval text with a literal trans. and interpretation.